Successful ICT Projects

in

Excel

P.M.Heathcote

B.Sc.(Hons), M.Sc.

Updated for Excel 2000 by:
Rosemary Richards

Published by
Payne-Gallway Publishers Ltd
76-78 Christchurch Street
Ipswich IP4 2DE
Tel 01473 251097
Fax 01473 232758
E-mail info@payne-gallway.co.uk
Web site www.payne-gallway.co.uk

2000

Acknowledgements

I am very grateful to Sue Clark for her valuable input and comments on the first draft, which have resulted in a much better book than it would otherwise have been. Thanks also to Tim Newling for teaching me how to lay out accounts for Chapter 14, Phil Holmes for material he supplied and Sylvia Langfield for testing the examples. Many thanks to Rosemary Richards who has updated the book for Excel 2000, and to Oliver for his patience and skill in getting the book ready for press.

Cover picture © "Music Series" reproduced with kind permission from Sarah Simpson
Cover photography © Mike Kwasniak, 160 Sidegate Lane, Ipswich

Cover design © by Tony Burton

Second edition 2000

10 9 8 7 6 5 4 3

A catalogue entry for this book is available from the British Library.

ISBN 1 903112 26 5
Copyright © P.M.Heathcote 2000

Printed in Great Britain by
W M Print Ltd, Walsall, West Midlands

Preface

Projects in Excel

Excel is a powerful and versatile spreadsheet program which is eminently suitable for project work at every level from GNVQ to degree work. Parts 1 to 3 of the book take the reader through a crash course in Excel which need last only a few sessions, using numerous different examples to give a flavour of what can be achieved. Part 4 gives advice on all stages of project work, giving students plenty of ideas which could form the basis of their own projects. It also covers the stages of the systems life cycle so that students are well equipped to write about each stage of project development.

The intended audience

The book was written primarily for 'AS' and 'A' Level Information and Communications Technology students and contains in Appendix B the AQA mark scheme for a Minor Project. However, the book contains enough information on the advanced features of Excel to make it suitable for work on the Major Project in the second year of an A Level course. It will also be suitable for students on many other courses at different levels since the mark scheme, with minor variations, is one which applies to projects in 'A' Level Computing and many Business and ICT courses.

Working on a network

Students working on a school or college network will have no difficulty in completing any of the exercises, as alternative instructions are given when necessary to cope with restricted access to files held on a file server.

Version of Excel

The book is primarily for Excel 2000 and Excel 97 users. However, instructions are given throughout the book to assist Excel 7 users where differences arise, and Excel 5 users should have very little difficulty in following the instructions for Excel 7, since differences are generally very minor. This means that the book is quite suitable for users of Excel 5, 7, 97 and 2000.

The sample project

A sample project is included to show students how a complete project report may be laid out. Students should not assume that this is the only way to write a project report, and above all should use their own ideas and originality and check the mark scheme for their particular course. Moderators will not take kindly to seeing barely disguised versions of the sample project turning up on their desks!

Contents

Table of Contents

Chapter 15 – The Systems Life Cycle   143

Chapter 16 – Writing the Project Report   150

APPENDIX A:
Sample Project

APPENDIX B:
AQA Project Mark Scheme

INDEX

Part 1
Excel Basics

Chapter 1 – Workbooks and Worksheets

Introduction

Microsoft Excel is a powerful spreadsheet program that can be used to store and work with lists of data, perform calculations and create charts and reports. It has a large number of advanced features which this book will help you to master and put to use in a project for an I.T. or Computing course. The version used in the book is Excel 2000, but if you are using an earlier version you will easily be able to follow the exercises and examples.

The Excel environment

An Excel file is referred to as a *workbook*. A workbook can contain one or more *worksheets*, each worksheet being similar to a page in an accountant's ledger, with numbers, text and calculations held in rows and columns. A workbook could contain, for example, a list of students in a particular class. The workbook could contain separate worksheets for the marks obtained by each student in different subjects, with a final worksheet showing overall grades, calculated from the marks in individual subjects. The facility to have several worksheets in a single workbook allows the concept of a *three-dimensional* workbook; you can look at all Andrews' marks for Computing in Term 1, or all the class's marks for Week 1 in Computing, or going through the separate worksheets, all the marks scored by Andrews in Week 1.

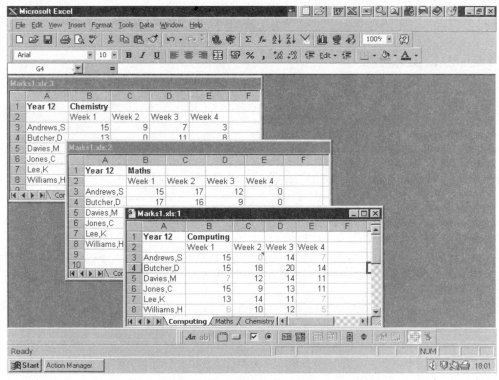

Figure 1.1: Several worksheets make up one workbook

Opening a new workbook

- To start Excel and open a new workbook, double-click the Excel icon on the Office toolbar or click **Start** in the bottom left-hand corner of the screen and select **Programs, Microsoft Excel**.

A new workbook opens. By default, the workbook has 3 worksheets named **Sheet1**, **Sheet2** and **Sheet3** (The default number of worksheets may be different on your computer.)

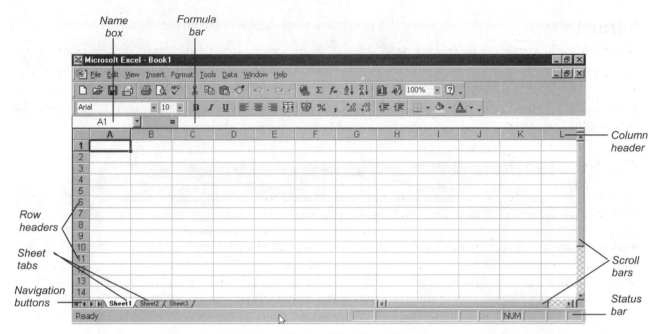

Figure 1.2: A new Excel workbook

Anatomy of a worksheet

A worksheet consists of *columns* and *rows*. Columns run vertically and are identified by letters called *column headers* which run across the top of the worksheet. Rows are identified by numbers called *row headers*. The intersection of a row and column is called a *cell*. Cells are identified by the column and row they are in.

When you select a cell by clicking in it, it becomes the *active cell*, surrounded by a heavy border – in the diagram above, the active cell is **A1**, at the intersection of column A, Row 1. The cell reference for the active cell appears in the Name box and the corresponding column and row headers become bold and raised.

You can also change the active cell by pressing the **Enter** key, **Tab** key or any of the Arrow keys.

Scroll bars on the right and bottom side of the worksheet are used to view different parts of the worksheet. You can only see a small portion of the worksheet in the window – an entire worksheet is 256 columns by 65536 rows.

- Try scrolling down and clicking in a cell in the worksheet.

You can return to cell A1 at any time by pressing **Ctrl-Home**.

You can also use the **Page Up** and **Page Down** keys to move up and down a page at a time.

- Select cell Z50. Press the **Home** key. What does this key do? Return to cell A1 now.

Task 1.1: Create a spreadsheet to hold student marks

In this task you will create a workbook consisting of several sheets similar to the one shown in Figure 1.1, and add an extra sheet to hold average marks.

Opening a new workbook and saving it

- Load Excel if it is not already loaded. A new blank worksheet will automatically appear.

- If you have not got a new blank worksheet on your screen, select **File, New** and click the Workbook icon to open a new worksheet. Alternatively, click the **New File** icon. By default, a new workbook contains 3 sheets; otherwise change this in **Tools**, **Options**, **General**.

- Select **File, Save** to save it immediately as *Marks* in your usual folder (directory), or a new folder specially created for Excel exercises. Excel adds the extension **.xls** to the name.

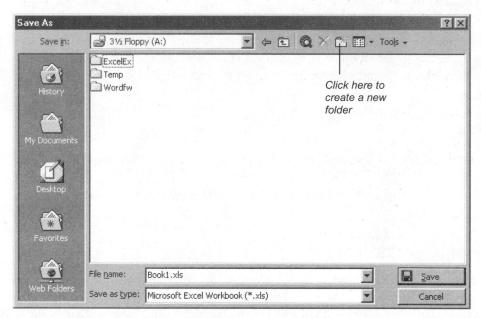

Figure 1.3: Saving a worksheet

Adding, deleting and naming sheets

- To insert an extra sheet, click the **Sheet3** tab at the bottom of the worksheet. Select **Insert, Worksheet** from the menu bar. A new sheet named **Sheet4** is inserted in front of **Sheet3**. To move it so that it appears after **Sheet3**, drag the tab to the right of **Sheet3**.

- You can also insert a new sheet by right-clicking a sheet tab, selecting **Insert** and then double-clicking the **Worksheet** icon.

- To delete a worksheet, right-click its tab and select **Delete**. Try deleting sheets 1 and 2.

- You should now have three worksheets in your workbook. Right-click the tab for the first worksheet and select **Rename**. The sheet name will be highlighted. Type its new name, *Computing*.

- Name the other two worksheets *Maths* and *Chemistry*.

Inserting the same information in several worksheets at once

We now want to create the class list on each sheet. For the purposes of this exercise we will assume that we are entering data for only three subjects – you could of course have sheets for every subject and enter marks for each student for the subjects that they study.

- Click on the tab for the **Computing** worksheet.

- Hold down the Ctrl key while you click the tab for **Maths** and then for **Chemistry**. All three worksheets are now selected and whatever you type in the current worksheet will appear in all three sheets.

- In cell B2, type *Week 1*. Instead of typing *Week 2, Week 3* etc along the row, you can use a useful shortcut. With the right mouse button, drag the small square at the bottom right of cell B2 across the next 3 cells. From the pop-up menu, select **Fill Series**. The labels are automatically filled in for you.

- In cell A3 down to A8 type a list of names as shown in Figure 1.1. After typing the name, press **Enter** or the Down Arrow key to move to the next cell. (If you make a mistake and need to change a name, double-click the cell and then you can edit it; press **Enter** to finish editing.)

- *Andrews, S* is too long to fit in the cell. You can adjust the column width so that it exactly accommodates the longest entry in the column. Double-click the column header between A and B. (You can also adjust a column width by dragging the boundary between column headers.)

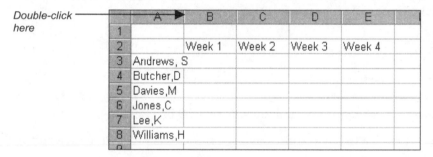

Figure 1.4: Adjusting column width

- You can also make columns B to E narrower. Select the four columns by dragging across the column headers. Now double-click the column header between B and C. All four column widths will adjust.

- Type the label *Year 12* in cell A1.

Moving cell contents

To move the contents of one or more cells to a new location, select the range to be moved by dragging across it, and then drag one of the boundaries, keeping away from the corner handle.

- Try moving the list of names down one row.

- Move the headings right by 1 column.

- Undo the two moves now using the **Undo** button. *(Excel 7 will only undo one.)*

Copying and pasting cells between worksheets

Check that the same information has been inserted into each of your 3 worksheets. If it hasn't, you didn't have all three sheets selected all the time. Never mind – you can quickly copy and paste the entries to each worksheet later, using the technique described below.

- First, use the right mouse button to click a worksheet tab and insert an extra worksheet. Rename it *Averages* and drag the sheet tab so that it is the rightmost sheet in the list.

- Click the **Computing** worksheet tab to make it the active sheet, and drag across cells A1 to E8 to select all these cells. (Note that another way of selecting a range is to click in Cell A1, then shift-click in cell E8. To select an entire worksheet, click the intersection of the column and row headers.)

- From the menu bar select **Edit, Copy** or click the **Copy** icon on the Standard toolbar. The selected cells are surrounded by a moving dotted line.

- Click the **Averages** worksheet tab and with the cursor in cell A1, select **Edit, Paste** or click the **Paste** icon on the Standard toolbar.

Copying a worksheet

You can copy an entire worksheet very quickly.

- Click the tab for the **Averages** worksheet. Hold down the Ctrl key while dragging the tab to the right and releasing it. A new sheet called **Averages (2)** is created.

- Rename this sheet *SortList*.

Selecting cells in a worksheet

- In the current worksheet, select cell A3 containing **Andrews, S** by clicking in it.

- You can select the last item in a list by double-clicking the bottom border of the selected cell. Try this now.

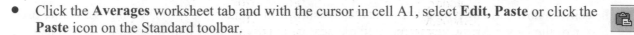

Figure 1.5: Selecting the last cell in a list

- Double-click the top border of the cell containing **Williams, H**. This will take you back up to **Andrews, S**.

- Try moving from the cell containing **Week 1** to the cell containing **Week 4** by double-clicking its right-hand border.

- Click in any of the cells containing data, and then click **Ctrl-Shift-***. This selects all adjoining cells, which in this case will be cells A1 to E8.

- Save your workbook at regular intervals – now would be a good time! The shortcut key **Ctrl-S** is a convenient way of saving.

Entering and editing data and comments

You can enter text, numbers and formulae into a worksheet.

- Click the tab for the **Computing** worksheet.

- Starting in cell B3, enter the marks as shown below. The quickest way is to enter the marks row by row; e.g. enter *15* in B3, tab to C3 and enter *11*, and so on across the top row. Then press **Enter** and the cursor will automatically go to cell B4, ready to enter the next row. *(Excel 7 goes to E4.)*

Note that numbers are automatically right-aligned in a cell, whereas text is automatically left-aligned. Later we will look at various ways of formatting cells.

	Week 1	Week 2	Week 3	Week 4
Andrews, S	15	11	14	7
Butcher,D	15	18	20	14
Davies,M	7	12	14	11
Jones,C	15	9	13	11
Lee,K	13	14	11	7
Williams,H	8	10	12	5

Figure 1.6: Worksheet data

To delete the contents of a cell, click it and press the Delete key. To delete the contents of several cells, first select them and then press the **Delete** key.

- Delete the last mark for **Williams,H**.

- Delete all the marks for **Jones,C**.

- Now undo those changes by clicking the **Undo** button twice. *(Excel 7 only undoes one action.)*

To alter the contents of a cell, double-click it and the cursor remains in the cell waiting for it to be edited. (You can also edit the contents of a cell by selecting it and typing the changes in the Formula bar – see Figure 1.2.)

- Double-click the mark for **Andrews** in Week 2 and change it to *0*. Press **Enter**.

- You can add a comment to any cell. Right-click the cell you have just changed and select **Insert Comment.** *(In Excel 7 don't right-click, choose **Note** from the **Insert** menu.)*

- A box appears for you to enter the comment. Delete any existing comment and type *Stephanie was ill and missed the test*, as shown in the figure below. You can size the comment box by dragging on a handle.

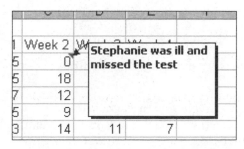

Figure 1.7: Attaching a comment to a cell

- Move the cursor away from the cell and the comment disappears. Any time you leave the cursor over the cell, the comment reappears. A red triangle in the top right corner of a cell indicates that there is a comment attached to the cell.

- You can edit or delete the comment by right-clicking the cell and choosing the appropriate option.

Freezing panes to keep column labels visible

The list of names that you have typed is short and easily fits on one screen. However, if you have a longer list of say 30 or 40 names, the column headings will disappear as you scroll down the list. You can freeze the top two rows so that this does not happen.

- Select cell A3.

- From the **Window** menu, select **Freeze Panes**.

The top two rows will now remain in view as you scroll down the worksheet. You can unfreeze them again by selecting **Window**, **Unfreeze Panes**.

Viewing several worksheets simultaneously

Sometimes it is convenient to be able to see several worksheets on screen, as in Figure 1.1. To do this you need to open extra windows.

- From the **Window** menu, select **New Window**. Not a lot appears to happen as the new window sits on top of the original one, showing the same worksheet.

- Click the **Maths** tab to display the Maths worksheet in the current window. Select **Window, Arrange**. A dialogue box appears asking how you want the windows arranged. Select **Tiled** and click **OK**. The windows appear side by side.

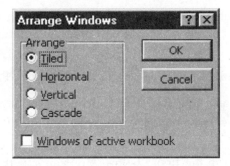

Figure 1.8: Options for arranging windows

- Open a third new window and this time arrange them using the **Cascade** option.

- Click the **Chemistry** tab to display the Chemistry worksheet in the new window.

- You can now size the windows by dragging inwards from the corner of each window, and arrange them to your liking.

- Add a title to each worksheet – *Computing* in the cell B1 of the Computing worksheet, *Maths* in cell B1 of the Maths worksheet, etc. Click the Row 1 headers and click the **Bold** button to make all the headings in row 1 bold.

Entering simple formulae

Spreadsheets were specifically designed for calculating numbers. You can enter numbers in some cells, and in others write formulae to tell Excel what calculation to perform to get the required results. Formulae usually consist of a combination of cell references, numbers and specially written Excel functions such as Sum, Average, Count etc.

To write a formula in a cell, it must be preceded by an equal (=) sign.

- Make sure you have only the **Computing** worksheet selected. (Click one of the other tabs, then click the **Computing** tab. Maximise this worksheet using the **Maximise** icon in the top right hand corner of the worksheet.)

- In cell G3, type *=B3+C3+D3+E3* and press **Enter**. (You can use upper or lower case letters.) The sum of the values in cells B3 to E3 is calculated and entered.

- There is a quicker way of summing a row or column. With cell G4 as the active cell, click the **AutoSum** button on the Standard toolbar. Excel suggests a range, which you can either accept or drag through a different range. In this case, you need to change the range to *B4:E4*, and then press **Enter**.

- To copy the formula to the cells below, simply drag the small square in the corner of the cell G4 down to cell G8. The formula is copied, and cell references automatically adjusted so that the sum of the correct row is calculated each time.

- In F3 we'll try another Excel function, **Average**. With the cursor in cell F3, type *=average(*

- Now drag across cells B3 to E3. In the formula bar, type a closing bracket to complete the formula and press **Enter**. The average of the cells is calculated. (You could of course type the whole formula instead of dragging across the cells you want to average, but this way is quicker and less error-prone.)

- Copy the formula down to the other rows by dragging the corner of the cell. You'll notice that some figures are shown as whole numbers, and some are shown to two decimal places. In the next chapter we'll discuss formatting.

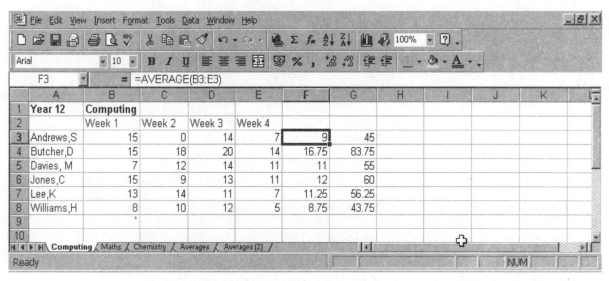

Figure1.9: Using the Average function

- We don't need the figures in column G, so select cells G3 to G8 and press the **Delete** key.
- Type a heading *Avg Mark* in cell F2.
- Save your spreadsheet.

Printing a worksheet

You don't really need to print this worksheet, but if you are going to, first type your name in cell F1 if you are using a network printer.

- Drag across cells A1 to F8 to select them, or select any occupied cell and press **Ctrl-Shift-*.**
- From the **File** menu select **Print Area, Set Print Area**. *(In Excel 5, use **Options, Set Print Area**.)*
- From the **File** menu, select **Print Preview**. This shows you what your worksheet will look like when printed. It is a good idea to do a Print Preview before you print to make sure it all fits on the page, and that you have correctly selected the print area.
- Click the **Zoom** button to have a closer look at the print preview.
- If you want to print, select **Print**. A dialogue box appears. By default you will print only the current worksheet. Leave this as the default.

Caution: Always check that the Preview Status Bar indicates the correct number of sheets, in this case **Page 1 of 1**, *before printing, otherwise you might inadvertently send dozens of pages to the printer by setting the wrong print area.*

- If you decide not to print, click **Close** to return to the worksheet.
- Select **File, Close** to close the worksheet, and click **Yes** when asked if you want to save changes.
- Bring the spreadsheet with you to the next session as you'll be working on it some more.

Chapter 2 – Editing and Formatting

Enhancing the appearance of a worksheet

In this chapter we'll be looking at ways of smartening up a worksheet. We'll also cover topics such as adding and deleting columns, and ways of copying formatting as well as data to other parts of a workbook.

You'll need the workbook **Marks.xls** which you created in Chapter 1. If you haven't got it with you, open a new workbook and name the first worksheet *Computing* by right-clicking the tab for Sheet1 and selecting **Rename**. Enter data as shown in Figure 2.1.

We'll only be using one worksheet in this chapter.

	A	B	C	D	E	F	G
1	**Year 12**	**Computing**					
2		Week 1	Week 2	Week 3	Week 4		
3	Andrews,S	15	0	14	7	9	
4	Butcher,D	15	18	20	14	16.75	
5	Davies,M	7	12	14	11	11	
6	Jones,C	15	9	13	11	12	
7	Lee,K	13	14	11	7	11.25	
8	Williams,H	8	10	12	5	8.75	
9							

*Figure 2.1: The **Computing** worksheet in the **Marks.xls** workbook*

Task 2.1: Improve and format the Computing worksheet

In this task you will work on the **Computing** worksheet shown in Figure 2.1 to make it look like Figure 2.2.

Page 1							Marks.xls
Computing							
	Week 1	Week 2	Week 3	Week 4	Week 5	Week 6	Week 7	Avg Mark
	04/01/99	11/01/99	18/01/99	25/01/99	01/02/99	08/02/99	15/02/99	
Andrews, S	15	0	14	7				9.0
Butcher,D	15	18	20	14				16.8
Davies,M	7	12	14	11				11.0
Jones,C	15	9	13	11				12.0
Lee,K	13	14	11	7				11.3
Williams,H	8	10	12	5				8.8

*Figure 2.2: The improved **Computing** worksheet*

Adding and deleting rows and columns

We'll start by inserting three rows at the top of the worksheet.

- Open the **Marks.xls** workbook and make sure that the **Computing** tab is selected. We will use just this worksheet to practise formatting techniques, but remember that if you want the changes to apply to every worksheet in the workbook, you can select all the worksheets before you start.

- Drag down across the row headers 1, 2 and 3.

- Click with the right mouse button and select **Insert**. Three rows will be inserted.

- Use a similar technique to add three columns to the left of the **Avg Mark** column. You'll soon find out which column headers you need to drag across – use the **Undo** button if the columns get inserted in the wrong place.

- Insert another row just above **Andrews, S**.

Deleting rows and columns is achieved in a similar way. You can also select **Insert, Row** or **Insert, Column** from the menu bar or **Edit, Delete** to delete rows and columns.

Copying series

You can perform different kinds of copying operations simply by dragging the corner square of a cell across one or more adjacent cells. Excel makes its own best guess at what you actually want to do. For example, if you use the left mouse button to drag the corner of the cell containing **Williams,H** down to the cell below it, the text Williams,H is copied to this cell. If you drag the corner of cell E5 (containing **Week 4**) across the next 3 adjacent cells, the cells are filled with **Week 5, Week 6** and **Week 7**. If you wanted them filled with **Week 4, Week 4, Week 4** you would need to drag with the right mouse button and select **Copy Cells**.

- Use the left mouse button to copy cell E5 to cells F5 to H5.

- Enter the date *04/01/99* in cell B6, just below Week 1. If your system has been correctly set up for British dates, this will be interpreted as January 4th. If it is set up for dates in American format, it will be interpreted as April 1st. You'll find out which it is in a minute.

- Use the left mouse button to copy cell B6 to cells C6 to H6 to continue the series.

- Your column widths may not be wide enough to accommodate the dates, so drag across the column headers of any columns containing ###### and double-click the border between any two column headers.

The date series has been inserted as consecutive days, whereas it is wanted in consecutive weeks. You have to enter dates in 2 adjacent cells to get the series started correctly.

- Delete the contents of cells C6 to H6.

- Enter the date *11/01/99* in cell C6.

- Now select both the cells B6 and C6, and drag the corner across D6 to H6. This time, the dates are inserted correctly, one week apart. Your worksheet should now appear as in Figure 2.3.

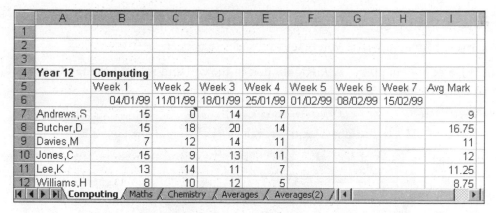

	A	B	C	D	E	F	G	H	I
1									
2									
3									
4	Year 12	Computing							
5		Week 1	Week 2	Week 3	Week 4	Week 5	Week 6	Week 7	Avg Mark
6		04/01/99	11/01/99	18/01/99	25/01/99	01/02/99	08/02/99	15/02/99	
7	Andrews,S	15	0	14	7				9
8	Butcher,D	15	18	20	14				16.75
9	Davies,M	7	12	14	11				11
10	Jones,C	15	9	13	11				12
11	Lee,K	13	14	11	7				11.25
12	Williams,H	8	10	12	5				8.75

Figure 2.3: Series of dates copied

Adjusting the system date settings

If your dates are being interpreted as April 1st instead of January 4th, this has to be altered in the Control Panel. You probably won't be able to do this on a network but you can do it on your home machine or get the network manager to correct the settings.

- Select **Start, Settings, Control Panel**.

- Choose **Regional Settings**. Click the **Regional Settings** tab and make sure **English (British)** is selected.

- Click the **Date** tab. A dialogue box appears as shown below.

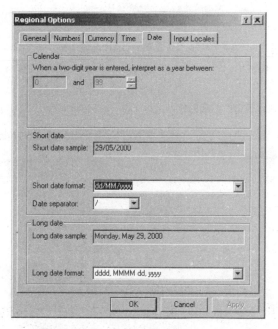

Figure 2.4: Altering the date settings

- Click **OK** and then **Apply** in the next window. You will have to restart your computer before any new settings take effect, so be sure and save your work before you restart.

Formatting dates

You can choose the format in which you want your dates to appear.

- Select Cell B6 containing 04/01/99. Right-click in the cell and select **Format Cells**. A dialogue box appears as shown below.

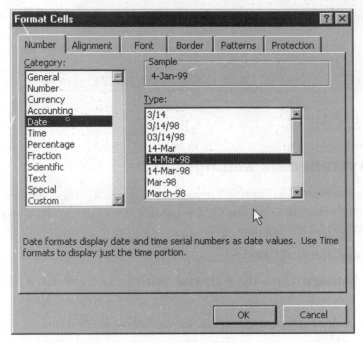

Figure 2.5: Formatting the date

- Click the **Number** tab and select **Date**. In the right hand list, select **14-Mar-98**, and click **OK**. *(In Excel 5, choose **dd-mmm-yy**.)*

Copying formats to other cells

You could have selected all the date cells and formatted them all together, but this way gives you a chance to see how to copy formats to other cells.

- Select the date cell you have just formatted, and drag its corner handle across the other dates with the right mouse button.

- Select **Fill Formats**.

Editing a formula

We've added extra columns since the formula for Average Mark was calculated. If you click in cell I7, you will see that the formula in the Formula bar reads **=Average(B7:E7).**

- Double-click in cell I7. The cells that are averaged are shown outlined in blue. *(Not in Excel 7.)*

- Drag the corner handle of cell E7 to extend the range to cell H7. Press **Enter**.

- Copy the amended formula to the cells below in the column by dragging the corner handle with the left mouse button.

Formatting numbers

The column containing averages looks a mess because some results come out as whole numbers and others are shown to 2 decimal places. All the cells in the column need to be formatted to one decimal place.

- Click the column header with the right mouse button and select **Format Cells**. The Format Cells dialogue box appears as in Figure 2.5. Make sure the **Number** tab is selected, and choose **Number** in the left-hand list.

- Enter **1** for the number of decimal places. Click **OK**.

(Alternatively click the **Increase/Decrease Decimal** buttons on the Formatting toolbar.)

Conditional formatting

(Excel 2000 and 97 only.) You can apply a format to a cell conditional on, say, the value being below a given number. For example, we will make marks appear in red if they are 8 or less.

- Select all the cells containing marks (B7 to H12).

- From the **Format** menu select **Conditional Formatting**. The Conditional Formatting dialogue box appears.

- Under **Condition 1**, make sure that **Cell Value** appears in the first drop-down list.

- In the second drop-down list box select **less than or equal to**.

- In the right hand box, type *8*.

The dialogue box should appear as shown below.

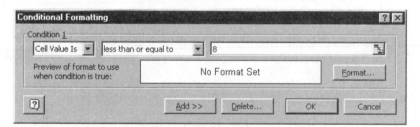

Figure 2.6: The Conditional Formatting dialogue box

- Click **Format**.

- In the Format Cells dialogue box, make sure that the **Font** tab is selected and in the **Color** list, select red. Click **OK**.

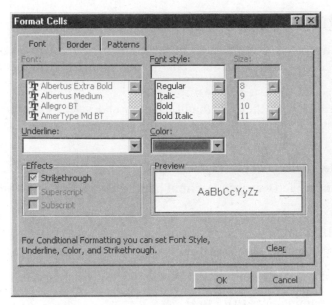

Figure 2.7: The Format Cells dialogue box

- Click **OK** in the Conditional Formatting dialogue box.

Formatting headings

There are many ways of smartening up a worksheet for example by centering headings, changing font size or using white text on a black background. You can also print column headings vertically or at an angle. All of these techniques are covered below.

- In cell A1 type the heading *Barchester College.*

- Select the text and use the Formatting toolbar droplists to make it 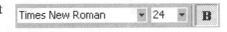 **Times New Roman, 24 point, Bold**.

- Drag across cells A1 to I1 to select them, and click the **Merge and Centre** button on the Formatting toolbar. *(Centre across Columns in Excel 7.)*

- Select cell A4 which contains the subheading **Year 12**. Drag its upper border to cell A2 to move it.

- You can use the **Format Painter** to copy a format from one cell to other cells. Click cell A1 containing the heading **Barchester College**, click the **Format Painter** tool and then click cell A2. The subheading **Year 12** will now take on the same formatting as **Barchester College.**

Note: To apply the same format to several non-adjacent cells, first select a cell whose format you want to copy. Then double-click the Format Painter, and click in each destination cell. Click the Format Painter again when you are finished.

- Using the same techniques, make the heading **Computing** 14 point Bold and centred across columns A-I.

- Drag the border between the row headers 4 and 5 down so that the row is twice the depth of the other rows.

- Right-click in cell A4, and select **Format Cells**. Click the **Alignment** tab, and the following window appears.

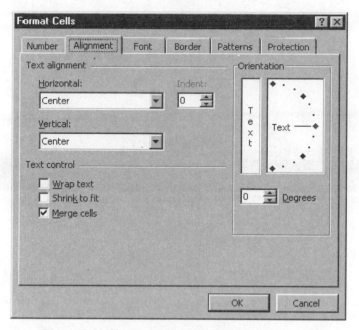

Figure 2.8: Changing the alignment of text in a cell

You'll notice that there are many different ways of aligning text in a cell. For the moment just select **Center** in the **Vertical** alignment list box. Click **OK**.

You can wrap text in a cell if you want narrower columns. For example, if you make column I narrower, part of the heading **Avg Mark** will not fit in the cell. Make the text occupy two rows as follows:

- Right-click the cell I5 and select **Format Cells**.

- Click the **Alignment** tab and click the **Wrap text** check box. In the **Horizontal** alignment list box, select **Right**. Click **OK**.

- Align all the cells in Row 5 to the right and make the row deeper.

Adding borders and colours

- Right-click in cell A4, and select **Format Cells**. Click the **Border** tab in the **Format Cells** window, which should still be open. *(In Excel 7, select cells A4 toI4 before right-clicking.)*

- Click the **Outline** border button, and select a suitable border from the list on the right.

- Now click the **Patterns** tab and select a suitable colour for the cell background.

You can also have white text on a black background. Select cells A5 to I5 and use the **Fill Colour** and **Font Colour** buttons to do this.

Your worksheet should now look like the one shown below:

	A	B	C	D	E	F	G	H	I
1	**Barchester College**								
2	**Year 12**								
3									
4	**Computing**								
5		Week 1	Week 2	Week 3	Week 4	Week 5	Week 6	Week 7	Avg Mark
6		04-Jan-99	11-Jan-99	18-Jan-99	25-Jan-99	01-Feb-99	08-Feb-99	15-Feb-99	
7	Andrews,S	15	0	14	7				9.0
8	Butcher,D	15	18	20	14				16.8
9	Davies,M	7	12	14	11				11.0
10	Jones,C	15	9	13	11				12.0
11	Lee,K	13	14	11	7				11.3
12	Williams,H	8	10	12	5				8.8
13									

Figure 2.9: The formatted worksheet

You can use the other worksheets in this workbook to try out some of the other alignment options: for example you can angle the headings *(or in Excel 7, make them vertical)*:

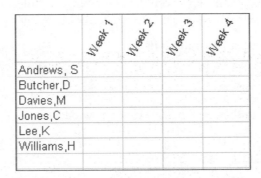

Figure 2.10: Another formatting option

Headers and footers

Headers and footers contain information that will appear on every page of a worksheet such as page number, current date, file name, author and so on. If you are used to using headers and footers in Word you will look in vain on the **View** menu for the **Header and Footer** option – it is under **File, Page Setup**.

- Select **File, Page Setup** and click the **Header/Footer** tab. The following window will appear.

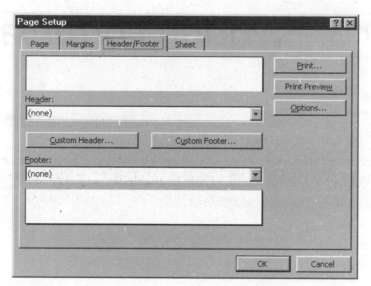

Figure 2.11: Inserting a header and footer

- Click in the **Header** list box and Excel suggests various options that it thinks you might like to have as your header. There are three tab positions, separated by commas.

- Select one of the options for the header – for example **Page1, Marks xls**.

- Select **Custom Footer** and type your own footer as in the figure below. Click **OK**, and **OK** in the next window.

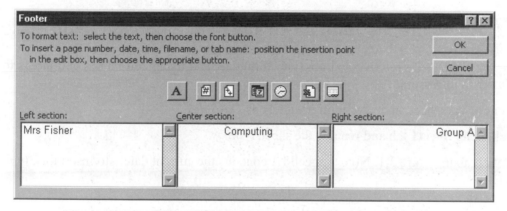

Figure 2.12: Entering a custom footer

Printing the worksheet

You will not see the header and footer in Normal view. Click the **Print Preview** tool to see how the page will appear. If all is well, select **File, Print** and accept the defaults.

Note that the top 3 rows in the worksheet do not print. That is because the Print Area is still as it was set earlier. You can reset this if you want the whole sheet to print.

- Save and close the worksheet.

Chapter 3 – Writing Formulae

Formula basics

The power of Excel lies largely in its ability to accept and manipulate various kinds of formula that refer to other cells either on the same or different worksheets.

There are various things you need to know straight away about writing formulae:

1. All formulae start with an = sign to identify them as a formula.

2. Formulae can contain the mathematical symbols

    +   Addition

    -      Subtraction

    *   Multiplication

    /   Division

    ^   Exponentiation (e.g. $7\char`^2 = 49$)

    ( )   Parentheses

3. Formulae can be entered into a spreadsheet either by typing the formula, or by using the mouse to 'point' at cells referred to in a formula.

In this chapter we'll use as an example of these techniques, a college shop that stocks (among other things) a small range of clothing emblazoned with the college logo. They stock T-shirts and sweatshirts each in 3 different sizes, Small, Medium and Large.

Task 3.1: Calculate the total day's sales for a college shop

In this task you'll be using relative and absolute formulae, and using cell names and labels to make the formulae easier to understand.

- Open a new worksheet, and save it immediately as *DaySales*.

- Right-click the **Sheet1** tab and rename the sheet *T-shirts*.

- Enter labels as in Figure 3.1. Note that cell E1 contains the current date – to insert this, type *=Today()* in cell E1.

	A	B	C	D	E	F
1	Sales of T-Shirts				06/10/98	
2						
3		Price	Qty	Value		
4	Small					
5	Medium					
6	Large					
7						
8	TOTAL					
9						

Figure 3.1: Beginning the DaySales worksheet

- Use buttons in the Formatting toolbar to make all the labels bold, right-align column headers in columns B to D, merge and centre cells A1 to D1, change the font and font size of the headings. You should end up with headings more like those shown in Figure 3.2.

- Enter Sales prices of *8, 8.5* and *9*.

- Enter quantities of *7, 10* and *2*.

- Format the currency amounts by selecting cells B4 to B6 and D4 to D8, and clicking the **Currency** tool.

- The worksheet should look something like Figure 3.2. (The font used in the heading is **Avant Garde Bk BT** but you can substitute anything suitable.)

	A	B	C	D	E	F
1	Sales of T-Shirts			06/10/98		
2						
3		Price	Qty	Value		
4	Small	£ 8.00	7			
5	Medium	£ 8.50	10			
6	Large	£ 9.00	2			
7						
8	TOTAL					
9						

Figure 3.2: Formatted headings in DaySales

Entering formulae

- Enter the formula for **Value** in cell D4 by clicking in the cell and typing the formula *=B4*C4*. Press Enter.

- Try the 'pointing' method of entering formulae. In cell D5, type = and then click the mouse in cell B5. Type * and click in cell C5. Press **Enter**.

- Instead of pressing the **Enter** key on the keyboard you can click the **Enter** button, which is the second button in a little threesome **Cancel, Enter** and **Edit Formula**. *(In Excel 7, the third button is f_x the **Function Wizard**.)*

- Drag the corner handle of cell D5 down to cell D6 to copy it.

- Select cell D8 and click the **AutoSum** button. Excel guesses (in this case correctly) which cells you want to sum, so click the **Enter** button or click **AutoSum** again.

Using labels and editing formulae

The formulae in column D are not particularly easy to read. It would be preferable to use formulae such as **=Price*Qty** instead of **=B4*C4**. When you have labels at the head of a column, Excel automatically recognises these as labels when you use them in formulae (however, check on **Tools** menu, **Options**, **Calculation** tab, that the **Accept Labels in Formulas** box is checked)

*(In Excel 7, you must define the cell names. Select B3:D6, **Insert, Name, Create, TopRow**.)*

- Double-click in cell D4 to edit it. Notice that Excel indicates which cells are involved in the formula by colour-coding and outlining the relevant cells.

- Double-click **B4** in the formula. Type *Price*.

- Double-click C4 in the formula, and type *Qty*. Click the **Enter** button or press **Enter**.

- Double-click the corner handle of the cell. This formula is copied automatically to cells D5 and D6.

- Double-click the total in cell D8. Edit this cell so that it reads *=Sum(Value)* and press **Enter**.

Naming individual cells

As well as using cell references or labels to identify cells, you can give a name to any cell. We'll name cell D8 *Total*.

- Click in cell D8 to select it.

- Click in the Name box (see below) and type the name *Total*. Press **Enter**.

You can now use the name **Total** to refer to this cell instead of its cell reference D8. Note however that this is an *absolute*, not a *relative*, cell reference. This point is discussed further later in the chapter.

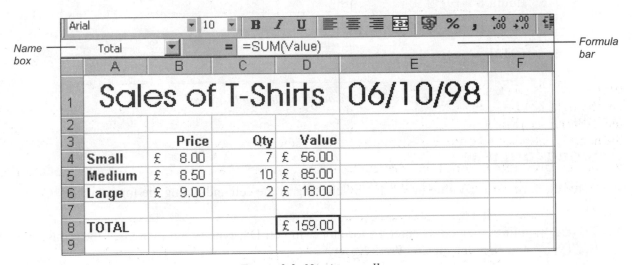

Figure 3.3: Naming a cell

Using names on different sheets

When you define a name, it becomes global to the workbook. This means that if you create a name in one worksheet, you can still refer to it in another worksheet. Try this by moving to **Sheet2** and typing *=Total* in cell A1. The figure **159** appears.

Creating duplicate names in a workbook

If you copy a worksheet, Excel will create special versions of the name that are specific to the new worksheet.

- Create a clone of the **T-Shirts** worksheet by holding down the Ctrl key as you drag the sheet tab to the right over **Sheet2**. Right-click the new tab and rename it **Sweatshirts**.

- Edit the heading to **Sales of Sweatshirts**. It may not fit in the cell – if not, move the date to the next cell and merge and centre the new heading over an extra cell.

- Click in cell D4 of the new worksheet. You will see that the formula still appears as **Price*Qty**.

- Click in the Total cell, D8. This is still named **Total**.

The names in this sheet are *local* rather than *global* names. To see the full name of the cell, click **Insert** on the menu bar, then select **Name**, then **Define**. The following window appears:

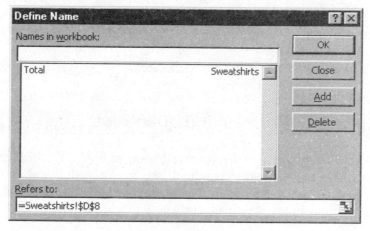

Figure 3.4:Local name

*(In Excel 7, the name appears as **Sweatshirts!Total**.)*

On the right hand side the worksheet name **Sweatshirts** appears. Click **Close**, and try the same thing in the **T-Shirts** worksheet. No worksheet name will appear on the right, because this is the worksheet where the name was first created and it is therefore a global rather than a local name.

- In the **Sweatshirts** worksheet, change the figures for **Price** and **Qty** as shown in Figure 3.5. The formulae for **Value** and **Total** adjust automatically.

	A	B	C	D	E	F
1	Sales of Sweatshirts					06/10/98
2						
3		Price	Qty	Value		
4	Small	£ 12.00	6	£ 72.00		
5	Medium	£ 13.00	4	£ 52.00		
6	Large	£ 14.00	8	£ 112.00		
7						
8	TOTAL			£ 236.00		
9						

Figure 3.5: The cloned worksheet

Writing formulae which refer to other sheets

In cell A1 of **Sheet2**, we will write a formula which adds together the totals in the other two sheets.

- Click the **Sheet2** tab. Delete the value in A1 if you have not already done so.

- In cell A1, type =

- Click the tab for the **T-shirts** worksheet and click in cell D8.

- In the formula bar (see Figure 3.3), type a + sign.

- Click the **Sweatshirts** worksheet tab and click in cell D8. Press **Enter**.

- The figure **395** appears. In the formula bar you will see the formula **=Total + Sweatshirts!Total**.

The first argument reads **Total** and not **T-Shirts!Total** because it is a global name, whereas the second argument is local to the **Sweatshirts** worksheet.

*(In Excel 7, the formula will appear as **T-Shirts!D8 + Sweatshirts!D8** even though you have named these cells.)*

That concludes this exercise so save and close this worksheet.

Task 3.2: Create a list of prices and quantities

In this task you will be exploring many of the advanced features of Excel which can be used in creating and analysing formulae. The task involves creating a list, for budgeting and comparison purposes, of various alternative prices and sales quantities for a new proposed line of jackets which the college hopes to include in its new Autumn range. The manager wants to get an idea of possible sales income for various different scenarios.

Creating row and column headings consisting of static values

- Open a new workbook and save it as *Jackets*.

- In cell A1 type a heading *Budget figures for Jackets*.

- Enter *Price1* in cell C3 and drag its handle across the next 3 columns to copy it.

- Enter *Qty1* in cell A5 and drag its handle down the next 4 rows to copy it.

- Enter *£20* in cell C4 and *£22* in cell D4. Select these two cells and drag the corner handle across to cell F4.

- Enter *10* in B5, *20* in B6 and copy these cells down to B9.

- Right justify the Price headings, embolden the row and column headings and colour the text maroon to distinguish it from the entries in the table. Your worksheet should look like the figure below.

	A	B	C	D	E	F	G
1	Budget figures for Jackets						
2							
3			Price1	Price2	Price3	Price4	
4			£20	£22	£24	£26	
5	Qty1	10					
6	Qty2	20					
7	Qty3	30					
8	Qty4	40					
9	Qty5	50					
10							

Figure 3.6: A range of prices and quantities is entered first

The numbers that you have entered and copied are static – in other words, if you change the value in say, cell C4, the other values in the row will not automatically change. Try it, and then undo your change.

Using relative addresses

To create a list that changes automatically when the first value is changed, all the values except the first must be replaced by formulae.

- Double-click cell D4 and change it to =*C4 | 2*. Press **Enter**.

- Copy this formula along the row.

- Similarly, edit B6 to read =*B5+10* and copy it down the column.

- Now try changing the values in C4 and B5. As soon as you press **Enter**, the other values in the row or column change automatically. Undo your changes after you have experimented.

Using absolute addresses

The worksheet can be made even more flexible by allowing the user to enter different increments for both the quantity and the price.

- In the block of cells H3-I4, enter labels and values as shown in the figure below.

- Format the worksheet as shown. (Word-wrap has been applied to cells H3 and I3 using **Format, Cells, Alignment, Wrap text**, and a border put round the block of 4 cells to separate it from the list.) Cells A1 to F1 have been merged and the text centred using the **Merge and Center** button on the Formatting toolbar. (Other cells have had column widths adjusted using **Format**, **Column**, **Autofit Selection**.)

- Format cells C5:F9 as currency.

	A	B	C	D	E	F	G	H	I	J
1			Budget figures for Jackets							
2										
3			Price1	Price2	Price3	Price4		Quantity Increment	Price Increment	
4			£20	£22	£24	£26		5	3	
5	Qty1	10								
6	Qty2	20								
7	Qty3	30								
8	Qty4	40								
9	Qty5	50								
10										

Figure 3.7: Setting up variable quantity and price increments

- In cell D4, instead of the formula **=C4+2**, you need **=C4+I4**. Edit it to make this change now. Price2 changes to £23.

- Drag the corner handle to copy the cell to E4 and F4. Oh dear! They also read £23.

This is because Excel by default uses relative addressing, so the formula in cell E4 reads **=D4+J4**, and of course J4 is empty. I4 has to be made into an *absolute* address, i.e. one that will not change whenever it is copied to another cell.

You have already seen one way of doing this – actually a very good way. You could name cell I4 **Price_Increment**, and use this name in the formula.

- Select cell I4.

- From the **Insert** menu select **Name**, **Define**. Excel uses the label above the cell as the name, replacing the space with an underscore.

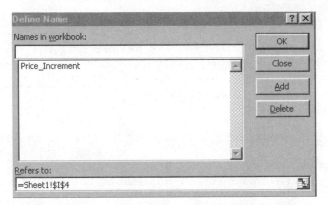

Figure 3.8: Assigning an absolute name to a cell

Note that the box at the bottom of the window tells you that the name refers to **Sheet1!$I$4**. The $ signs in front of the column and row names tell you that this is an *absolute* cell reference.

- Click **OK** to accept the name.

- Name cell H4 **Quantity_Increment** in a similar way.

- Note that when you select cell H4, the new cell name appears in the name box.

- Now edit the formula in cell D4 to read *=C4+Price_Increment* and copy it across the row. The prices should now increment correctly.

- Edit cell B6 to read *=B5+Quantity_Increment*. (You can do this quickly by double-clicking cell B6, double-clicking **10** in the formula to select it, and then clicking in H4, the cell named **Quantity_Increment**. Then press **Enter**.)

- Copy the formula to the other rows in column B.

- Save your worksheet!

Using mixed references in a formula

The next stage is to fill in the table.

- First of all, change the Quantity and Price increments back to 10 and 2 respectively. This will make the test results easier to calculate manually to verify that we are getting the right answers!

- In cell C5, enter the formula **=B5*C4** to get the sales value for 10 jackets at £20 each.

- You can probably already see that copying this formula to the rest of the row is not going to give the correct result, but do it anyway. You'll get something like Figure 3.9; the formula in D5, for example reads **=C5*D4** which is not what we want. We want **B5*D4**. In other words, the B5 needs to be an absolute reference and D4 a relative reference.

- Double-click cell C5, double-click **B5** in this cell and then press the function key F4. This turns **B5** into an absolute reference, **$B$5**. Press **Enter**.

- Copy the cell across the row.

D5				=	=C5*D4					
	A	B	C	D	E	F	G	H	I	J
1			Budget figures for Jackets							
2										
3			Price1	Price2	Price3	Price4		Quantity Increment	Price Increment	
4			£20	£22	£24	£26		10	2	
5	Qty1	10	£200	£4,400	######	######				
6	Qty2	20								
7	Qty3	30								
8	Qty4	40								
9	Qty5	50								
10										

Figure 3.9: Problems with relative references

- Copy C5 down the column. More problems!

- You need a mixture of absolute and relative references. The formula you need in cell C5 is shown in the formula bar of Figure 3.10. See if you can work out why!

C5				=	=$B5*C$4					
	A	B	C	D	E	F	G	H	I	J
1			Budget figures for Jackets							
2										
3			Price1	Price2	Price3	Price4		Quantity Increment	Price Increment	
4			£20	£22	£24	£26		10	2	
5	Qty1	10	£200	£220	£240	£260				
6	Qty2	20	£400	£440	£480	£520				
7	Qty3	30	£600	£660	£720	£780				
8	Qty4	40	£800	£880	£960	£1,040				
9	Qty5	50	£1,000	£1,100	£1,200	£1,300				
10										

Figure 3.10

Note that $B5 and C$4 are mixed addresses. $B means 'stay in column B' while 5 is not absolute so means 'the current row' in this situation. We are always looking for the quantities in column B and the prices in row 4 so these need to be absolute.

- To edit the formula in C5 (currently **$B$5*C4**), double-click it and then double-click **$B$5**. Each time you press F4, the dollar signs toggle on or off on either the row or column reference. Change the reference to **C4** in this formula in a similar way to *C$4*.

Alternatively, you can simply edit the $ signs instead of pressing F4.

- Copy the contents of cell C5 by first dragging the corner handle across the columns (to F5), then clicking it again and dragging it down across all the rows.

Checking your formulae

- Double-click various cells in the grid. As you click each cell, one Range Finder box is always in the Quantity column and the other is always in the Price row. *(Excel 7 does not have Range Finder.)*

- Now introduce a couple of inconsistencies just to see the effect. In cell D7 edit the formula to read *=$B7*22* and press **Enter**.

- Now double-click the formula. The Range Finder only highlights the Quantity column.

3			Price1	Price2	Price3	Price4	
4			£20	£22	£24	£26	
5	Qty1	10	£200	£220	£240	£260	
6	Qty2	20	£400	£440	£480	£520	
7	Qty3	30	£600	=$B7*22		£780	
8	Qty4	40	£800	£880	£960	£1,040	
9	Qty5	50	£1,000	£1,100	£1,200	£1,300	

Figure 3.11: The Range Finder

- In cell F9 enter *£1300* instead of the formula. Everything looks fine but if you change the Quantity or Price increments, you will get wrong results in the cells you have just changed. It would be very difficult to detect these errors without carefully examining every cell. Luckily, Excel provides the means for the job in the form of tools on the Auditing toolbar.

The Auditing toolbar

The Auditing toolbar is not on the shortlist of toolbars that appears when you right-click a toolbar. You have to use the Customize dialogue box to turn it on. *(In Excel 7 select it from the toolbar list.)*

- Right-click a toolbar and select **Customize**. The following window appears.

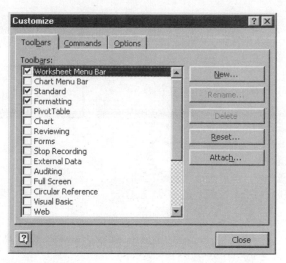

Figure 3.12: The Customize Toolbars window

- Check the **Auditing** option and then click **Close**. The Auditing toolbar appears:

Figure 3.13: The Auditing Toolbar

An important tool on this toolbar is the **Trace Dependents** button, which shows all the cells which use a value from a selected cell.

- Click cell B5 to select it.

- Click the **Trace Dependents** button on the **Auditing** toolbar.

- Arrows show which cells are dependent on the active cell, as shown in the figure below.

	A	B	C	D	E	F	G	H	I	J
1			Budget figures for Jackets							
2										
3			Price1	Price2	Price3	Price4		Quantity Increment	Price Increment	
4			£20	£22	£24	£26		10	2	
5	Qty1	10	£200	£220	£240	£260				
6	Qty2	20	£400	£440	£480	£520				
7	Qty3	30	£600	£660	£720	£780				

Figure 3.14: Using the Trace Dependents tool

- Click the **Trace Dependents** button several times more until you reach the last row and nothing more happens when you click it again. You will see all the cells that depend on Cell B5.

	A	B	C	D	E	F	G	H	I	J
1			Budget figures for Jackets							
2										
3			Price1	Price2	Price3	Price4		Quantity Increment	Price Increment	
4			£20	£22	£24	£26		10	2	
5	Qty1	10	£200	£220	£240	£260				
6	Qty2	20	£400	£440	£400	£520				
7	Qty3	30	£600	£660	£720	£780				
8	Qty4	40	£800	£800	£960	£1,040				
9	Qty5	50	£1,000	£1,100	£1,200	£1,300				
10										

Figure 3.15: Showing cells which depend on B5

Notice that cell F9 does not depend on B5. You also made a change in another cell, which doesn't show up this time.

- Click the **Remove All Arrows** button.

- Select cell C4 and repeat the exercise. You will see two cells which are different from the others.

- Remove the arrows. Try selecting cell H4 and tracing its dependents!

Detecting whether cells contain values or formulae

You can use another useful tool, the **Go To** option, to help analyse your worksheet.

- Select any cell in the worksheet.

- Press **Ctrl-G** or select **Go To** from the **Edit** menu, and in the dialogue box click the **Special...** button.

- In the next dialogue box select the **Constants** option, as shown in the figure below. Click **OK**.

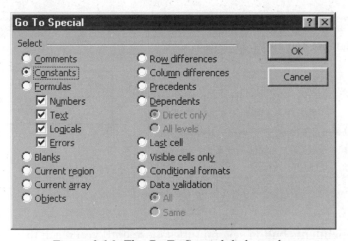

Figure 3.16: The Go To Special dialogue box

All the cells containing labels and constants, rather than formulae, are selected.

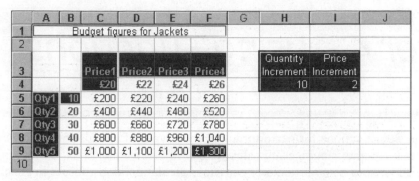

Figure 3.17: Labels and constants selected

That completes this exercise. You have had a glimpse of the power of Excel – try some more of the options yourself.

Chapter 4 – Using Functions

Introduction

Excel has well over 200 functions for performing different types of calculations from summing a column of figures to the most complex engineering calculations. In this chapter we'll be looking at just a few of them – but when you need to do a particularly complex calculation, don't forget to check whether there is a ready-made function available to do the job for you!

Task 4.1: Use functions to enhance the Marks workbook

In this task you will be enhancing the original **Chemistry** worksheet to provide additional information on each student's average mark, the number of assignments they have handed in, their overall grade (A-E, N, U) and whether they need to have a note sent to their personal tutor informing them of problems. You will be creating test data automatically using a random number generator instead of typing in each individual mark.

You will be trying out the following functions:

RAND	Calculates a random number
TRUNC	Truncates a number to an integer by removing the decimal part of the number
ROUND	Rounds a number to a specified number of decimal places
COUNT	Counts the number of values in a range
SUM	Sums the values in a range
VLOOKUP	Calculates a value based on another value in a Lookup table
IF	If..Then..Else

Setting up the Chemistry worksheet

- Load up the **Marks** workbook and save it as *Marks4* using the **File, Save As** command.

- Click the **Chemistry** tab and make sure your worksheet looks like the one shown in Figure 4.1. If you haven't got this workbook or worksheet handy, open a new workbook, name the first sheet *Chemistry* and enter data as shown.

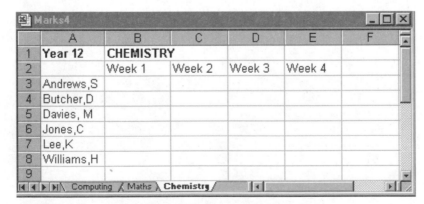

Figure 4.1: The Chemistry worksheet

The Chemistry teacher sets assignments every week but the maximum mark available varies – sometimes the assignment may be out of 20, other times out of 50, for example. We need an extra row to specify the maximum marks available.

- Right-click the Row3 header and click **Insert** to insert a new row.

- In cell A3 type the label *MaxMark*.

- Add extra columns and data to the worksheet and format it so that it looks like Figure 4.2.

*Note: Drag the handle in cell E2 over rows F and G to extend the Weeks to Week 6. Use **Format, Cells, Alignment, Wrap text** to word-wrap headings in columns H to L. Embolden the row and column headings. Use the **Borders** tool to put a border at the top and bottom of A3 to L3. You can adjust column widths manually or by double-clicking between column headers.)*

- Select cells A3 to G3 and from the **Insert** menu select **Name, Create**. Check **Left Column** in the dialogue box, and make sure no other box is checked. Naming cells in this way by using labels means that you can refer to any of the cells B3 to G3 as **MaxMark**. In cell B3 **MaxMark** has the value 20; in cell C3, **MaxMark** has the value 15, and so on.

	A	B	C	D	E	F	G	H	I	J	K	L
1	Year 12	CHEMISTRY										
2		Week 1	Week 2	Week 3	Week 4	Week 5	Week 6	No of Assignments handed in	Total Mark	Percent	Grade	Note to Tutor
3	MaxMark	20	15	20	50	10	20					
4	Andrews,S											
5	Butcher,D											
6	Davies,M											
7	Jones,C											
8	Lee,K											
9	Williams,H											
10												

Figure 4.2

Generating random numbers as test data

Generating test data to test all the formulae and functions in a worksheet can be time-consuming and tedious, but you can shorten this process considerably by using a random number generator.

- Select cell B4. Click the **Edit Formula** button (the = sign on the Formula bar) and the Formula Palette appears as shown in Figure 4.3. The name box changes to a list of common functions.

(In Excel 7, type an = sign or double-click in cell B4 and click the Function Wizard button (fₓ) near the formula bar. You will find the method of choosing a function slightly different from Excel 97 but easy to follow!)

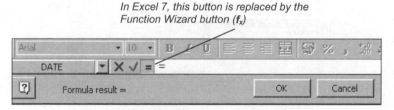

Figure 4.3: The Formula Palette

- Click the down arrow next to **Date** (or whatever function name is displayed) to see a list of functions.

- Click **More Functions...**

- The **Paste Function** window appears. Click **All** in the left-hand list box, and scroll down to find **RAND** in the right-hand list box.

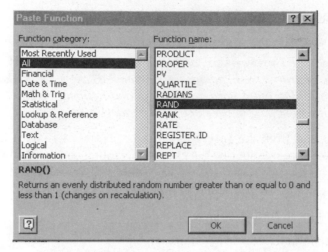

Figure 4.4: The Paste Function dialogue box

- This function returns a random number greater than or equal 0 and less than 1 – not exactly what we want but it's a start. Click **OK**. *(Click* **Finish** *in Excel 7.)*

- We want a random number between 0 and **MaxMark**. In the formula bar, type **(MaxMark+1)* and click **OK**.

- This produces a random number to several decimal places, between about 0.0001 and 20.9999. All we need to do now is to truncate the number so that only the integer part is used and we have what we want – a random number between 0 and 20.

- Double-click the formula in cell B4 to edit it.

- Leave the = sign and highlight the rest of the formula. Copy it to the clipboard using **Edit, Cut**.

- Click the down arrow next to the function name in the **Name** box again, selecting **More Functions**.

- This time select **Math & Trig** in the left-hand list and **TRUNC** on the right.

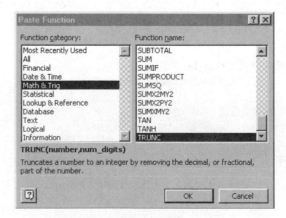

Figure 4.5: The TRUNC function

- Click **OK**. A new dialogue box appears asking you to enter the arguments for the **TRUNC** function. In the **Number** box, click **Edit, Paste** to paste the formula you just cut.

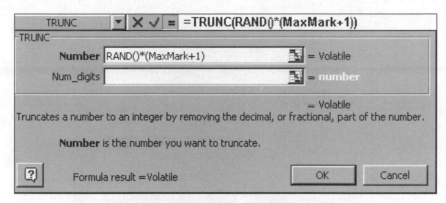

Figure 4.6: Entering arguments for the TRUNC function

- Leave the second box for **Num_digits** blank and click **OK**.

- This gives you a whole number between 1 and 20.

- Drag the handle of cell B4 down to cell B9. A column of random numbers appears.

2		Week 1	Week 2
3	**MaxMark**	20	15
4	Andrews, S	11	
5	Butcher,D	5	
6	Davies,M	12	
7	Jones,C	5	
8	Lee,K	14	
9	Williams,H	4	
10			

Figure 4.7. Random numbers between 0 and 20

- Copy this column across to the columns for Weeks 2 to 6 to generate test data for these weeks.

- Do you notice the marks keep changing every time you do something to the formula in the cell? (Try double-clicking in cell B4 and then pressing **Enter**.) This could be very inconvenient if you want to give test data and expected results in your project! Every time you close the workbook and reopen it you will have a different set of marks.

Converting formulae to values

Having got a satisfactory set of test data, you can convert all the formulae to values. Before you do this, it would be a good idea to make a copy of your worksheet so that if later you want to add more students to it, you will have a copy of the formula in the extra worksheet and won't have to work it all out again. Also, you may need it for documentation purposes.

- Click the **Chemistry** worksheet tab, and hold down Ctrl while you drag the tab to the right. Right-click the new tab **Chemistry(2)** and rename it **Chemistry(Formulae)**.

- Click the **Chemistry** worksheet tab again to return to your original worksheet.

- Select cells B4 to G9 containing all the marks, and click the **Copy** button. Then right-click cell B4 and click **Paste Special**. In the dialogue box select the **Values** option as shown below.

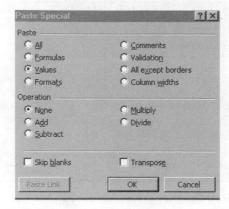

Figure 4.8: Converting formulae to values

- Click **OK**, and press **Esc** to end the operation.

Click in any cell now and you will see that the formulae have been replaced by values.

Counting the number of values in a range

Before you do this, amend your test data by deleting the contents of various cells so that some students don't have a mark for every assignment. Have at least one student who has handed in all assignments, and one student who has missed 3 assignments. (Leave these cells completely blank.)

To count the number of assignments:

- Click in cell H3. In the formula bar, type =*Count(MaxMark)* and press **Enter**.

- Copy the formula to cells H4 to H9. You'll probably get unwanted borders – leave them for now, and we'll remove them shortly.

You will see that the result is 6 in every row, even if some students have not handed in every assignment. Examine the formula in each row and you will see that in every case it is **=Count(MaxMark)**, and that is where the error lies. We'll cure that in a minute!

Naming cells is an excellent practice but it is not always straightforward. Some guidelines are given below.

Naming cells and ranges

There are several ways of assigning a name to a cell or a range of cells.

Method 1: Typing the name in the Name **box**

Select the cell or range, and type the name in the **Name** box to the left of the Formula bar. You must press **Enter** for the name to register.

- Try this now by naming cell I3. Select cell I3, type *TotalPossible* in the **Name** box and press **Enter**. This creates an *absolute* cell reference.

Method 2: Using existing labels as names

Select the range you want to name, including the row or column labels and from the **Insert** menu select **Name, Create**. In the **Create names in** box, designate the location that contains the labels by selecting the **Top row**, **Left column**, **Bottom row**, or **Right column** check box.

This method is useful for quickly assigning names to a number of cells without having to name each cell individually.

Note that the name created by using this procedure refers only to the cells that contain values and does not include the existing row and column labels. Spaces in labels are replaced with underscores.

- Try this now by selecting the range H2 to L9 and selecting **Insert, Name, Create, Top Row**. Cells in column H, for example, will be given the name **No_Of_Assignments_Handed_In**.

Method 3: Using Insert, Name, Define

Select the range you want to name and from the **Insert** menu select **Name, Define**. Type the name in the dialogue box and click **OK**. You can use this menu option to check what cell names you have already allocated to various cells. It is also particularly useful when you want to change the existing definition of a name.

For example, when you used **MaxMark** in the formula for counting the number of assignments each student has handed in, it didn't work when you copied it down the column because **MaxMark** always referred to the top row. We can cure this by making the name into a *relative* reference.

- Select cells B3:G3.

- From the **Insert** menu select **Name, Define**.

- Select the name **MaxMark** from the list of names. The **Refers To** box at the bottom of the dialogue box contains **=Chemistry!$B$3:$G$3**.

- Edit the reference so that it reads *Chemistry!$B3:$G3* (see Figure 4.9). You can click in the **Refers to** box and use the F4 key, or simply type the corrections.

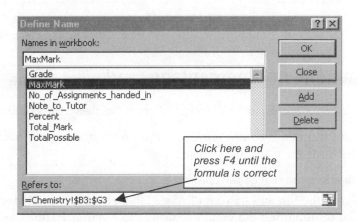

Figure 4.9: Creating a relative reference

You've now created a name that is relative to the particular row that is being referred to, while keeping the column references absolute.

- Click **OK**.

You should now find that the formula for counting the number of assignments handed in gives the correct result!

Method 4: Use automatic naming

Excel 2000 and 97 will automatically name cells for you using row or column labels (however, check on **Tools** menu, **Options**, **Calculation** tab, that the **Accept Labels in Formulas** box is checked). For example try the following:

- In cell B14, type *=Williams,H* and press **Enter**. Williams' mark appears. Copy this cell to cells C14 to G14. All Williams' marks appear. (You can delete this row after the experiment!)

If you don't want to use these default names, you can of course name the cells yourself using one of the other methods. *(Excel 7 does not support automatic naming.)*

Rules for valid names

Given below is a list of the rules for names reproduced from Excel's Help system.

Guidelines for naming cells, formulas, and constants in Microsoft Excel

What characters are allowed?   The first character of a name must be a letter or an underscore character. Remaining characters in the name can be letters, numbers, periods, and underscore characters.

Can names be cell references?   Names cannot be the same as a cell reference, such as Z$100 or R1C1.

Can more than one word be used?   Yes, but spaces are not allowed. Underscore characters and periods may be used as word separators — for example, Sales_Tax or First.Quarter.

How many characters?   A name can contain up to 255 characters.

Note   If a name defined for a range contains more than 253 characters, you cannot select it from the **Name** box.

Are names case sensitive?   Names can contain uppercase and lowercase letters. Microsoft Excel does not distinguish between uppercase and lowercase characters in names. For example, if you have created the name Sales and then create another name called SALES in the same workbook, the second name will replace the first one.

Figure 4.10: Rules for naming cells

Calculating the total and percentage marks

- In cell I3, type the formula *=Sum(MaxMark)* and copy this down the column.

- In cell J3, type the formula *=Total_Mark/TotalPossible%* and press **Enter**. Note that typing the % sign automatically turns the result into a percentage.

- Copy the formula down the rest of the column.

If you've got a border at the top and bottom of row 3, this gets copied too, and you don't want it. There are two quick ways of reformatting the columns: using the **Format Painter** or selecting the range G4 to G9, dragging the corner handle across the next two columns using the right mouse button and selecting **Fill Formats** from the shortcut menu. Try each of these methods as follows:

- Try the **Fill Formats** method and then click **Undo**. Now for the second method: select cell G4 and then click the **Format Painter** button. Then select cells H4 to J9 to make these cells adopt the formatting of G4.

- Format the numbers in column J to zero decimal places.

	A	B	C	D	E	F	G	H	I	J	K	L
1	Year 12	CHEMISTRY										
2		Week 1	Week 2	Week 3	Week 4	Week 5	Week 6	No of Assignments handed in	Total Mark	Percent	Grade	Note to Tutor
3	MaxMark	20	15	20	50	10	20	6	135	100		
4	Andrews,S	15		3	23	6	15	5	62	46		
5	Butcher,D	4	3	17			13	4	37	27		
6	Davles,M	9		18	26	1	6	5	60	44		
7	Jones,C	6			13		3	3	22	16		
8	Lee,K	15	13	12	39	8	7	6	94	70		
9	Williams,H	14	12	18	50	8	14	6	116	86		
10												

Figure 4.11: Percent is calculated from a mixture of absolute and relative cell references

Creating a Lookup table

The next step is to create a table of grades that Excel can look up to insert the correct grade in column K based on the percent obtained.

- In cell P2, type the heading *Grade Lookup Table*. Make it bold and centre it across P2 and Q2.

- Enter the figures as shown in Figure 4.12. This is a *range lookup*, and to find the correct grade, Excel looks first at the value in the first row and asks "Is the percentage grade greater than or equal to 0?" It is, so it moves down a row and asks "Is the percentage grade greater than or equal to 35?" If it is not, (suppose it is equal to 34), then Excel backs up one row and assigns the grade U.

In other words, according to this table, 0-34 = U

35-39 = N

40-46 = E

… and so on to 70-100 = A

Grade Lookup Table	
0	U
36	N
40	E
47	D
55	C
63	B
70	A

Figure 4.12: Grades table

- Select a cell inside the table and press **Ctrl-Shift-*** to select the entire table. Click in the **Name** box and name the table *Grade_Lookup_Table*. Press **Enter**.

Naming a Lookup table has several benefits – it makes the Lookup formula easier to read, it simplifies referring to the table as an absolute reference, it allows you to easily move the table to a different worksheet and it eliminates the need to change formulae if you change the size of the lookup table.

Using the Lookup table

Excel has a useful function called **Vlookup** which enables you to look up values from a table.

- Select cell K4 and click the **Edit Formula** button (the = sign). *(In Excel 7 type = in the formula bar and click the **Function Wizard** button f_x).*

- Click the arrow next to the list of functions and select **More Functions**.

- In the **Function** category select **Lookup & Reference**, and in the **Function name** list select **VLOOKUP**. Click **OK**.

The VLOOKUP dialogue box appears as shown below. It has three required arguments and one optional argument.

Read the explanatory text in the dialogue box, and note particularly that the table must be sorted in ascending order. VLOOKUP will not work on an unsorted table.

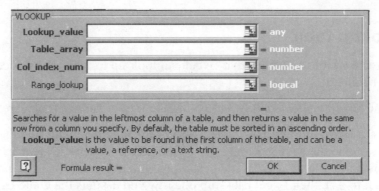

Figure 4.13: The VLOOKUP dialogue box

- In the **Lookup_value** box, type *Percent*, the label at the top of the column containing the value you want to look up.

- In the **Table-array** box, type *Grade_Lookup_Table*.

- In the **Col_index_num** box, type *2*, the number of the column that contains the grades.

- Click **OK**.

- Copy the formula down the column, get rid of any unwanted borders and make the grades bold type.

Creating effective test data

The most likely places to get things wrong are the boundaries between grades. Therefore you should adjust the marks in your test data so that at least two of them are on the boundaries, e.g. exactly 46% or exactly 35%, and also make sure that at least one grade is in the U and A grade ranges. Then you should check the results carefully to make sure that they are what you expected.

If for example you arrange for Andrews' total mark to equal 63, his percentage mark will appear as 47. However, it is held internally as 46.7 – less than the mark required for a D, so his grade appears as E. How will you cure this?

One way is to edit the formula for **Percent** in column J to read *=ROUND(Total_Mark/TotalPossible%,0)*. This rounds the percentage to a whole number.

A typical set of reasonable test data is shown below.

	A	B	C	D	E	F	G	H	I	J	K	L
1	Year 12	CHEMISTRY										
2		Week 1	Week 2	Week 3	Week 4	Week 5	Week 6	No of Assignments handed in	Total Mark	Percent	Grade	Note to Tutor
3	MaxMark	20	15	20	50	10	20	6	135	100		
4	Andrews,S	15		3	23	6	15	5	62	46	E	
5	Butcher,D	4	3	17			13	4	37	27	U	
6	Davies,M	9		18	26	1	6	5	60	44	E	
7	Jones,C	6			13		3	3	22	16	U	
8	Lee,K	15	13	12	39	8	7	6	94	70	A	
9	Williams,H	14	12	18	50	8	14	6	116	86	A	
10												

Figure 4.14: Testing the Vlookup function

You might also consider, for example, how you are going to test whether your random number formula is correct. Are you sure that all numbers between 0 and **MaxMark** can be generated? One way to test it would be to use a spare part of the worksheet and copy the formula for generating a random number between 0 and 20 to say, two or three hundred cells. If you never get 0 or 20 you should look at it again!

The IF function

The IF conditional function is used to put a value in a cell depending on the value in some other cell. In this example we'll use it to put an asterisk in column L if the student has completed only 4 or fewer assignments.

- Select cell L4 and click the **Edit Formula** button (the = symbol near the Formula bar). *(In Excel 7 type = and click the Function Wizard button f_x.)*

- Press the down arrow next to the list of functions. In the list of functions, click **IF**. (If this function is not in the shortlist, click **More Functions**, select **Logical** in the left-hand list, and **IF** in the right-hand list.)

- A dialogue box appears. In **Logical_test**, type the condition that you are testing, using the cell name instead of the cell reference for ease of reading – i.e., *No_of_Assignments_handed_in <= 4*. In **Value_if_true**, type "*" (including the quotes), the text that you want to appear if the condition is met. In **Value_if_false** type "", i.e. opening and closing quotes with nothing between them, since nothing is to be entered into the cell in this case. Click **OK**.

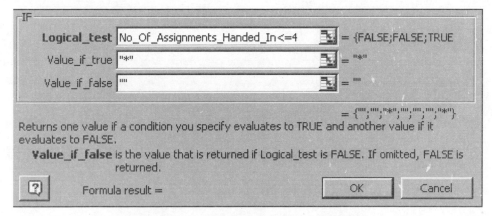

Figure 4.15: The IF function dialogue box

- Copy the formula down to the rest of the column. Check the results – your test data needs to contain at least two students who have completed only 4 or fewer assignments. Make sure that at least one student has missed 3 assignments before going on to the next paragraph.

Notice that in the formula bar, the formula is written

=IF(No_of_Assignments_handed_in<=4 ,"*","")

IF this condition is true...   THEN return this value...   ...ELSE return this value

Nested IF statements

Suppose we want to put one asterisk in the cell if a student has missed 2 assignments, and three asterisks if the student has missed 3 or more assignments. What is required is a 'nested if'.

First of all, name cell H3 *No_Of_Assignments* and press **Enter**.

The logic goes:

    IF   No_of_Assignments_handed_in <= No_Of_Assignments-2
    THEN
            IF No_of_Assignments_handed_in <= No_Of_Assignments-3
            THEN write 3 asterisks
            ELSE write 1 asterisk
    ELSE leave cell blank

The formula is written:

    =IF(No_of_Assignments_handed_in <= No_Of_Assignments-2,
            IF(No_of_Assignments_handed_in <= No_Of_Assignments-3,"***","*"),"")

Notice that the middle argument is itself a complete **IF** statement, 'nested' within the outer IF statement. (50p says you can't type it correctly first time – hand the money to your teacher at the end of the lesson.)

- Save the workbook. You have reached the end of the task!

Don't close the workbook just yet as you have another short task to complete.

Task 4.2: Use Goal Seek to determine a result

Letters have been sent to tutors, and students have been given a bit of a talking-to. The **Marks** worksheet looked like Figure 4.16 at half-term, and Butcher and Jones have come to the teacher to find out how they can redeem themselves.

	A	B	C	D	E	F	G	H	I	J	K	L
1	Year 12	CHEMISTRY										
2		Week 1	Week 2	Week 3	Week 4	Week 5	Week 6	No of Assignments handed in	Total Mark	Percent	Grade	Note to Tutor
3	MaxMark	20	15	20	50	10	20	6	135	100		
4	Andrews,S	15		3	23	6	15	5	62	46	E	
5	Butcher,D	4	3	17			13	4	37	27	U	*
6	Davies,M	9		18	26	1	6	5	60	44	E	
7	Jones,C	6			13		3	3	22	16	U	***
8	Lee,K	15	13	12	39	8	7	6	94	70	A	
9	Williams,H	14	12	18	50	8	14	6	116	86	A	
10												

The shaded cell shows which mark will be looked at – it's not shaded in your worksheet.

Figure 4.16: The completed Marks worksheet

Butcher, who missed the test in Week 4 through illness ('a bit of a cold coming on') wants to know whether he can take it now, and how many marks he would have to get to push his grade up to an E, or even a D.

The teacher calls Williams over. "Here's my worksheet. Can you help Butcher here?"

"No problem, I'll use Goal Seek." (Rest of class looks sick.)

Using Goal Seek

Goal seek is used to change the value in a specified cell until a formula of your choice evaluates to a specified value.

- Select cell J5, containing Butcher's percentage grade. (You may have to use a different cell, according to your test data.)

- Select **Tools, Goal Seek**.

- Enter values in the dialogue box as shown below. You can enter the value in the **By changing cell** box simply by clicking in cell E5.

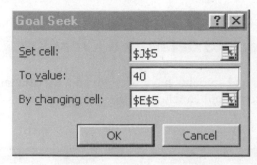

Figure 4.17: Using Goal Seek

- Excel tries out random values, quickly homing in on a solution, which is displayed in the following box, and inserted into the worksheet:

	A	B	C	D	E	F	G	H	I	J	K	L
1	Year 12	CHEMISTRY										
2		Week 1	Week 2	Week 3	Week 4	Week 5	Week 6	No of Assignments handed in	Total Mark	Percent	Grade	Note to Tutor
3	MaxMark	20	15	20	50	10	20	6	135	100		
4	Andrews,S	15		3	23	6	15	5	62	46	E	
5	Butcher,D	4	3	17	16		13	5	53	40	E	
6	Davies,M	9		18	26	1	6	5	60	44	E	
7	Jones,C	6			13		3	3	22	16	U	***
8	Lee,K	15	13	12	39	8	7	6	94	70	A	
9	Williams,H	14	12	18	50	8	14	6	116	86	A	
10												
11												
12												
13												
14												
15												
16												
17												
18												
19												

Figure 4.18: Result found by Goal seek

Butcher is so staggered by this result he now wants to know what mark he needs in the test to get a B.

Using Goal Seek he will very quickly discover that he needs to get 52 – an impossible goal. He will have to settle for a C.

Try out some options on your own worksheet!

Chapter 5 – "What if" Scenarios

"What if.."

You have probably been told that spreadsheets are excellent for exploring different solutions to problems – for example, "What will be the effect on profits if we put the price of hamburgers down by 20p and sell 10% more of them as a result?"

You have already seen one tool, **Goal Seek**, that can be used to explore different possibilities to achieve a desired result. In this chapter we're going to look at an even more powerful tool, the **Scenario Manager**, which enables you to change not just one value but several, to reach a desired goal.

Task 5.1: Decide on ticket prices for theatre production

Imagine that you are the Treasurer for a Drama or Operatic Society. You have already worked out that this year's production will cost £3,000 taking into account scenery, costumes, orchestra and so on. Your task is to come up with a pricing structure for tickets that will ensure as far as possible that the organisation will not make a loss.

You have been given last year's seating plan and seat prices.

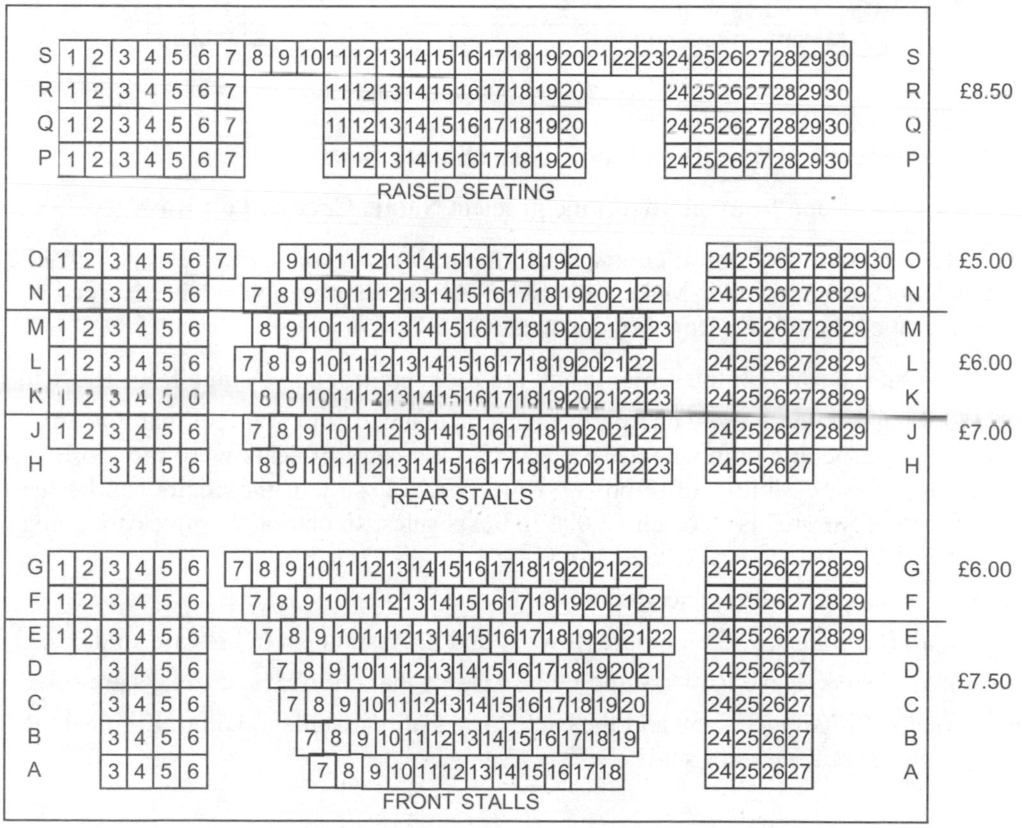

Figure 5.1: Theatre seating plan

Your first task is to calculate what the revenue will be if every seat is sold. Luckily the Treasurer did this in 1998 and has given you the following printout of the worksheet:

	A	B	C	D	E
1	**Seat Prices for 1998 Production**				
2					
3	Seats	Row	Number of seats	Price	Seat Revenue
4	Front Stalls(1)	A	20	£7.50	£150.00
5	Front Stalls(1)	B	21	£7.50	£157.50
6	Front Stalls(1)	C	22	£7.50	£165.00
7	Front Stalls(1)	D	23	£7.50	£172.50
8	Front Stalls(1)	E	28	£7.50	£210.00
9	Front Stalls(2)	F	28	£6.00	£168.00
10	Front Stalls(2)	G	28	£6.00	£168.00
11	Rear Stalls(1)	H	24	£7.00	£168.00
12	Rear Stalls(1)	J	28	£7.00	£196.00
13	Rear Stalls(2)	K	28	£6.00	£168.00
14	Rear Stalls(2)	L	28	£6.00	£168.00
15	Rear Stalls(2)	M	28	£6.00	£168.00
16	Rear Stalls(3)	N	28	£5.00	£140.00
17	Rear Stalls(3)	O	26	£5.00	£130.00
18	Raised seating	P	24	£6.50	£156.00
19	Raised seating	Q	24	£6.50	£156.00
20	Raised seating	R	24	£6.50	£156.00
21	Raised seating	S	30	£6.50	£195.00
22	**Maximum revenue**				**£2,992.00**

Figure 5.2: 1998 Seat prices

- Open a new worksheet and save it as *Theatre*. Name **Sheet1** *Seats*.

- Select cells B3 to E21 and from the **Insert** menu select **Name, Create, Top Row**.

- Enter the data as shown. Column E contains a formula, *Number_of_seats * Price*. Cell E22 contains the formula *Sum(Seat_Revenue)*. Make full use of all the shortcuts you have learned to copy and format cells. Notice there is no Row I in this theatre!

- If you can't see all the rows on the screen, click the zoom control and change from 100% to say 85%.

Things are not looking too good. Only one performance is planned, and you feel that it is unlikely to be a complete sell-out. Also, people complained last year that the rows of seats were too close together and you need to consider the possibility of removing rows A and L so that the chairs can be rearranged to allow more leg-room. Your goal is to reach £3,000 in ticket sales, so obviously prices are going to have to go up.

You'd like to look at several different scenarios.

1   Put 50p on all the tickets, and eliminate Rows A and L. Assume all tickets are sold.

2   Put 50p on all tickets, leave Rows A and L and assume that only 85% of tickets are sold.

3   Put the raised seating up to £7.50 and the back 2 rows of rear stalls to £6.00. Eliminate Rows A and L and assume 95% of seats are sold.

Creating and naming input cells

Before you create any scenarios, you should name all the cells that you might use in each scenario; then, when you generate a scenario summary, the cell names you defined are used and readability is improved. Also, it is going to be more convenient to have a price table so that if you want to change the price of the Front Stalls, for example, you only need to change one cell, not five.

- Create a table of proposed prices, as shown in Figure 5.3.

- Click anywhere in the table and press **Ctrl-Shift-*** to select the whole table. In the **Name** box, type *Proposed_Prices*. Press **Enter**.

- Select cells G4 to H9 and click **Insert, Name, Create**. Click **Left Column** in the Create Names dialogue box to name each cell using the labels in column G. Click **OK**.

	A	B	C	D	E	F	G	H	I
1	Seat Prices for 1998 Production								
2									
3	Seats	Row	Number of seats	Price	Seat Revenue		Proposed Prices		
4	Front Stalls(1)	A	20	£7.50	£150.00		FStalls1	£7.50	
5	Front Stalls(1)	B	21	£7.50	£157.50		FStalls2	£6.00	
6	Front Stalls(1)	C	22	£7.50	£165.00		RStalls1	£7.00	
7	Front Stalls(1)	D	23	£7.50	£172.50		RStalls2	£6.00	
8	Front Stalls(1)	E	28	£7.50	£210.00		RStalls3	£5.00	
9	Front Stalls(2)	F	28	£6.00	£168.00		Raised	£6.50	
10	Front Stalls(2)	G	28	£6.00	£168.00				

Figure 5.3: Table of proposed prices

- You now need to replace the prices that you typed in column D with formulae referencing the **Proposed Prices** table. Click cell D4, and type *=FStalls1* in place of the current contents. Copy this formula down the next 4 cells. In D9 and D10 you need the formula *=FStalls2*, and so on down the column.

- Add two row labels at the bottom of the list of seats, *Percentage sales* and *Probable revenue* which will be calculated as a percentage of the maximum possible revenue.

- Type 85% in cell E23.

- Name cells as follows, remembering to press **Enter** after selecting each cell and typing the name in the Name box.

C4	*Row_A*
C14	*Row_L*
E22	*Maximum_Revenue*
E23	*Percentage_Sales*
E24	*Probable_Revenue*

- Type the formula in cell E24, *=Percentage_Sales * Maximum_Revenue*

21	Raised seating	S	30	£6.50	£195.00	
22	**Maximum revenue**				**£2,992.00**	
23	**Percentage sales**				**85%**	
24	**Probable revenue**				**£2,543.20**	
25						

Figure 5.4: Final preparations

Creating a scenario of the current situation

Before experimenting with various scenarios, it is a good idea to create a scenario documenting the current situation so that you can refer back to it when comparing alternatives.

- On the **Tools** menu, select **Scenarios**. The **Scenario Manager** dialogue box appears.

- Click the **Add** button. The **Add Scenario** dialogue box appears.

- In the **Scenario Name** box, type **1998 Prices**, and then press **Tab** to highlight the entry in the **Changing Cells** box.

- Click cell H4, and then hold down the Ctrl key while you click in cells H5, H6, H7, H8, H9, (containing the seat prices) C4, C14 (containing the number of seats in rows A and L) and E23 (containing the percentage sales). (You'll have to drag the window aside to see them all.)

- Add a comment as shown in Figure 5.5.

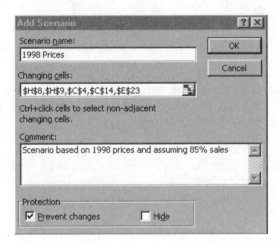

Figure 5.5: The Add Scenario dialogue box

- Click **OK**. The Scenario Values dialogue box appears containing the cell names and values.

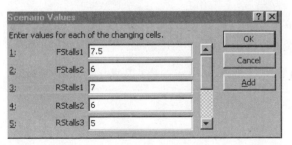

Figure 5.6: The Scenario Values dialogue box

48

- As this is the scenario based on current values, you don't want to make any changes in this box. Click **OK**.

- The Scenario Manager dialogue box appears with your first scenario listed in the scenarios list.

Creating additional scenarios

Now the fun starts! You're ready to enter all the other different scenarios you wanted to try out.

With the **Scenario Manager** dialogue box open:

- Click the **Add** button. The Add Scenario dialogue box appears.

- In the **Scenario Name** box, type *Option 1*, and then press **Tab** to highlight the entry in the **Changing Cells** box. Click **OK**.

- Enter data as follows:

Option 1

Fstalls1	*8.00*
Fstalls2	*6.50*
Rstalls1	*7.50*
Rstalls2	*6.50*
Rstalls3	*5.50*
Raised	*7.00*
Row_A	*0*
Row_L	*0*
Percentage_sales	*1.00*

- Click **OK**.

- Click **Add** to add your next scenario.

- Add scenarios for Option 2 and Option 3 as listed below:

Option 2		Option 3	
Fstalls1	*8.00*	**Fstalls1**	*7.50*
Fstalls2	*6.50*	**Fstalls2**	*6.00*
Rstalls1	*7.50*	**Rstalls1**	*7.00*
Rstalls2	*6.50*	**Rstalls2**	*6.00*
Rstalls3	*5.50*	**Rstalls3**	*6.00*
Raised	*7.00*	**Raised**	*7.50*
Row_A	*20*	**Row_A**	*0*
Row_L	*28*	**Row_L**	*0*
Percentage_sales	*0.85*	**Percentage_sales**	*0.95*

The **Option 3** values are shown in the figure below.

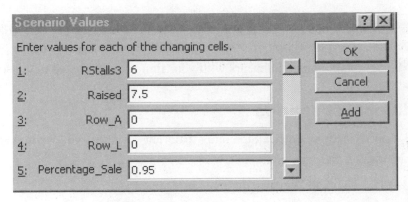

Figure 5.7: the Option 3 scenario

- Click **OK**. The Scenario Manager dialogue box appears again, listing all the scenarios.

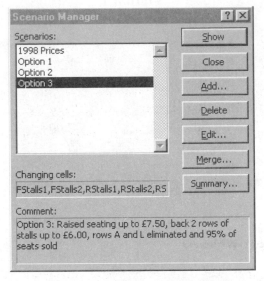

Figure 5.8: All the scenarios listed

Nearly there!

Viewing the scenarios

You've done all the work – now you want to enjoy the fruits of your labours. First of all you will view each scenario in turn and see what changes are made to your worksheet.

- Make sure the figures for **Maximum Revenue** and **Probable Revenue** are visible on screen.

- In the Scenario Manager dialogue box, click **Option 1** and click **Show**.

- Move the dialogue box to one side so that you can see the effect of the changes on the probable revenue. This gives a probable revenue of £2,881.

- It's not too promising, so click **Option 2** and view the changes. Even worse! The probable revenue is now only £2,739.55.

- Option 3 doesn't produce the desired result either – only £2688.50. You're going to have to take drastic action. Enter a fourth scenario, **Option 4**. Put all the seat prices up by £1, take out row A and assume 95% sales, as in the table below for Option 4.

Option 4	
Fstalls1	8.50
Fstalls2	7.00
Rstalls1	8.00
Rstalls2	7.00
Rstalls3	6.00
Raised	7.50
Row_A	0
Row_L	28
Percentage_sales	0.95

- Click **OK**.

- When you have entered the scenario, click **Show** in the **Scenario Manager** to see the result. You now have a Probable Revenue of £3119.80 but will you sell 95% of tickets? Maybe not!

- Edit the scenario, assuming only 90% sales. This results in probable sales of £2955.60, which is pretty close.

- Click **Close** in the **Scenario Manager** dialogue box.

- Save your worksheet.

Creating a scenario summary

The committee is clearly going to want to see a summary of your findings, and will probably want you to try out additional scenarios if you give them any inkling of just how easy it is. Best keep your mouth shut.

- On the **Tools** menu select **Scenarios**.

- In the Scenario Manager dialogue box click **Summary**. The Scenario Summary dialogue box appears. *(In Excel 7 the result cell shows as $E$24.)*

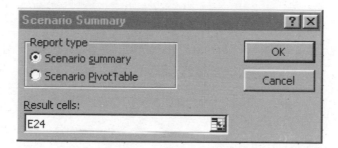

Figure 5.9: The Scenario Summary dialogue box

- Make sure that the **Scenario Summary** option button is selected and that the results cell reads E24, and click **OK**.

- A new worksheet named **Scenario Summary** is added to your workbook. It shows the changes and results for each scenario.

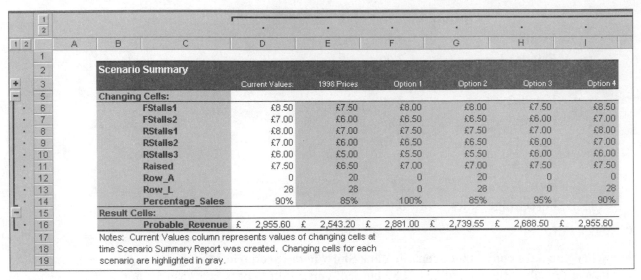

Figure 5.10: Scenario summary

- Click the + sign in the border near Row header 3 to see the comments that you added to each scenario displayed. You can edit these comments in the summary if you wish.

- You can widen columns, change the zoom factor, add notes at the top or bottom, or edit this sheet in any way you like before printing it out.

Using Solver

One final question – the Chairman wants to know exactly what percentage of seats need to be sold with prices as in **Option 4** in order to make exactly £3,000? **Solver** will provide a quick answer.

- Select **Tools**, **Scenarios**, **Option 4** to ensure that Option 4 data is showing.

- In the **Seats** worksheet select cell E24, and then on the **Tools** menu select **Solver**.

If it's not on the menu you may need to install it: refer to the Help system.

- Fill in the Solver parameters as shown in the figure below.

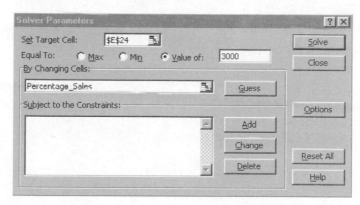

Figure 5.11: Entering Solver parameters

- Click **Solve**. You have your answer – 91%!

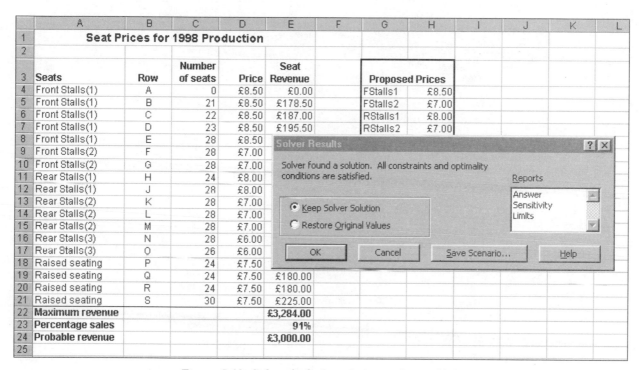

Figure 5.12: Solver finds the solution to the problem

That completes the task. I hope you're amazed and delighted by the power of Excel – spreadsheets have come a long way in the last 20 years!

Part 2
Data Analysis and Presentation

In this section:

Chapter 6 – Linking Workbooks

Introduction

In Part 2, we will be looking at how Excel can be used to store and analyse information held in list form. Many different applications use lists of one sort or another; lists of club members and their details, stock items, invoices, student records, questionnaire responses and expenses are just a few. Excel provides the means to reference, organise and summarise lists and to extract useful information from the raw input data.

Task 6.1: Store and look up data in different workbooks

Atlas Publications publishes a range of road atlases which are sold by three different methods: to wholesalers, who in turn sell them on to bookshops and service stations; to bookshops who place orders by phone, fax or mail; to members of the public who place orders normally for one book. They hold information on account customers, products and sales in three different workbooks.

In the **Sales** workbook, Atlas keeps a daily record on a spreadsheet of all invoices (each invoice corresponding to an order). A number of reports based on the data in this workbook help to keep the management informed on who their best customers are, which products are most successful and so on.

The data for the first 3 days in September is shown below.

	InvoiceDate	InvoiceNum	Customer	Type	Product	Quantity	RetailPrice	SalesPrice
1	**Road Atlas Sales**							
2								
3	**InvoiceDate**	**InvoiceNum**	**Customer**	**Type**	**Product**	**Quantity**	**RetailPrice**	**SalesPrice**
4	01/09/98	1001	Gardners	Wholesaler	A1	100	£ 1,000.00	£ 450.00
5	01/09/98	1001	Gardners	Wholesaler	A2	24	£ 168.00	£ 75.60
6	01/09/98	1002	Dragon	Retailer	A1	15	£ 150.00	£ 105.00
7	01/09/98	1002	Dragon	Retailer	A2	20	£ 140.00	£ 98.00
8	01/09/98	1002	Dragon	Retailer	A3	12	£ 60.00	£ 42.00
9	01/09/98	1003	Metcalfe Ltd	Retailer	A3	45	£ 225.00	£ 157.50
10	01/09/98	1004	Ballams	Retailer	A2	30	£ 210.00	£ 147.00
11	01/09/98	1004	Ballams	Retailer	A3	30	£ 150.00	£ 105.00
12	02/09/98	1005	Cash Sale	Direct	A3	2	£ 10.00	£ 10.00
13	02/09/98	1006	Smiths	Retailer	A1	18	£ 180.00	£ 126.00
14	02/09/98	1006	Smiths	Retailer	A2	10	£ 70.00	£ 49.00
15	02/09/98	1007	TES	Wholesaler	A3	50	£ 250.00	£ 112.50
16	02/09/98	1007	TES	Wholesaler	A3	40	£ 200.00	£ 90.00
17	03/09/98	1008	Gardners	Wholesaler	A1	75	£ 750.00	£ 337.50
18	03/09/98	1008	Gardners	Wholesaler	A3	40	£ 200.00	£ 90.00
19	03/09/98	1009	Ballams	Retailer	A2	17	£ 119.00	£ 83.30
20	03/09/98	1010	Cash Sale	Direct	A3	1	£ 5.00	£ 5.00
21	03/09/98	1011	Metcalfe Ltd	Retailer	A1	18	£ 180.00	£ 126.00
22	03/09/98	1012	Dragon	Retailer	A2	35	£ 245.00	£ 171.50
23	03/09/98	1012	Dragon	Retailer	A3	40	£ 200.00	£ 140.00

*Figure 6.1: Record of daily sales invoices in the **Atlas Sales** Workbook*

Note: You should make sure that the dates in your system are correctly displayed in British, not American, format as **dd/mm/yy**. If they are not, adjust the system date settings as described in Chapter 2 – or if you are working on a network, and can't alter settings, enter the dates as **01-Sep-98** etc and format the dates in the date column to appear in this format.

Organising data in different workbooks

Looking at Figure 6.1 above, you can see that there is a lot of repetitive information. It would be a tremendous nuisance to have to type **Wholesaler** or **Retailer** as well as the customer name, every time a new invoice was recorded, and the person entering the data might not even know which type of customer they were. Similarly, it should not be necessary to type in the retail price or the sales price on each line – there is a set retail price for each product, and the sales price will be determined by the level of discount each customer gets.

For these reasons, the application designer has decided that three separate workbooks are needed:

- A **Customer** workbook
- A **Product** workbook
- A **Sales** workbook

Creating the Customer, Product and Sales workbooks

- Open a new workbook and save it as *Atlas Customers*.

- Type in the data as shown in the figure below.

	A	B	C
1	**Customers**		
2			
3	**Name**	**Type**	
4	Gardners	Wholesaler	
5	TES	Wholesaler	
6	Dragon	Retailer	
7	Metcalfe Ltd	Retailer	
8	Ballams	Retailer	
9	Smiths	Retailer	
10	Cash sale	Direct	
11			

*Figure 6.2: The **Atlas Customers** workbook*

The data in this workbook will be used as a Lookup table. The table needs to be given a name. However, we must take into account that this table will grow as more customers are added, so we will define the table as occupying all of columns A and B.

- Drag across column headers A and B to select both these columns.

- In the Name box type the name *CustomerTable* and press **Enter**.

- Rename Sheet1 *CustomerList*. (Right-click the sheet tab and select **Rename**.)

- Save and close the workbook.

- Open a new workbook, and save it as *Atlas Products*.

- Type in the data as shown below.

	A	B	C	D
1	**Products**			
2				
3	**ProductCode**	**Description**	**RetailPrice**	
4	A1	Deluxe Edition	£10.00	
5	A2	Standard Edition	£7.00	
6	A3	Economy Edition	£5.00	
7				

*Figure 6.3: The **Atlas Products** workbook*

- Drag across column headers A to C to select these three columns..

- Name the range *ProductTable*.

- Rename Sheet1 *ProductList*.

- Save and close the workbook.

- Open a new workbook and save it as *Atlas Sales*. Enter headings and data in columns A, B, C, E and F as shown below. You'll notice that as you start to type *Gardners* on the second row of the table, Excel correctly guesses what you want to type as soon as you type *G*. Use shortcuts wherever possible to speed up data entry – don't forget, for example, that if you drag the corner of cell A4 down the next 6 cells using the right mouse button, you can choose **Copy Cells** rather than **Fill Series**. Note there may be more than one line per invoice number.

	A	B	C	D	E	F	G	H
1	**Road Atlas Sales**							
2								
3	**InvoiceDate**	**InvoiceNum**	**Customer**	**Type**	**Product**	**Quantity**	**RetailPrice**	**SalesPrice**
4	01/09/98	1001	Gardners		A1	100		
5	01/09/98	1001	Gardners		A2	24		
6	01/09/98	1002	Dragon		A1	15		
7	01/09/98	1002	Dragon		A2	20		
8	01/09/98	1002	Dragon		A3	12		
9	01/09/98	1003	Metcalfe Ltd		A3	45		
10	01/09/98	1004	Ballams		A2	30		
11	01/09/98	1004	Ballams		A3	30		
12	02/09/98	1005	Cash Sale		A3	2		
13	02/09/98	1006	Smiths		A1	18		
14	02/09/98	1006	Smiths		A2	10		
15	02/09/98	1007	TES		A3	50		
16	02/09/98	1007	TES		A3	40		
17	03/09/98	1008	Gardners		A1	75		
18	03/09/98	1008	Gardners		A3	40		
19	03/09/98	1009	Ballams		A2	17		
20	03/09/98	1010	Cash Sale		A3	1		
21	03/09/98	1011	Metcalfe Ltd		A1	18		
22	03/09/98	1012	Dragon		A2	35		
23	03/09/98	1012	Dragon		A3	40		

*Figure 6.4: Test data in the **Atlas Sales** workbook*

- Rename Sheet1 *Invoices*.

- Save the workbook.

Opening a group of files that share a common characteristic

We now want to open the two files **Atlas Customers** and **Atlas Products** so that we can look up information from them.

- On the Standard toolbar, click the **Open** button.

- In the **Open** dialogue box, click the arrow to the right of **Tools**, and then click on **Find**. *(in Excel 7 and 97, click the* **Advanced**..... *button)*

- In the **Property** box, make sure **File Name** is selected. (You could also select **Keyword**.)

- Make sure that **Includes** is specified in the **Condition** box, and type *Atlas* in the **Value** box.

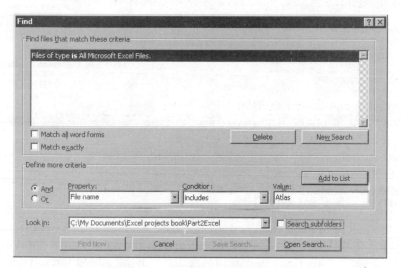

Figure 6.5: The Find dialogue box

- Click **Add to List**, and then click **Find Now**. The results of the search appear in the Open dialogue box.

*Figure 6.6: Finding files with **Atlas** in the file name*

- Click **Atlas Customers**, and then hold down the Ctrl key while you click **Atlas Products**. Click **Open** to open both the files.
- On the **Window** menu click **Arrange**, and then **Tiled** so that you can see all the workbooks at once. The arrangement is not entirely convenient – size and drag the windows so that you can see the Customer and Product tables as in the Figure below.

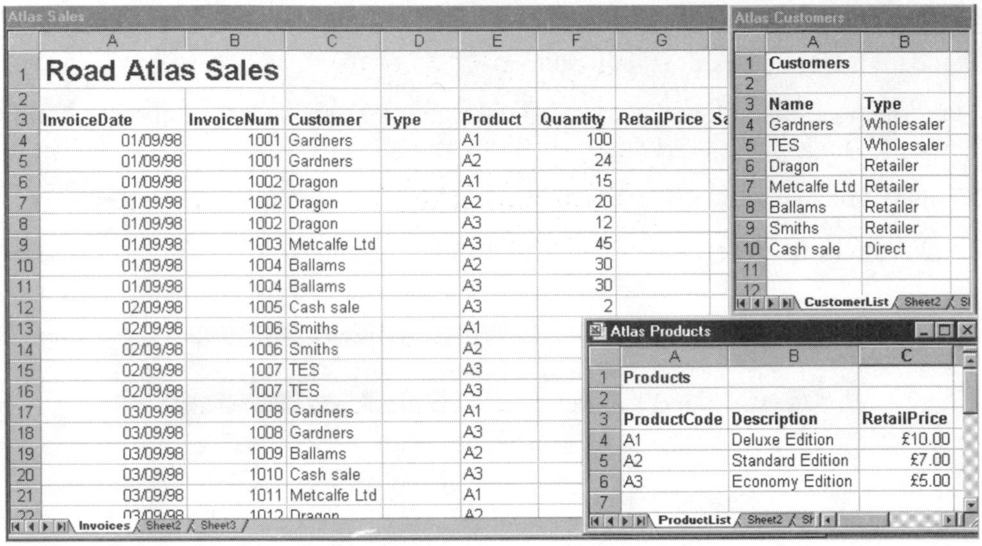

Atlas Sales

	A	B	C	D	E	F	G
1	Road Atlas Sales						
2							
3	InvoiceDate	InvoiceNum	Customer	Type	Product	Quantity	RetailPrice
4	01/09/98	1001	Gardners		A1	100	
5	01/09/98	1001	Gardners		A2	24	
6	01/09/98	1002	Dragon		A1	15	
7	01/09/98	1002	Dragon		A2	20	
8	01/09/98	1002	Dragon		A3	12	
9	01/09/98	1003	Metcalfe Ltd		A3	45	
10	01/09/98	1004	Ballams		A2	30	
11	01/09/98	1004	Ballams		A3	30	
12	02/09/98	1005	Cash sale		A3	2	
13	02/09/98	1006	Smiths		A1		
14	02/09/98	1006	Smiths		A2		
15	02/09/98	1007	TES		A3		
16	02/09/98	1007	TES		A3		
17	03/09/98	1008	Gardners		A1		
18	03/09/98	1008	Gardners		A3		
19	03/09/98	1009	Ballams		A2		
20	03/09/98	1010	Cash sale		A3		
21	03/09/98	1011	Metcalfe Ltd		A1		

Invoices / Sheet2 / Sheet3

Atlas Customers

	A	B
1	Customers	
2		
3	Name	Type
4	Gardners	Wholesaler
5	TES	Wholesaler
6	Dragon	Retailer
7	Metcalfe Ltd	Retailer
8	Ballams	Retailer
9	Smiths	Retailer
10	Cash sale	Direct
11		

CustomerList / Sheet2

Atlas Products

	A	B	C
1	Products		
2			
3	ProductCode	Description	RetailPrice
4	A1	Deluxe Edition	£10.00
5	A2	Standard Edition	£7.00
6	A3	Economy Edition	£5.00
7			

ProductList / Sheet2

Figure 6.7: The windows arranged conveniently

Naming columns as cell ranges

Later on it will be convenient to have each cell in each datasheet named. We must take into account that more data will be added to all three of the worksheets, and so the names must apply not only to cells that already have data in them, but also to any extra rows that may be added later. Therefore, the names we allocate must apply to entire columns, not just existing cell ranges.

- In the **Atlas Sales** workbook, select column A by clicking the column header and in the Name box type the name *InvoicesDate* and press **Enter**.
- Select column B and name it *InvoiceNum*.
- Name all the other columns in the same way, giving them the same names as their column headings.
- Similarly, name all the columns in the other workbooks after their column headers by selecting the columns one at a time and typing the name into the Name box. Remember to press **Enter** after naming each column.
- Save all three workbooks.

Copying sheets into a single workbook

If you decided you wanted all these workbooks combined into one, this is very easy to do. We will first open a second copy of **Atlas Sales** in a new window, and save it as *Atlas Backup*. Then we'll copy the **CustomerList** and **ProductList** sheets from the other workbooks into this one. This way, if anything goes wrong with the linking procedure you will have it as a backup.

- Click in the **Atlas Sales** workbook to make it the active workbook.

- From the **File** menu choose **Save As** and save the workbook as *Atlas Backup*.

- Click in the **Atlas Customers** workbook, hold down Ctrl and drag the **CustomerList** sheet tab to the right of the **Sheet3** tab in the **Atlas Backup** workbook. You now have a copy of the **Atlas Customers** worksheet in the **Atlas Backup** workbook. Check carefully that you have created a copy of **CustomerList** and not simply moved it – if you have lost the original sheet in **Atlas Sales**, try the operation again in reverse, or select the sheet tab, right-click and select **Move or Copy**.

- Now click in the **Atlas Products** workbook, hold down Ctrl and drag the **ProductList** sheet tab to the right of the **Sheet3** tab in the **Atlas Backup** workbook. You now have a copy of the **Atlas Products** worksheet in the **Atlas Backup** workbook.

- Delete sheets 2 and 3 in **Atlas Backup**. (Right-click the sheet name and select **Delete**.)

- Save and close **Atlas Backup**. We're not going to use it in this exercise.

- Open **Atlas Sales** and size the window as shown above.

In your project work, you should consider carefully whether you want to have separate linked workbooks, or separate sheets in the same workbook. The latter solution will avoid linkage problems which may arise if, for example, you transfer your work from a floppy disk to a hard disk and the pathnames in the links change.

Looking up values from other workbooks

We now need to fill in the rest of the **Atlas Sales** data. We'll start by writing the formula to insert the correct customer type in column D.

- Select cell D4, the first cell for customer type.

- Click the **Edit Formula** button (the = sign to the left of the formula bar), and select **VLOOKUP** from the function list. The Vlookup dialogue box appears. *(Excel 7: Type = and click the f_x button.)*

- With the cursor in the **Lookup_value** box, click in cell C4, which is the value you want to look up. (You may need to drag the dialogue box out of the way.) It would be preferable to use the field name that we have created for cells in this column, i.e. **Customer**. Delete **C4** and type *Customer*. *(In Excel 7, leave the **Lookup_Value** as C4.)*

- Tab to the **Table_Array** box. Click anywhere in the **Atlas Customers** worksheet and you will see that Excel automatically inserts '**[Atlas Customers]CustomerList**'!$A$1 or whatever cell reference you clicked in. Delete the cell address $A$1 or equivalent, and instead type the name of the table which you defined earlier, *CustomerTable*.

- Tab to **Col_Index_Num** and type *2*, since the value to be inserted is from the second column of the table.

- Now read the text in the dialogue box, which is shown below.

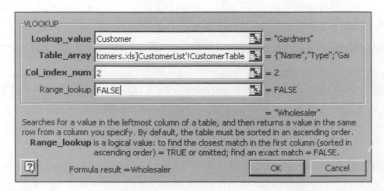

Figure 6.8: Finding an exact match

When we used Vlookup in Chapter 4, we were looking up a number which fell within a certain range. The table had to be sorted in ascending numerical order. This time, we want to find an exact match, and so we must specify **False** in the Range_Lookup box, because we are looking for a specific value, not a range.

- Type *False* in the Range_Lookup box and click **OK**.

The value **Wholesaler** should appear in cell D4. If it doesn't, you've made a mistake and you must edit the formula.

- Drag the corner handle down the rest of the column.

- Change cell C11 to introduce a deliberate spelling mistake. You will see **#N/A** appear as the Type. Undo your change, but take note that this is the sort of test you should include in your test data.

- Now you need to enter a formula in cell G4 by looking up the retail price in the **Atlas Products** workbook. Follow the same steps as you used to enter the Vlookup formula for Customer Type. Note that **Lookup_value** is *Product* (or *E4 in Excel 7*) and **Col_index_num** will be *3* this time because the retail price is in the third column of **ProductTable**. Remember to multiply the price by the Quantity so edit the formula to be:

    =VLOOKUP(Product,'Atlas Products.xls'!ProductTable,3,FALSE)*Quantity

    *In Excel 7, the formula is =VLOOKUP(E4,'Atlas Products.xls'!ProductTable,3,FALSE)*F4*

- Copy the formula down the rest of the column and click the **Currency** button to format it as currency.

Note: If you use the **Currency** button to format cells as Currency, the £ sign appears left justified as in Figure 6.9. If you format a cell by selecting **Format, Cells**, clicking the **Number** tab and selecting **Currency**, the £ sign appears next to the amount, as in Figure 6.13. Quirky!

Entering the sales price

To enter the sales price you can either use a nested IF formula, add an extra column to the CustomerTable in the Atlas Customers workbook to specify the discount for each customer, or make a new Discount table somewhere. This is the type of Design decision you will have to make and justify in your own project.

In this application, discounts are as follows:

Wholesalers:	55%
Retailers:	30%
Cash sales:	No discount

We will use a nested IF formula.

- In cell H4, type the following formula:

  =IF(Type="Wholesaler",45%*RetailPrice,IF(Type="Retailer",70%*RetailPrice,RetailPrice))

  *In Excel 7, the formula is **=IF(D4="Wholesaler",45%*G4,IF(D4="Retailer",70%*G4,G4))***

- Copy the formula down the rest of the column.

- Format column H as currency.

- Save all the workbooks.

Task 6.2: Test various aspects of the Atlas Publications application

Testing the application

This application needs very thorough testing because there are a multitude of things that can go wrong, and questions to which you probably don't know the answers without experimenting. You need to make a list of all the things that need testing. For example:

What happens if:

1. A new invoice is added?
2. The price of a product is changed?
3. The user opens the **Atlas Sales** workbook but does not open the two linked workbooks?
4. A new product is added, and then a new invoice for this product is added?
5. A new customer is added?

In your project work, you should write down a list like the one above of things that need testing, and try all your tests so that you know the answers. Also write down what the desirable end result is once you have sorted out any problems. For example, the desired result to test number 1 (Add a new invoice) is "The new invoice is added to the list and all the formulae are correctly calculated." You may have some doubts at the moment as to whether that will actually happen, so let's try it. We'll add a new invoice for October.

- In row 24, add a new invoice, date *04/10/98*, number *1013* to *TES*. Tab to cell D24. *Oh dear!* The customer type is not automatically displayed. In cell E24, type *A1* and in cell F24, *20*. Tab to cells G24 and H24. The retail and sales prices remain blank.

22	03/09/98	1012	Dragon	Retailer	A2	35	£ 245.00	£ 171.50
23	03/09/98	1012	Dragon	Retailer	A3	40	£ 200.00	£ 140.00
24	04/10/98	1013	TES		A1	20		
25								

Figure 6.9: Adding a new invoice

If you click in D24, you can see that the cell is completely blank, containing no formula. Not really surprising since you only copied the formula down as far as row 23. Now you have to find a way of curing this problem.

The first solution that may occur to you is to copy the formulae down for several hundred rows. This is a really bad idea because for a long time everything will appear to work perfectly, but sooner or later (probably after you have left the organisation) it will fail when someone enters an invoice in the first row below the row you copied the formulae to. The user, who has been entering invoices quite happily for weeks, will be totally flummoxed.

Remember, the purpose of testing is not to prove that you CAN get everything to work perfectly (most of the time) but that you CANNOT (under any circumstances) get it to fail. Luckily, in this instance there is a neat solution.

Using a built-in data form

Excel provides the means to quickly create a basic data entry form for entering data into a worksheet, and using a form has the advantage that formulae will be automatically calculated.

- Delete the new record you previously inserted in row 24.

- With the cursor anywhere in the table, from the **Data** menu select **Form...**

A data form appears as shown below:

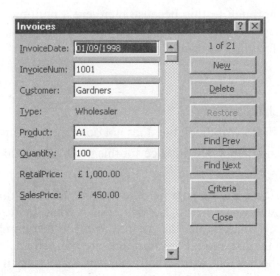

Figure 6.10: Using a data form

- Click **New** and a blank form appears.

- Enter the following data: Invoice date *04/10/98*, InvoiceNum *1013*, Customer *TES*, Product *A3*, Quantity *20*.

- Click **Close**. The new record is inserted with all the formulae correctly calculated. (Check this is so.)

In Chapter 10 we will be doing more work on customising data entry forms and validating input data.

Problems with links

You should be very careful when dealing with linked workbooks to avoid ending up with broken links or unusable workbooks. To create a link to a separate workbook, you can use any of the following methods:

1. Create the link in a sheet in the same workbook and then move the worksheet to a new workbook.

2. Type an = sign and then activate the other workbook by clicking in it, and clicking the required cell or range.

3. Type a cell reference, complete with square brackets around the workbook name.

As long as both workbooks are open when you move the worksheets or save the workbook with a new name, Excel can automatically adjust any links for you. If you change a file name when a workbook is not open, or use Windows Explorer to rename or move a file, you will end up with broken links.

In the worst case scenario you will get an error message like the one below and you will probably have to start from scratch.

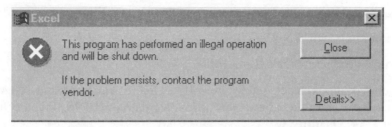

Figure 6.11: Problems with linked workbooks

A common source of problems is using the label names that are automatically assigned by Excel to columns, rather than creating names of ranges as we have done in this chapter. While the formulae that create links between workbooks appear to work at first when they are created, the links fail when the workbook is closed and reopened.

(Thanks to John Penrose, Head of Computing and IT at New College Pontefract for this insight!)

If you have difficulties during the implementation of Chapter 6, consider using only linked sheets in the same workbook.

Updating links to other workbooks

Currently you should have all three of the Atlas workbooks open. What happens if you change a price in the Product workbook?

- Note the sales price in H4 is £450.00.

- In the **Atlas Products** workbook, change the price of product A1 to *£12*. The sales price changes to £540. Fine. Change the price back to *£10*.

But what happens if just the **Products** workbook is open when the price is changed, and only the **Sales** workbook is open when new invoices are added?

- Save and close the **Sales** and **Customer** workbooks.

- Change the price of A1 to **£11**. Save and close the **Products** workbook.

- Open the **Sales** workbook (**Atlas Sales.xls**). You will get a message like the one below *(Or in Excel 7, a differently worded message asking a similar question.)*

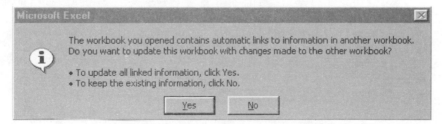

Figure 6.12: Links to another workbook

- Click **Yes**. Cell H4 now reads £495, as the price of product A1 has changed. If you had clicked **No**, nothing would have changed in the **Sales** workbook.

Adding a new product

What happens if a new product is added, and then a new invoice for this product is added?

- Open the **Atlas Products** workbook.

- In row 7 enter a new product: *A4, Pocket Edition, £4.00*

- In the Atlas Sales workbook, click anywhere in the table of invoices and select **Form...** from the **Data** menu. Click **New** and add a new record: Invoice date **05/10/98**, InvoiceNum **1013**, Customer **Cash sale**, Product **A4**, Quantity **1**.

- Click **Close**.

- Everything should work correctly.

- In the Atlas Products workbook, type the text END OF TABLE at the bottom of your table. The worksheet will now look like Figure 6.13.

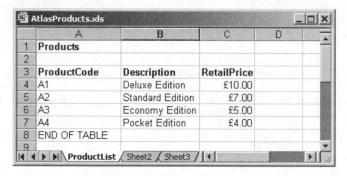

Figure 6.13: The edited Products worksheet

- Save and close all your worksheets.

Chapter 7 – Filtering, Sorting and Subtotalling Lists

Introduction

Excel provides many tools for finding out more information from tables of data. We'll use the **Atlas Sales** workbook to try out some of these capabilities.

- Use **File, Open** to open the three workbooks **Atlas Sales, Atlas Customers** and **Atlas Products**. Alternatively, open **Atlas Backup** if you completed the last exercise in Chapter 6.

- Delete the new rows you inserted when testing so that the data appears as in Figure 6.1.

(If you have not got these files, you will have to create a new workbook called **Atlas Sales** and enter data as shown in Figure 6.1. For the purposes of this exercise you don't need the links and the formulae used in the worksheet.)

Task 7.1: Analyse the Atlas Sales data to provide management information

The management would like answers to the following questions:

1. What orders have Ballams placed over the past month?
2. Which are the six highest sales values (per invoice line)?
3. What is the total daily value of all invoices?
4. What is the total value of each invoice?

Filtering to display a subset of records

To find all the invoices for Ballams:

- Click anywhere in the list of invoices in the **Atlas Sales** worksheet.

- From the **Data** menu select **Filter, Autofilter**. Filter arrows appear next to your column headers.

- Select all the column headers and double-click a boundary to increase the cell widths.

- In the **Customer** column, click the Filter arrow and select **Ballams**. The invoices for Ballams remain in view and the rest are hidden.

	A	B	C	D	E	F	G	H
1	Road Atlas Sales							
2								
3	InvoiceDate ▼	InvoiceNum ▼	Customer ▼	Type ▼	Product ▼	Quantity ▼	RetailPrice ▼	SalesPrice ▼
10	01/09/98	1004	Ballams	Retailer	A2	30	£210.00	£147.00
11	01/09/98	1004	Ballams	Retailer	A3	30	£150.00	£105.00
19	03/09/98	1009	Ballams	Retailer	A2	17	£119.00	£83.30
25								

Figure 7.1: Filtering a set of data

- To remove the filter, click the Customer filter arrow again, and select **All**. The filter is removed and all the records appear again.

Finding the top six values

(You can't do this in Excel 5.)

- Click the filter arrow in the **Sales Price** column.

- Select **Top 10**. A dialogue box appears and you can change 10 to *6* as shown below.

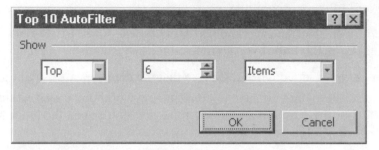

Figure 7.2: The Top 10 AutoFilter

- Click **OK**. The invoice lines with the 6 top sales values are displayed.

You can try out other filters such as the **Custom** filter. To remove the filter arrows, select **Filter** from the **Data** menu and deselect **AutoFilter**. Do this before you continue.

Sorting data

Simple sorts can be performed using the **Sort** buttons on the Standard toolbar. For example, to sort in alphabetical order of customer:

- Click anywhere in the **Customer** column.

- Click the **Sort Ascending** button.

Now we'll sort the list again, this time on a major key **Date** and a minor key **InvoiceNum**, which should get us back to the original list.

- On the **Data** menu, select **Sort**.

- Click the arrow in the **Sort by** box and select **InvoiceDate**.

- Select **InvoiceNum** in the next box, and click **OK**. (See figure below.)

If you wanted to sort on more than 3 keys, you need to run the Sort procedure twice. Sort first on the minor keys and then on the major key.

Figure 7.3: Sorting on more than one key

Summarising data with subtotals

Next we want to find the total daily value of all invoices.

● Select any cell in the list of invoices.

● From the **Data** menu select **Subtotals**. The Subtotal dialogue box appears.

● Fill it in as shown below, and click **OK**.

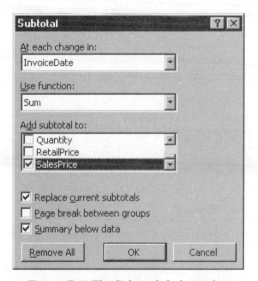

Figure 7.4: The Subtotal dialogue box

The subtotals are shown as in the figure below.

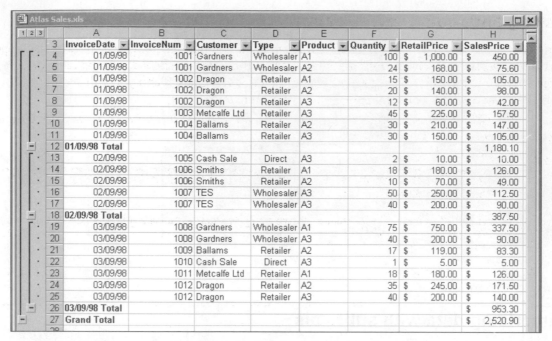

Figure 7.5: Daily Sales value Subtotals

Multiple levels of subtotals

To find the total value of each invoice, we can create a second level of subtotals. When you create multiple levels of subtotals, it is important to do the subtotalling in the right order. You need to create the larger subtotals first (in this case, by date, which we have already done) and then the nested subtotals.

- Select **Data, Subtotals** again.

- In the Subtotals dialogue box, specify **InvoiceNum** in the **At Each Change In** box, **Sum** in the **Use Function** box, and **SalesPrice** in the **Add Subtotal to** box. Deselect **Replace Current Subtotals** and click **OK**.

The subtotals for each invoice appear as shown below.

1 2 3 4		A	B	C	D	E	F	G	H
	1	**Road Atlas Sales**							
	2								
	3	InvoiceDate	InvoiceNum	Customer	Type	Product	Quantity	RetailPrice	SalesPrice
	4	01/09/98	1001	Gardners	Wholesaler	A1	100	£ 1,000.00	£450.00
	5	01/09/98	1001	Gardners	Wholesaler	A2	24	£ 168.00	£75.60
	6		**1001 Total**						£525.60
	7	01/09/98	1002	Dragon	Retailer	A1	15	£ 150.00	£105.00
	8	01/09/98	1002	Dragon	Retailer	A2	20	£ 140.00	£98.00
	9	01/09/98	1002	Dragon	Retailer	A3	12	£ 60.00	£42.00
	10		**1002 Total**						£245.00
	11	01/09/98	1003	Metcalfe Ltd	Retailer	A3	45	£ 225.00	£157.50
	12		**1003 Total**						£157.50
	13	01/09/98	1004	Ballams	Retailer	A2	30	£ 210.00	£147.00
	14	01/09/98	1004	Ballams	Retailer	A3	30	£ 150.00	£105.00
	15		**1004 Total**						£252.00
	16	**01/09/98 Total**							£1,180.10
	17	02/09/98	1005	Cash Sale	Direct	A3	2	£ 10.00	£10.00
	18		**1005 Total**						£10.00
	19	02/09/98	1006	Smiths	Retailer	A1	18	£ 180.00	£126.00

Figure 7.6: Nested subtotals

70

Showing and hiding levels of detail

You can select how much detail to show by clicking the outline buttons in the new column that appears to the left of the worksheet. The buttons are numbered to allow you to show a specific level of detail – for example if you click **1**, you will see only the grand total level. Click **2** and you will see the total invoice value for each date. Click **3** to see the total value of each invoice.

(In Excel 7 the Grand Total will appear in column 39, not 40, and there won't be another Grand Total line as shown below.)

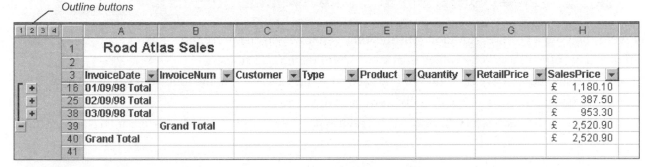

Figure 7.7: Level 2 detail

Pasting subtotals into a Word document

If you wanted to paste these totals into a word-processed report you could do as follows:

- Start Word and open a new or existing report document.

- In the spreadsheet, select cells A1 to H40 in the summary as shown in Figure 7.7 (Outline button 2) and select **Edit**, **Copy**.

- Move back to the Word document, make sure the insertion point is in the correct place and select **Paste** from the **Edit** menu. The cells appear as shown below (without the borders, which can be added):

Road Atlas Sales							
InvoiceDate	InvoiceNum	Customer	Type	Product	Quantity	RetailPrice	SalesPrice
01/09/98 Total							£ 1,180.10
02/09/98 Total							£ 387.50
03/09/98 Total							£ 953.30
	Grand Total						£ 2,520.90
Grand Total							£ 2,520.90

Figure 7.8: Cells pasted into a Word document

You can then edit this as required using Word's **Table** functions.

Removing subtotals and filters

- To remove all the subtotals in your worksheet, click in the worksheet and select **Data, Subtotals**. In the dialogue box, click **Remove All**.

- To remove the filter arrows, select **Data, Filter**, and deselect **Autofilter**.

Task 7.2: Use a PivotTable to create dynamic summaries

PivotTables are a powerful tool for consolidating, summarising and presenting data.

In this task you will use PivotTables to answer the following questions:

1. How many books have been ordered by each customer, and what is the total value of their orders?
2. What is the average sale quantity for each customer?
3. How many books have been ordered by each type of customer, and what is the total value of their orders?

Creating a PivotTable

- Click any cell in the list of invoices and from the **Data** menu select **PivotTable And PivotChart Report**. The PivotTable And PivotChart Wizard appears. (*In Excel 7 and 97, select Pivot Table Report.*)

- Make sure that the **Microsoft Excel List or Database** option button is selected, and then click **Next**. The Step2 dialogue box shows the range that Excel has selected as the data for the PivotTable. (If the whole table is not selected with a moving dotted line around it, select the table, including headings, manually before clicking **Next**.)

- Click **Next**. The Step3 dialogue box appears.

- In Excel 2000, make sure that the **New Worksheet** option button is selected, and then click **Finish**. The PivotTable And PivotChart Wizard dialogue box closes.

The PivotTable toolbar appears, and the PivotTable report is displayed on the new worksheet. Your screen should look something like Figure 7.9 below.

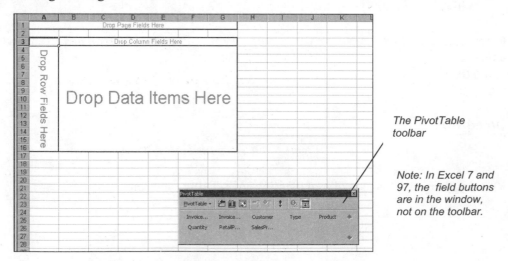

Figure 7.9: PivotTable layout diagram

The table is created by dragging the field buttons from the PivotTable toolbar (or window) into the PivotTable layout. We want to find how many books have been ordered by each customer.

- Drag the **Customer** button into the area indicated by the text 'Drop Row fields here' (the **Row** box).

- Drag the **Product** button into the **Column** box.

- Drag the **Quantity** button into the **Data** box.
  *(In Excel 97 and 7, click **Next**, check that **New Worksheet** is selected and click **Finish**.)*

Your worksheet should look similar to the figure below.

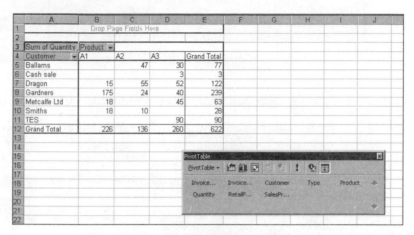

Figure 7.10: The PivotTable

You can rearrange the data in any way you like. Try dragging the **Product** button to the boundary between A3 and B3. Or, if you decide you would rather have products down the side and customers along the top, drag the **Customer** button to the boundary between B1 and C1.

Editing the PivotTable

As well as finding how many books have been ordered by each customer, we want to know the value of each customer's orders.

- First of all restore the PivotTable to its original state by clicking **Undo** or by dragging the buttons to their original locations, as in Figure 7.10. The PivotTable toolbar appears automatically when you create a PivotTable.

Figure 7.11: The PivotTable toolbar

- Select any cell in the PivotTable and click the PivotTable Wizard tool. The Step 3 dialogue box appears.

- Click on **Layout**, *(not Excel 97 or 7)* and the following dialogue box appears:

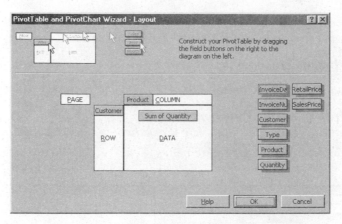

Figure 7.12: The PivotTable wizard layout

- Drag the **SalesPrice** button into the data area under **Sum of Quantity**. Click **OK.**

- In Excel 2000, in step 3 of the wizard, make sure that the **New Worksheet** option button is selected.

- Click **Finish**.

- In Excel 2000, right-click the row headers for rows 1 and 2 and select **Delete** to delete these two rows so that the screen appears as in Figure 7.13.

	A	B	C	D	E	F	G
1			Product ▾				
2	Customer ▾	Data ▾	A1	A2	A3	Grand Total	
3	Ballams	Sum of Quantity		47	30	77	
4		Sum of SalesPrice		230.3	105	335.3	
5	Cash Sale	Sum of Quantity			3	3	
6		Sum of SalesPrice			15	15	
7	Dragon	Sum of Quantity	15	55	52	122	
8		Sum of SalesPrice	105	269.5	182	556.5	
9	Gardners	Sum of Quantity	175	24	40	239	
10		Sum of SalesPrice	787.5	75.6	90	953.1	
11	Metcalfe Ltd	Sum of Quantity	18		45	63	
12		Sum of SalesPrice	126		157.5	283.5	
13	Smiths	Sum of Quantity	18	10		28	
14		Sum of SalesPrice	126	49		175	
15	TES	Sum of Quantity			90	90	
16		Sum of SalesPrice			202.5	202.5	
17	Total Sum of Quantity		226	136	260	622	
18	Total Sum of SalesPrice		1144.5	624.4	752	2520.9	
19							

Figure 7.13: Pivot table showing Sales Price and Quantity

The PivotTable is difficult to read because the currency amounts need formatting.

- Click cell B4 (or whichever cell in your worksheet represents Sum of SalesPrice for Ballams).
  *(In Excel 7, select cell B4, select **Data, Pivot Table field**, click the **Number** button and select **Currency**. Click **OK** in both dialogue boxes.)*

- On the PivotTable toolbar, click the **Field Settings** button.

- In the PivotTable Field dialogue box, click the **Number** button. The Format Cells dialogue box appears.

- In the category list, select currency, and click **OK**.

- In the PivotTable Field dialogue box, click **OK**.

Showing more detail in a PivotTable

To show more detail in the PivotTable:

- Select cells A3 to F18 and click the **Show Detail** button on the PivotTable toolbar.

- In the Show Detail dialogue box, select **InvoiceDate** and click **OK**.

An extra level of detail appears, which you can hide again by clicking the **Hide detail** button.

*(In Excel 7, select the whole Pivot Table before clicking **Hide Detail**.)*

Showing average sales quantities

To answer question 2 ("What is the average sale quantity for each customer?"), we need to find the Average quantity instead of the Sum.

- Use the right mouse button to click any cell in the PivotTable, and then select **Wizard...**
  *(In Excel 7, click the **Pivot Table Wizard** button on the Query and Pivot toolbar.)*

- In Excel 2000, in the step 3 dialogue box, click **Layout.**

- Double-click **Sum of Quantity** and a dialogue box appears as shown below. Select **Average** from the list as shown.

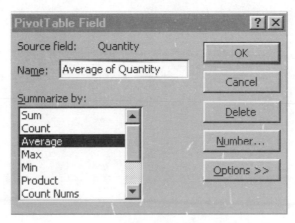

Figure 7.14: Changing the Summary function

- Click **OK**, and (in Excel 2000) **OK** in the layout dialogue box.

- Click **Finish** in the next dialogue box.

Figures appear as shown below. You can format the averages to appear to one decimal place by clicking cell B3 (or whichever cell contains **Average of Quantity**) and using the **Field Settings** button on the PivotTable toolbar as before.

*(In Excel 7, format the cells as described on the previous page. You will get the error **#DIV/0!** For Average Quantity wherever the quantity is equal to 0. There's not much you can do about this!)*

Atlas Sales.xls

	A	B	C	D	E	F	G
1			Product				
2	Customer	Data	A1	A2	A3	Grand Total	
3	Ballams	Average of Quantity		23.5	30.0	25.7	
4		Sum of SalesPrice		£230.30	£105.00	£335.30	
5	Cash Sale	Average of Quantity			1.5	1.5	
6		Sum of SalesPrice			£15.00	£15.00	
7	Dragon	Average of Quantity	15.0	27.5	26.0	24.4	
8		Sum of SalesPrice	£105.00	£269.50	£182.00	£556.50	
9	Gardners	Average of Quantity	87.5	24.0	40.0	59.8	
10		Sum of SalesPrice	£787.50	£75.60	£90.00	£953.10	
11	Metcalfe Ltd	Average of Quantity	18.0		45.0	31.5	
12		Sum of SalesPrice	£126.00		£157.50	£283.50	
13	Smiths	Average of Quantity	18.0	10.0		14.0	
14		Sum of SalesPrice	£126.00	£49.00		£175.00	
15	TES	Average of Quantity			45.0	45.0	
16		Sum of SalesPrice			£202.50	£202.50	
17	Total Average of Quantity		45.2	22.7	28.9	31.1	
18	Total Sum of SalesPrice		£1,144.50	£624.40	£752.00	£2,520.90	
19							

Figure 7.15: Finding Average quantities

Now see if you can create PivotTables to answer question 3 of this task! (Click the **Invoices** sheet tab, click in the table and select **Data, PivotTable And PivotChart Report…**)

If there's a message that using existing data will save memory, answer **Yes** if the data has not changed.

- Finally, save the workbook.

Chapter 8 – Creating Charts

Charts and graphs

Excel has excellent tools for creating charts, which are invaluable for presenting data in an easily understandable format. In addition to drawing bar charts, line graphs, pie charts and other types of chart, trend lines can be added to show a trend or forecast sales for the next few months, for example. Charts can either be embedded in an existing worksheet or placed in a chart sheet – a sheet in a workbook that contains only a chart. You can easily make an embedded sheet into a chart sheet, or a chart sheet into an embedded chart, at any time.

Charts can be created from raw data or from summaries held, for example, in a pivot table. Before we start work on charts, we'll create a reasonable amount of test data and do a little more work on pivot tables so that we have some figures to chart.

Task 8.1: Create test data and pivot table to chart

In this task we're going to generate a lot of sales data very quickly, and then create a PivotTable to summarize it.

- Use **File, Open** to open the **Atlas Sales** workbook. You can click **No** if a message appears asking if you want to update this workbook with changes made to the other workbook.

- Make sure your worksheet has data in columns A, C, E and F as in Figure 6.4 – it doesn't matter what data is in the other columns. Delete any extra rows you may have added. (If you have not got this workbook handy, create it now, entering figures as in Figure 6.4. You only need columns A, C, E and F for this exercise; leave the other columns blank.)

- Open a new workbook.

- From the **Window** menu select **Arrange, Tiled**.

- Click in the Zoom control and change the view to 85% in both workbooks.

- In the Atlas Sales workbook, select cells A3 to A23. With your finger on the Ctrl key, select C3 to C23, E3 to E23 and F3 to F23. Click the **Copy** button.

- Move to cell A3 in the new workbook and click the **Paste** button.

- Close the *Atlas Sales* Workbook.

- Save the new workbook as *Atlas Monthly Sales*.

Using Edit, Replace

Next, you're going to copy the data, change the dates to October and increase the sales quantities.

- Copy all the data from A4 to D23, to cells starting in A24. Press **Esc** to exit **Copy** mode and delete the dotted outline.

- Select cells A24 to A43 (all the newly copied dates) and from the menu select **Edit, Replace**.

- In the **Find What** box, type *09*.

- In the **Replace** with box, type *10*. Click **Replace All**. All the dates change to dates in October.

- Next, select cells D24 to D43 (all the newly copied quantities). Replace *1* by *2* throughout.

- Paste cells A24 to D43 to cells starting in A44.

- This time select all the date cells and replace 10 by 11. In the Quantity column, replace 2 by 3.

We'll also shuffle the products ordered a little.

- Delete the contents of cell C43.

- Move all the products from C44 to C63 up one cell by selecting the cells and dragging the boundary.

- In cell C63, type *A1*.

- Rename the sheet *Invoice Data*. (When you look back at an old workbook months later, it is useful to be able to immediately identify which sheet contains data.)

You now have 3 months worth of sales! Save the worksheet. The sales from Rows 22-63 should appear as follows:

Atlas Monthly Sales.xls:2

	A	B	C	D	E
2					
3	InvoiceDate	Customer	Product	Quantity	
4	01/09/98	Gardners	A1	100	
5	01/09/98	Gardners	A2	24	
6	01/09/98	Dragon	A1	15	
7	01/09/98	Dragon	A2	20	
8	01/09/98	Dragon	A3	12	
9	01/09/98	Metcalfe Ltd	A3	45	
10	01/09/98	Ballams	A2	30	
11	01/09/98	Ballams	A3	30	
12	02/09/98	Cash Sale	A3	2	
13	02/09/98	Smiths	A1	18	
14	02/09/98	Smiths	A2	10	
15	02/09/98	TES	A3	50	
16	02/09/98	TES	A3	40	
17	03/09/98	Gardners	A1	75	
18	03/09/98	Gardners	A3	40	
19	03/09/98	Ballams	A2	17	
20	03/09/98	Cash Sale	A3	1	
21	03/09/98	Metcalfe Ltd	A1	18	
22	03/09/98	Dragon	A2	35	
23	03/09/98	Dragon	A3	40	
24	01/10/98	Gardners	A1	200	
25	01/10/98	Gardners	A2	24	
26	01/10/98	Dragon	A1	25	
27	01/10/98	Dragon	A2	20	
28	01/10/98	Dragon	A3	22	
29	01/10/98	Metcalfe Ltd	A3	45	
30	01/10/98	Ballams	A2	30	
31	01/10/98	Ballams	A3	30	
32	02/10/98	Cash Sale	A3	2	
33	02/10/98	Smiths	A1	28	

Atlas Monthly Sales.xls:1

	A	B	C	D	E
34	02/10/98	Smiths	A2	20	
35	02/10/98	TES	A3	50	
36	02/10/98	TES	A3	40	
37	03/10/98	Gardners	A1	75	
38	03/10/98	Gardners	A3	40	
39	03/10/98	Ballams	A2	27	
40	03/10/98	Cash Sale	A3	2	
41	03/10/98	Metcalfe Ltd	A1	28	
42	03/10/98	Dragon	A2	35	
43	03/10/98	Dragon	A1	40	
44	01/11/98	Gardners	A2	300	
45	01/11/98	Gardners	A1	34	
46	01/11/98	Dragon	A2	35	
47	01/11/98	Dragon	A3	30	
48	01/11/98	Dragon	A3	33	
49	01/11/98	Metcalfe Ltd	A2	45	
50	01/11/98	Ballams	A3	30	
51	01/11/98	Ballams	A3	30	
52	02/11/98	Cash Sale	A1	3	
53	02/11/98	Smiths	A2	38	
54	02/11/98	Smiths	A3	30	
55	02/11/98	TES	A3	50	
56	02/11/98	TES	A1	40	
57	03/11/98	Gardners	A3	75	
58	03/11/98	Gardners	A2	40	
59	03/11/98	Ballams	A3	37	
60	03/11/98	Cash Sale	A1	3	
61	03/11/98	Metcalfe Ltd	A2	38	
62	03/11/98	Dragon	A3	35	
63	03/11/98	Dragon	A1	40	
64					
65					

Figure 8.1: Monthly sales data

Note: Check the last two lines – have you shuffled the products as described above?

Summarising using a PivotTable

- Click anywhere in the table and select **Data, PivotTable and PivotChart Report**. *(In Excel 97 and 7, select **Pivot Table Report…**)*

- Accept the defaults in Steps 1 and 2.

- In Excel 2000, in Step 3, click **Finish.**

- From the PivotTable toolbar *(or the window in Excel 97 and 7)* drag the field buttons onto the Page, Row, Column and Data areas in that order as shown in Figure 8.2 .

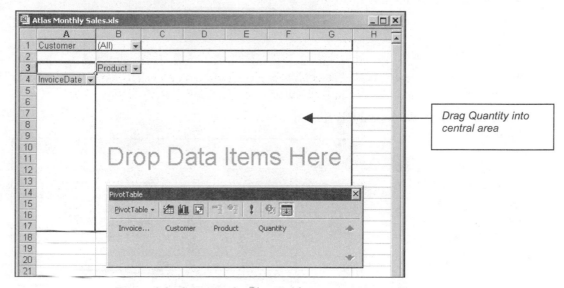

Figure 8.2: Creating the PivotTable

- Your PivotTable will appear on a new worksheet as shown below.

	A	B	C	D	E	F
1	Customer	(All)				
2						
3	Sum of Quantity	Product				
4	InvoiceDate	A1	A2	A3	Grand Total	
5	01/09/98	115	74	87	276	
6	02/09/98	18	10	92	120	
7	03/09/98	93	52	81	226	
8	01/10/98	225	74	97	396	
9	02/10/98	28	20	92	140	
10	03/10/98	143	62	42	247	
11	01/11/98	34	380	123	537	
12	02/11/98	43	38	80	161	
13	03/11/98	43	78	147	268	
14	Grand Total	742	788	841	2371	
15						

Figure 8.3: The PivotTable

Creating a monthly summary

To create the monthly summary, the dates need to be grouped.

- Select cell A4 containing the **InvoiceDate** button. *(Select A5 in Excel 7. If the toolbar is not displayed, right-click a toolbar, select **Query & Pivot**, and click **OK**.)* From the **Data** menu Select **Group and Outline** and then **Group**.

- The Grouping dialogue box appears. Select **Months** in the list box and click **OK**.

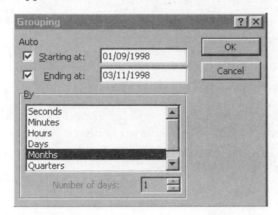

Figure 8.4: Grouping the data by month

The PivotTable now appears as shown below:

	A	B	C	D	E	F
1	Customer	(All) ▼				
2						
3	Sum of Quantity	Product ▼				
4	InvoiceDate ▼	A1	A2	A3	Grand Total	
5	Sep	226	136	260	622	
6	Oct	396	156	231	783	
7	Nov	120	496	350	966	
8	Grand Total	742	788	841	2371	
9						

Figure 8.5: The data grouped by months

- Note that by clicking the arrow in cell B1, you can look at the monthly sales for any individual customer.

- Rename the worksheet containing the PivotTable *Pivot Table*. (Right-click the sheet tab and select **Rename**.)

- Save your worksheet, and then save it again as *Atlas Sales Charts*. This is the workbook we'll use for the next task.

We're now ready to do some charting!

Task 8.2: Use a chart to present monthly sales and forecast a trend

In this task you will look at some of the options Excel offers for a visual presentation of data. You'll also be looking at how to create a trendline to forecast sales over the next few months based on the figures for the past months.

Creating a PivotChart report

- Open the workbook *Atlas Sales Charts* if it is not already open. The chart is to be based on the Pivot table, so click the *Pivot Table* worksheet tab.

- Right-click a cell within the PivotTable, point to **Select**, and if the **Enable Selection** command looks pushed in, click it. *(Omit this step in Excel 7.)*

- Select cells D7 to A4 by dragging from D7 up to A4 so that the Invoice date stays in the PivotTable. (You can't select A4 to D7, because as soon as you click A4 (the **InvoiceDate** button), Excel automatically selects the InvoiceDate column ready to change the structure of the PivotTable.)

   (In Excel 7, drag out an area covering cells B10 to G22. The Chart Wizard steps are somewhat different from those described below but you should have no difficulty in following them to create a chart.)

- On the PivotTable toolbar, double-click the **Chart Wizard** button. (If you single-click in Excel 2000, you get a chart without going through the Wizard steps, which we don't want to omit here.) *(In Excel 97 and 7, click the Chart wizard button on the Standard toolbar.)*
   The Chart Wizard appears as shown below:

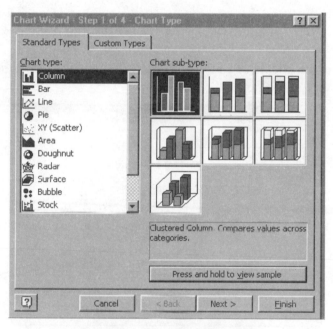

Figure 8.6: Chart Wizard, Step 1

- Make sure that **Column** is selected in the **Chart Type** list. You can get a preview of what the chart will look like by pressing the button marked **Press and hold to view sample**. Have a look at various column subtypes, and then select the first subtype before clicking **Next**.

- In the Step3 dialogue box, make sure the **Titles** tab is selected and enter *Current Sales by Product* in the **Chart Title** box. (See figure below.)

- Type *Quantity* in the **Value:(Y) axis** box.

- Have a look at the options available on the other tabs, but leave the defaults for now. Click **Next**.

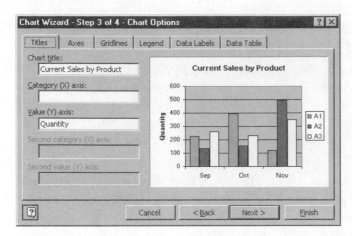

Figure 8.7: Chart Wizard, Step 3

- In the Step 4 dialogue box, make sure that the **As Object In** option button is selected and that the list box reads *PivotTable*, and then click **Finish**.

The new chart is created in the middle of your worksheet. It should look something like the figure below.

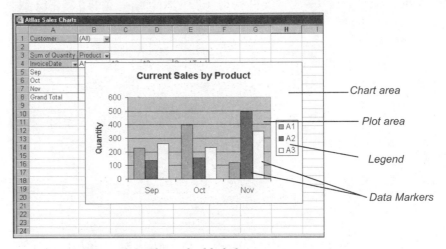

Figure 8.8: The embedded chart

Note: If the field buttons are displayed on the chart, click the arrow next to PivotChart on the PivotTable toolbar. Then click the **Hide PivotChart Fields** button.

Customising the chart

You can customise all aspects of the chart. We'll start by moving and enlarging it.

- Click in an empty area of the chart background (the chart area) so that handles appear, showing that it is selected. A Chart tip showing **Chart Area** will appear when your cursor is in this area. *(Not in Excel 7.)*

- Drag the corner handles so that the chart covers cells G2 to L17.

- Double-click the **Plot Area** (the inner grey box). The **Format Plot Area** dialogue box appears. Change the colour, or select **None**. (See figure below.)

- Click **OK**.

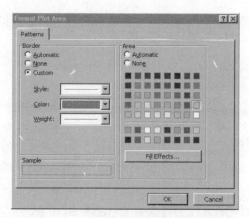

Figure 8.9: Formatting the Plot Area

- Double-click one of the A1 Data Markers in the chart (see Figure 8.8).

- Click **Fill Effects...** *(Not available in Excel 7.)*

- In the **Fill Effects** box, try out a few of the options!

- Click **OK** when you are happy with your effect, and **OK** in the next dialogue box.

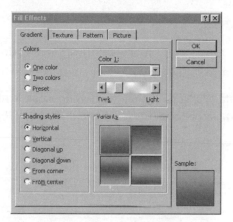

Figure 8.10: Fill effects

Printing the chart

- Click the chart to select it.

- On the Standard toolbar click the **Print Preview** button. Click **Print** if you want a hard copy, then **Close**.

Creating different charts by changing the PivotTable

You can create charts for each individual customer.

- Click the down arrow in cell B1, and select Gardners. The chart changes to show only the data for Gardners. Clever, isn't it! (*It's not quite so clever in Excel 7 as you get unwanted labels for **Sum of Quantity** and **Invoice Date**. Oh, well, that's progress for you.*)

You can also revise the data in the PivotTable report, which in turn updates the PivotChart report.

- Click anywhere in the PivotTable report, and then on the **Data** menu, click **PivotTable And PivotChart report.**

- In the PivotTable And PivotChart wizard, Step 3 of 3 appears. Be sure that the **Existing Worksheet** option is selected, and then click **Layout.** *(In Excel 97 and 7, drag the field buttons to exchange the positions of **Invoice Date** and **Product**.)*

- In Excel 2000, in the Layout dialogue box drag the field buttons to exchange the positions of **Invoice Date** and **Product**. Click **OK**.

- Click **Finish**. The sales are now shown by product rather than by date.

Making the embedded chart into a chart sheet

If you decide you would like to have the chart on a sheet of its own, you can move it as follows:

- Right-click in the chart area and select **Location**. *(Not available in Excel 7. Make a new chart with **Insert, Chart, As New sheet**.)*

- In the Chart Location dialogue box, click the **As New Sheet** option. Click **OK**.

The embedded chart is moved onto a separate chart sheet. You can rename, move, copy and delete a chart sheet in the same way as you would a worksheet.

Forecasting a sales trend

We can add a trend line to a chart to forecast sales quantities. We'll add it to the sales of product A2.

On the **Pivot Table** sheet of the current Sales by Product chart as shown in Figure 8.8:

- Right-click any of the A2 Data Markers in the chart, and select **Add Trendline**. *(In Excel 7, double-click the chart and select a bar in the data series. On the **Insert** menu, click **Trendline**.)*

- In the Add Trendline dialogue box, click **Linear**.

- Click the **Options** tab, and in the **Forward** box click the up arrow until it shows 2. This will give a trendline showing a two-quarter (6 month) forecast. Click **OK**.

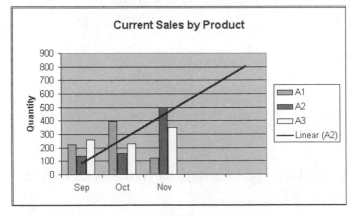

Figure 8.11: Adding a trendline

This is encouraging as it shows sales quantities for product A2 increasing. See if you can add trend lines to the other 2 data series in the chart.

Chapter 9 – Printing

Introduction

In this chapter you'll be looking at some of Excel's printing capabilities such as

- printing a multiple-page worksheet;
- setting print titles on every page;
- fitting information neatly onto a page;
- printing only selected information;
- centering text on the page;
- printing charts while maintaining their original dimensions.

First of all you need to quickly create a large worksheet to use as test data.

Task 9.1: Creating worksheet test data to print

- Open a new worksheet and save it as *Large Worksheet*.

- In cell A1 type *Large Worksheet* and make it **18 point Bold**.

- Enter headings and the first few lines of data as shown below. Widen the columns as necessary to accommodate all the headings and data.

	A	B	C
1	**Large Worksheet**		
2			
3	**Student Number**	**Name**	**Address**
4	1001	James Carter	5 Brentwood Avenue, Colchester, Essex CO6 4FR
5	1002	Neil Humphries	63 Charles Street, Edgeware, Middlesex HA6 8JM
6	1003	Eleanor Barrington	29 Crawford Avenue, Loughborough, Leics
7	1004	(xxx)	(Address)

	D	E	F	G
1				
2				
3	**Course code**	**Course Title**	**Tutor**	**Start date**
4	GNVQ1111	Advanced GNVQ in Computer Studies	David Billington	05/09/97
5	AL5555	A Level Programme	Priscilla Cameron	12/09/97
6	BTECNC99	BTEC National Certificate in Childcare	Barbara Lewis-Jones	03/01/98

Figure 9.1: Creating the large worksheet

- Use the right mouse button to drag the corner handle of cell A4 down to cell A200 and click **Fill Series** on the shortcut menu.

- Select cells B7 and C7 and drag the corner handle down to C200 using the left mouse button.

- Select cells D4 to G6 and drag the corner handle down to cell G200.

Your worksheet should look something like Figure 9.2 if you view it at 70%. Return to 100% view before continuing.

	A	B	C	D	E	F	G
1	**Large Worksheet**						
2							
3	**Student Number**	**Name**	**Address**	**Course Code**	**Course Title**	**Tutor**	**Start date**
4	1001	James Carter	5 Brentwood Avenue, Colchester, Essex CO6 4	GNVQ1111	Advanced GNVQ in Computer Studies	David Billington	05/09/97
5	1002	Neil Humphries	63 Charles Street, Edgeware, Middlesex HA6 8J	AL5555	A Level Programme	Priscilla Cameron	12/09/97
6	1003	Eleanor Barrington	29 Crawford Avenue, Loughborough, Leics	BTECNC99	BTEC National Certificate in Childcare	Barbara Lewis-Jones	03/01/98
7	1004	(xxx)	(Address)	GNVQ1112	Advanced GNVQ in Computer Studies	David Billington	05/09/97
8	1005	(xxx)	(Address)	AL5556	A Level Programme	Priscilla Cameron	12/09/97
9	1006	(xxx)	(Address)	BTECNC100	BTEC National Certificate in Childcare	Barbara Lewis-Jones	03/01/98
10	1007	(xxx)	(Address)	GNVQ1113	Advanced GNVQ in Computer Studies	David Billington	05/09/97
11	1008	(xxx)	(Address)	AL5557	A Level Programme	Priscilla Cameron	12/09/97
12	1009	(xxx)	(Address)	BTECNC101	BTEC National Certificate in Childcare	Barbara Lewis-Jones	03/01/98

Figure 9.2: Test data

Task 9.2: Preview and print the data in a variety of ways

Several problems are commonly encountered when printing a large worksheet:

1. The sheet may be printed with 6 columns on one page and only one on the second, when you would rather have three columns on each page.

2. The column headings only appear on the first page.

3. Several pages of the left side of a long worksheet may print out first, followed by the right hand side pages, when you would rather print the left side followed by the right side.

4. The worksheet almost fits on a page and you would like to avoid it printing a few lines on the second page.

In this task you'll learn how to overcome all these problems.

Previewing the worksheet

Before you print anything it is a good idea to look at it in Print Preview mode to make sure you are happy with the way it will appear on the printed page.

- On the Standard toolbar click **Print Preview**. Page 1 appears in Print Preview mode, showing that 4 columns will be printed on Page 1.

- On the button bar, click **Page Break Preview**.

   *(In Excel 7, close the Print Preview and click column header D. From the **Insert** menu select **Page Break** to insert a vertical page break between columns C and D.)*

- The **Welcome to Page Break Preview** dialogue box appears, as shown below. Click **OK** to close it.

The Page Break Preview shows you how the worksheet is broken up into pages, and the order in which the pages will be printed. All the pages on the left hand side of the worksheet will be printed first, and then the right hand pages. This order is called *Down, Then Over*.

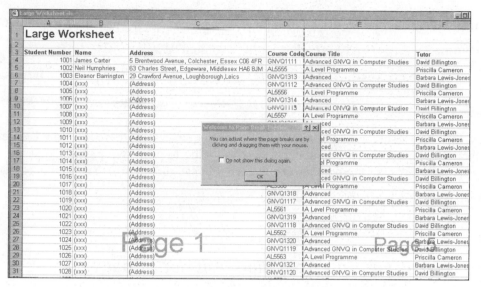

Figure 9.3: Page Break Preview

- Point to the vertical page break line and when the mouse pointer becomes a two-headed arrow, drag the line one column to the left. The page break line becomes a solid line to indicate that this is now a manual page break rather than an automatic one.

- Click the **Page Preview** button and scroll down to look at page 2. You will notice that the column headings do not appear.

- Click **View, Normal View** to return to Normal view.

Setting print titles

As well as having column headings appear on every page, it might be convenient to have the Student Number appear in the first column of both pages.

- From the **File** menu select **Page Setup**, and in the dialogue box click the **Sheet** tab.

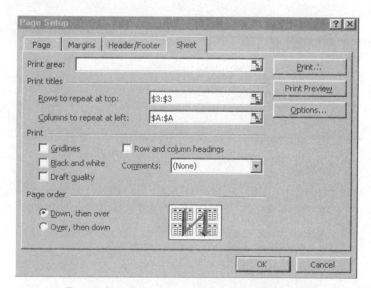

Figure 9.4: Setting print titles and print order

- Under **Print Titles**, click in the **Rows to Repeat At Top** box, and then click any cell in row 3.

- In the **Columns To Repeat At Left**, click a cell in column A.

- You can change the print sequence in this dialogue box to **Over, Then Down**. *(Across, Then Down in Excel 7.)* Click **OK**.

- Click the **Print Preview** button.

Unfortunately this has resulted in two undesirable consequences: part of the title **Large Worksheet** appears on page 2 and 3, and the worksheet is now too wide to print two pages across. (If it isn't, your columns may be narrower than the ones shown. Widen them slightly if so.) The first is easily fixed.

- Press **Esc** to return to Normal view.

- Move the title **Large Worksheet** to cell B1.

Printing a worksheet on a specified number of pages

The worksheet can be scaled so that it fits onto a specified number of pages. At the moment it is 3½ pages long and 3 pages wide. It could be conveniently fitted into fewer pages.

- From the **File** menu select **Page Setup**.

- Click the **Page** tab.

- In the **Fit to** box enter *2* pages wide by *3* tall. Click **OK**.

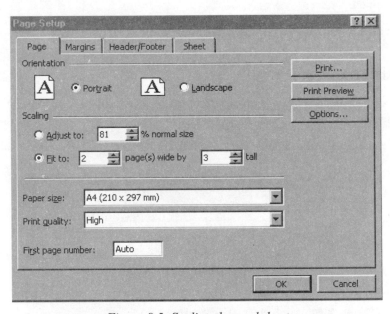

Figure 9.5: Scaling the worksheet

Note: Excel automatically adjusts to 81% of normal size, or whatever percentage is required to fit the worksheet in the specified number of pages. You may get a different percentage figure here.

- Click the **Print Preview** button. The status bar tells you that the worksheet will fit onto 6 pages.

Centering data on the page

At the moment the data is left aligned on the page. You can centre it as follows.

- Click the **Print Preview** button, then click the page to zoom out so that you can view the whole page.

- On the Button bar, click **Margins**. Margin lines appear, showing that the worksheet print area is left aligned. (The heading of the first column is against the lefthand margin.

- On the button bar, click **Setup**.

- In the Page Setup dialogue box, click the **Margins** tab.

- Check the **Horizontally** option under **Center on Page**. (If the data occupies the whole width of the page, the difference won't be obvious, so look at the next page which contains fewer columns.)

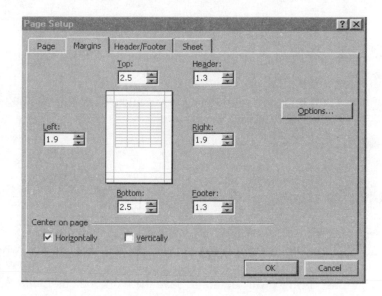

Figure 9.6: Centering text

Printing headers and footers

In the same dialogue box, you can set headers and footers. This topic was covered in Chapter 2.

Printing selected areas of the worksheet

Suppose you wanted to print just the **Student Number, Name** and **Course Title** for the first 20 students. One way to do this is to first hide the intervening columns that you don't want printed.

- In Normal View, drag across the column headers C and D. Select **Format**, **Column**, **Hide**.

- Now select cells A1 to E23.

- From the **File** menu select **Print**.

- In the **Print Dialogue** box click **Selection** instead of **Active Sheet**.

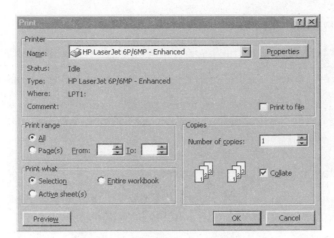

Figure 9.7: Printing a selection

- Click the **Preview** button in this dialogue box. Your previous settings will still apply and you may want to readjust them.

- When you have finished printing, you can unhide the columns again by selecting columns A to E and then selecting **Format, Column, Unhide**.

- Save and close the workbook.

Task 9.3: Printing charts

For this task you'll need the **Atlas Sales Charts** workbook created in Chapter 8. If you have got this handy, open it now and click the **PivotTable** sheet tab. If you have not got this workbook, open a new workbook and enter the text and numbers as shown in Figure 8.5, from A4 to D7. Then use the chart wizard to create a bar chart, accepting all the defaults. Save the workbook as *PrintChart*.

Printing an embedded chart

- To print the chart without the workbook, first click anywhere in the chart area to select it. *(Double-click in Excel 7.)*

- Click the **Print Preview** button. The sheet is scaled so that it occupies the whole page.

- To maintain the chart's original proportions, click the **Setup** button on the print preview page. Click the **Chart** tab.

- On the **Chart** tab, ensure the **Scale to Fit Page** option button is selected, then click **OK**. The chart will be displayed in the same proportions that it was on the worksheet.

- Click **Close** to return to normal view.

Printing a sheet and the embedded chart together

- Deselect the chart and then click the **Print Preview** button. You will see both the figures and the chart. You will need to position the chart in the worksheet so that it does not overlap the figures, and you can experiment with centering the text on the page, etc.

Part 3

Customising an Application

In this section:

Chapter 10 – Online Forms and Templates

Introduction

In Part 3, we will be looking at how to create a complete application. This may typically involve creating a template which will be used for data entry, transferring data entered by a user to an Excel database and performing some processing on it. The application may contain customised menus and toolbars, with buttons that run macros to perform certain tasks when a user clicks them.

There are many minor differences between Excel 2000, 97 and earlier versions which affect instructions or screenshots. Where necessary, these are pointed out but in cases where it is obvious what alternative to select, differences will not be pointed out and you will be expected to use your common sense!

Task 10.1: Create an online form for entering expenses

Bigco is a large company employing a number of people who regularly travel to meetings in other towns in the course of their duties. Each time an employee attends a meeting they fill in an online claim form detailing their expenses. This form is held as a template, so that an employee can open a new blank form based on the template and save the claim form as a worksheet. The claim form is shown below:

EXPENSES FORM

Name:

Meeting:		**Number:**
Place:		**Date:**

Travelling Expenses

Journey from:		From:		
To:		To:		

Rail Fare				
Tube/Bus Fares				
Car miles:	**miles @**	**£0.50**	**Car Mileage**	£0.00

Incidental Expenses

Subsistence	
Other Expenses	
(Specify other expenses)	
Total Claimed	£0.00

Figure 10.1: Expenses Claim Form

Creating the basic form

- Open a new worksheet and save it as *BigCo Expenses*.

- Enter headings in cells as shown in Figure 10.2.

	A	B	C	D	E	F	G	H	I	J
1		**EXPENSES FORM**								
2		Name:								
3		Meeting:					Number:			
4										
5		Place:					Date:			
6										
7		**Travelling Expenses**								
8										
9		Journey from:			From:					
10		To:			To:					
11										
12		Rail Fare								
13		Tube/Bus Fares								
14		Car miles:		miles @	£0.50		Car Mileage		£0.00	
15										
16		**Incidental Expenses**								
17		Subsistence								
18		Other Expenses								
19		(Specify other expenses)								
20		**Total Claimed**							£0.00	
21										

Figure 10.2: The basic Bigco Expenses worksheet

- Format cells E14 and the cells in column I as **Currency, 2 decimal places**.

- Format cell H5 as a date.

- In cell I14 enter a formula *=C14*E14*

- In cell I20 enter a formula *=Sum(I7:I19)* and format I12 to I20 as Currency. Note that if you do so using the **Currency** button, I14 for example will appear as **£ -** , whereas if you use **Format, Cells, Currency**, it will appear as shown in the figure above. Just another of Bill's little jokes.

- *(Skip this step in Excel 7.)* Use **Format, Cells**, click the **Alignment** tab and select **Merge cells** to merge cells as shown in the figure. Cells C3 to F3, C5 to F5, C9 to C10, F9 to F10, B12 to H12, B13 to H13, B17 to H17, B18 to H18, D19 to H19 and B20 to H20 are merged.

  (This step is important for the next task, where each entry needs a label immediately to its left for Excel's Automatic Naming to work properly – but you can't do it in Excel 7 without centering the labels, so don't even bother to try in that case.)

Data validation

*(This is not available in Excel 7. Skip to **Protecting the worksheet**.)*

You can specify that the contents of various cells must conform to given criteria. We will specify the following validations:

- The meeting number must be a whole number of up to 6 digits;

- The car miles must be between 1.0 and 500.00;
- The specified 'other expenses' must be one of *Parking*, *Taxis* or *Telephone calls*.

- Select cell H3 for the meeting number.
- Select **Data, Validation**. The following window is displayed.

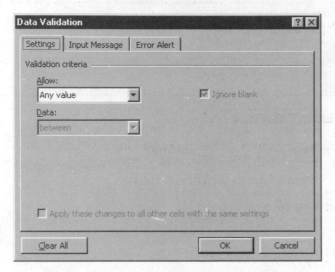

Figure 10.3: The Data Validation window

- Click the arrow in the **Allow** box and select **Whole Number**. Type *0* in the **Minimum** box and *999999* in the **Maximum** box. Click **OK**.

- Test out the validation by typing a letter in cell H3. The following message is displayed:

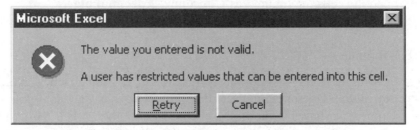

Figure 10.4: Error message when invalid data is entered

- Set the validation in cell C14 to **Decimal** between **1.00** and **500.00**.

- Click the **Input Message** tab in the Data Validation window. In the **Input message** box, type: *Input a value between 1.00 and 500.00.*

- Click the **Error Alert** tab in the Data Validation window. In the **Error message** box, type a customised error message: *The value must be between 1 and 500.*

- Click **OK**. Test your validation by putting in an invalid number of miles.

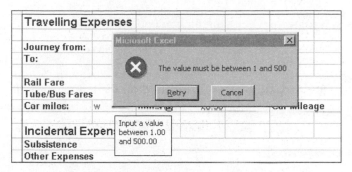

Figure 10.5: Customised prompt and error message

Selecting valid data from a list

The entry in cell D19 (Other Expenses) has to be one of three values: *Parking, Taxis* or *Telephone calls*. First of all, these three items need to be stored in a table and given a name. Then you can create a dropdown list in cell D19 from which to select a valid entry.

- In cell L1, type a heading *Allowable Expenses.*

- Below this heading, list the three items as shown in Figure 10.6.

- Select the range L2 to L4 and in the **Name** box, type the name *OtherExpenses*. Press **Enter**.

	K	L	M
1		**Allowable Expenses**	
2		Parking	
3		Taxis	
4		Telephone calls	
5			

Figure 10.6: List of valid 'other expenses'

- Select cell D19 for Other expenses, and select **Data, Validation**. On the **Settings** tab, select **List** in the **Allow** box, and type *=OtherExpenses* in the **Source** box. Check **In-cell Dropdown** and click **OK**.

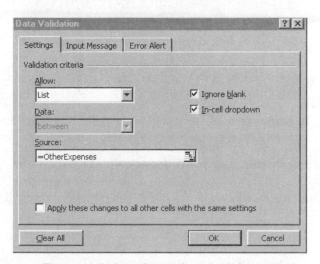

Figure 10.7: Specifying a list of valid entries

95

- The dropdown list arrow appears when you click in cell D19.

- Time to save your worksheet again! Save it by clicking the **Save** button.

- Save it again as *BigCoBak.xls*, using **File, Save As**. Then close this backup file, and reopen **BigCo Expenses.xls**. If you have any problems with protection, such as forgetting your password, you can use the backup file.

Protecting the worksheet

The next thing is to protect the worksheet so that the user cannot accidentally (or deliberately) change any headings or formulae. By default all cells will be automatically locked if you protect the worksheet. Therefore you must first unlock any cells in which data entry is allowed, and then protect the worksheet. You may not be able to do this on a college or school machine with restricted access but it should certainly be mentioned in your project and tried out at home if you have your own computer.

- Click in C2, the first cell where the user will enter data, and from the **Format** menu select **Cells**.

- Click the **Protection** tab and clear the **Locked Cells** box.

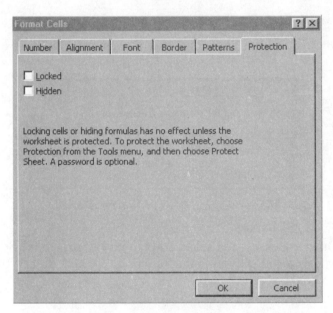

Figure 10.8: Unlocking cells for the user to enter data

- You might like to shade the cells where the user can enter data, or else shade the cells where the user cannot enter data, to make the form easier to fill in. Click the **Patterns** tab and choose a colour.

- Repeat this for all the cells in which the user will enter data. The quickest way is to hold down the Ctrl key as you select each cell. Then select **Format**, **Cells** and set the protection and shading.

- Now protect the worksheet by selecting **Tools, Protection, Protect Sheet**. You will be asked to enter a password and confirm it. Be very careful here – if you forget the password, you will not be able to edit your worksheet. Just for the record I've chosen the password *manager*. (The password is case-sensitive.)

  Note that if you leave the **Password** box blank, the worksheet is still protected against accidental changes. It's a good idea to leave it blank at least while you are working on implementing your project to avoid any possibility of forgetting the password.

Figure 10.9 – Setting a password

- Test your worksheet by making an entry in every unprotected cell, and attempting data entry in other cells as well.

Editing a protected sheet

You won't be able to make any changes without first unprotecting the sheet.

- Select **Tools, Protection, Unprotect sheet**. You will be asked to enter the password.

Hiding gridlines

Your form might look better without gridlines.

- Right-click any toolbar, and a list of toolbars appears. *(The list will be different in Excel 7.)*

Figure 10.10: List of toolbars

- Check **Forms**. The Forms toolbar appears.

Figure 10.11: The Forms toolbar

- Click the **Toggle Grid** button on this toolbar, and the gridlines disappear.

Hiding columns

You don't really want the user to see your list of valid expenses, so hide this column. *(Excel 7 users: You can do this even if you haven't entered anything in Column L.)*

- Click the column header for column L.

- Select **Format, Column, Hide**, or right-click in the column header and select **Hide**.

- Finally, name the sheet *Expenses*, delete all the unwanted sheets, and delete any test data you have put in the form. Save the workbook in its unprotected form, just in case you do forget the password!

- Now protect the worksheet again by selecting **Tools, Protection, Protect Sheet**.

Note that **Tools, Protection, Protect Workbook** does not prevent users from making entries in locked cells. It protects the structure of the entire workbook, so that users cannot, for example, add, delete or rename worksheets. To prevent data entry in locked cells, select **Tools, Protection, Protect Sheet**.

Saving the workbook as a template

When you have created a workbook such as an input form that will be used over and over again with different data each time, it is a very good idea to save it as a template.

The template will contain all the headings, formula and formatting for the form but no data. To use the template, a user opens a new workbook using **File, New** and selects the template instead of the more general **Workbook** template which simply contains 4 empty sheets (see Figure 10.13).

- Select **File, Save As**.

- In the **Save as Type** box, select **Template (*.xlt)**. The default folder automatically changes to the **Templates** folder. Click **Save**.

Figure 10.12: Saving a workbook as a template

- If you are working on a school or college machine you may not be able to save anything in the **Templates** folder. In that case, change the folder to your normal working drive and folder and save the template there as *Bigco Expenses.xlt*.

- Close the template.

Using the template

When you store a template in the default Templates folder, it will automatically appear in the list of templates when you select **File, New**. You can then select the template and click **OK**.

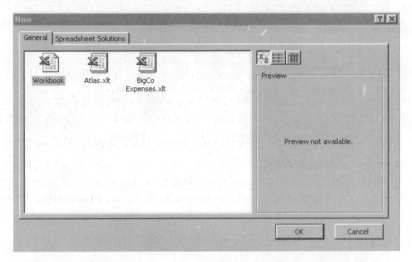

Figure 10.13: Opening a new workbook using a custom template

If, however, you have had to save your template on your own disk, you can open a new workbook based on this template from **Explorer** as follows.

- Load **Explorer** and find your template in the list of files on whichever drive you have saved it.

- Right-click the file name and select **New**. A new workbook based on your template opens.

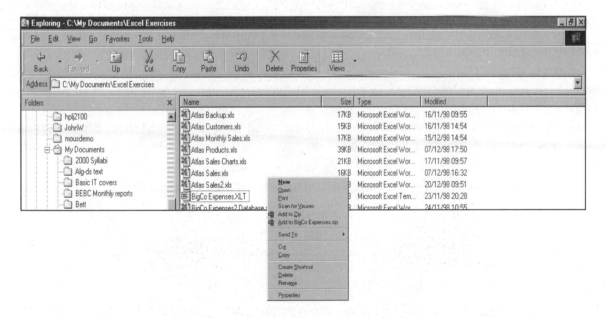

Figure 10.14: Opening a new file from Explorer

*(If you are using Windows 3.1, when you open a file with a .xlt extension, you get a document based on the template. To open the template itself, select the file name, then hold down the **Shift** key and click **OK**.)*

- Test out your new form. Pressing the **Tab** key should take you to each unlocked cell in turn. The form should look something like the figure below.

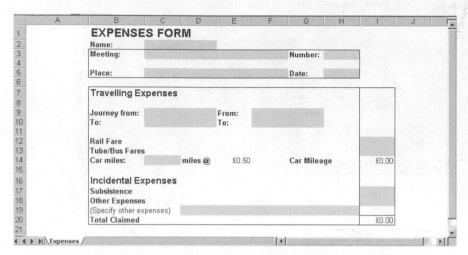

Figure 10.15: The finished Expenses form

In the next task, you'll learn how to transfer data from the form to another workbook which will act as a database.

- Delete any test data you have entered, and save the workbook as *BigCo Expenses2*.

Task 10.2: Transfer data from an input form to a database workbook

In order to do this task you need to have the **Template Wizard with Data Tracking** add-in installed on your system. Click the **Data** menu – if you do not see the **Template Wizard** command, then you cannot proceed without first installing the add-in.

The **Template wizard** can be used to transfer data from Excel to an Access database – useful in a major project where you need to link two packages. Once in Access, you can query the data in all sorts of ways to produce different reports.

Assuming you have the necessary add-in installed, you need to have the worksheet **BigCo Expenses2** open for this task, so if you have not still got it on your screen, open it now. The template wizard will create a new template from this worksheet.

- Select **Template Wizard** from the **Data** menu. The following screen appears:

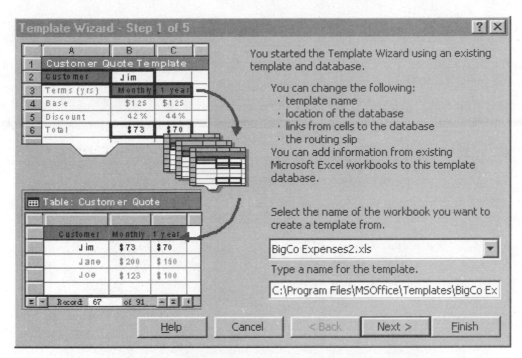

Figure 10.16: Step 1 of the Template Wizard

- You may want to change the destination folder of the template – you will need to do so if you are working on a restricted access network. Click **Next**.

- Step 2 of the Template Wizard appears, asking you for the name of the database workbook that you want to have created. Amend the pathname if necessary. *(If the window contains an additional list box **Select the type of database you want the wizard to create**, select **Microsoft Excel workbook**.)*

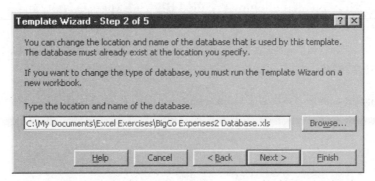

Figure 10.17: Step 2 of the Template Wizard

- Click **Next**.

- Step 3 of the Template Wizard appears as shown below. With the cursor in the first **Cell** box, click cell H3 in the **Expenses** worksheet which contains the meeting number. Press the **Tab** key, and the field name **Number:** is automatically assigned. Delete the colon, which you don't want as part of the field name.

Note that in this exercise we are not going to transfer the contents of *every* field to the database. We will transfer **Number, Date, Rail Fare, Tube/Bus Fares, Car Miles, Car Mileage, Subsistence, Other Expenses** and **Total Claimed**. This will enable the management to analyse the data to find out, for example, the total amount of expenses for each meeting, or total expenses claimed per month. The database will not be used to gather information on each individual employee's claims.

● Tab to the next **Cell** box and click in cell H5 for the **Date** field. Tab again, and delete the colon at the end of the Field Name **Date**.

● In the next **Cell** box, click in I12 for **Rail Fare**, and press **Tab**. Continue like this until you have entered all the required fields, when the Step 3 window will look like the figure below. Click **Next**.

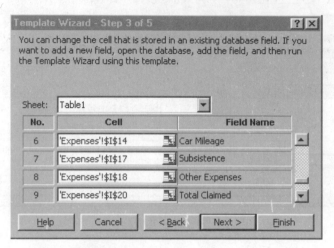

Figure 10.18: Fields to be added to the database

● Click **Next** in the Step 4 dialogue box.

● Click **Finish** in the Step 5 dialogue box.

● Save and close the workbook.

Excel has now automatically created a template called **BigCo Expenses2.xlt**, and a new workbook called **BigCo Expenses2 Database.xls.**

Testing the template

● Open a new file based on the **BigCo Expenses2** template. (Use **Explorer** if necessary, right-clicking the template name and selecting **New**.) A message appears:

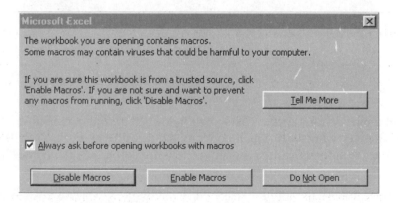

Figure 10.19: Warning message alerting you to danger from macro viruses

- In this particular case, you know there is a macro in this worksheeet that transfers the data to the database. Viruses are a real problem in many schools, colleges and workplaces, however, so first click the **Tell Me More** button and read about macro viruses. Then click the **Enable Macros** button, leaving the **Always ask before opening workbooks with macros** box checked.

- Fill in some test data for a meeting number *111* in Birmingham, a number of miles for a car journey, *£16* subsistence and *£5.00* in taxi fares.

- Select **File, Save** to save the worksheet. You may see the following message:

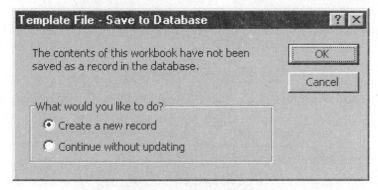

Figure 10.20: Creating a new database record.

- Select **Create a new record** and click **OK**. Give your workbook a name *Birmingham Expenses*.

- Close the workbook.

Viewing the database

- Open the workbook **BigCo Expenses2 Database.xls.** You will see that a record has been added corresponding to the data you entered into the form.

- You can format the columns in the database and widen them as required.

- You may see an extra column which is created automatically by Excel. Leave it if so.

- You can add test data straight into the database without going via the input form – note that there are no formulae in the database as everything is pasted as values.

	A	B	C	D	E	F	G	H	I	J
1	Number	Date	Rail Fare	Tube/Bus Fares	Car miles	Car Mileage	Subsistence	Other Expenses	Total Claimed	WT_RECID
2	111	18/11/98			230	£115.00	£16.00	£5.00	£136.00	-2.62E+08
3										

*Figure 10.21: The data inserted into the database **BigCo Expenses2 Database.xls***

Note that once several expenses forms have been entered, various analyses can be performed on the data in the database – you could, for example, use a PivotTable to calculate the total claimed for each meeting, or in each month.

- Save and close the workbook when you have finished experimenting.

In your project work, it is important that the input data is processed in some way to produce a result in the form of a report or graph – preferably using something more than a simple sum or pie chart. You might also consider using conditional formatting in the database so that all claims over a certain amount are highlighted in red, for example. You can write a macro to do this as shown in Chapter 12, or do it by using **Format, Conditional Formatting** in Excel 2000 and 97.

An Excel system for inputting and analysing expenses makes a good project but you must have a real user who can explain real requirements to you – it is no good making up your own rules.

Task 10.3: Create a mortgage repayment calculator

In this task you'll use some of the other tools on the Forms toolbar to create a simple model which calculates the repayments on a loan taken out to buy a house (or a car, 3-piece suite, washing machine, holiday etc).

- Open a new workbook and save it as *Mortgage Repayments*.

- Enter labels, values and a formula *=C3-C4* in C5, and format cells as shown in the figure below.

	A	B	C	D
1		Mortgage Repayments		
2				
3		Purchase Price	£50,000	
4		Down Payment	£3,000	
5		Loan	£47,000	
6		Interest Rate	8.25%	
7		Years	25	
8		Monthly Payment		
9				

Figure 10.22: Starting the Mortgage Repayments worksheet

- Name the cells by selecting cells B3 to C8 and selecting **Insert**, **Name**, **Create**. Select **Left Column**. Note that the names given to cells C3 and C4, for example, are **Purchase_Price**, **Down_Payment** as no spaces are allowed in a name.

- In cell C8 we need the **PMT** function to calculate the repayment. Select cell C8 and click the **Edit Formula** button (the = sign next to the Formula bar). *(In Excel 7, type = in the Formula bar and then click the **Function** button. Select **Financial** in the **Function Category** list.)*

- Select **PMT** from the list of functions for the periodic payment. A dialogue box is displayed.

- Fill in the boxes as shown below.

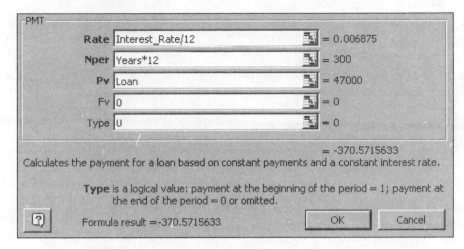

Figure 10.23: Using the Pmt function to calculate mortgage repayments

- Click **OK**. The monthly repayment of **£370.57** is shown in red as a negative value.

Displaying the formulae in a worksheet

When you document your project you will need to show all the formulae you have used. This is easily done:

- Select **Tools, Options** and click the **View** tab. Check the **Formulas** box as shown below, and click **OK**.

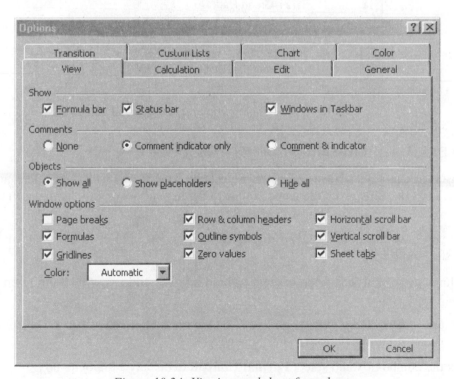

Figure 10.24: Viewing worksheet formulae

The spreadsheet now appears as shown below. You may need to widen column C.

	A	B	C
1		Mortgage Repayments	
2			
3		Purchase Price	50000
4		Down Payment	3000
5		Loan	=C3-C4
6		Interest Rate	0.0825
7		Years	25
8		Monthly Payment	=PMT(Interest_Rate/12,Years*12,Loan,0,0)
9			

Figure 10.25: The worksheet with formulae displayed

- Select **Tools, Options** again and deselect **Formulas** to return to Normal view. While you're in this window, notice some of the other options you could use if you needed to!

Adding a combo box control

Instead of simply typing the purchase price into cell C3, we will create a list of houses with their purchase prices from which the user will choose: the purchase price will then automatically be inserted into cell C3.

- Type a list of houses into cells as shown below.

	D	E	F	G
1				
2		House	Price	
3		32 Foxhall Road	£48,000	
4		121 Green Park Rd	£29,000	
5		7 Wood Grove	£68,000	
6		68 Park Rd	£129,995	
7		7 Tye Lane	£76,000	
8		95 Frederick Close	£99,995	
9				

Figure 10.26: List of houses and purchase prices

- Select cell E2 and press **Ctrl-Shift-*** to select the whole table.

- On the **Insert** menu select **Name, Create**. Select the **Top Row** check box, clear any other check boxes and click **OK**. This gives the name **House** to the list of houses and the name **Price** to the list of prices.

- Make sure you have the Forms toolbar displayed. If it is not, right-click a toolbar and select **Forms** from the list of toolbars.

- Widen column A so that it is wide enough to hold a house address with room to spare (see Figure 10.28).

- Click the **Combo Box** *(Drop Down in Excel 7)* button on the Forms toolbar. Drag from the top left corner of cell A3 to the bottom right of the cell.

- Right-click the combo box and select **Format Control** to display a dialogue box.

- Enter *House* as the Input range and *D4* as the cell link. Click **OK**.

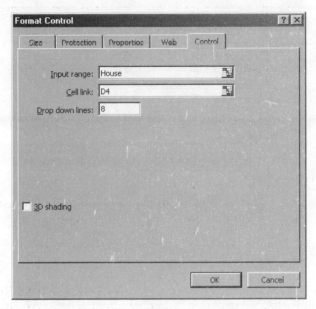

Figure 10.27: Defining cells for the combo box control

- Press **Esc** to deselect the combo box.

- Click the arrow next to the combo box control, and select **121 Green Park Rd**. The name appears in the combo box and the number **2** appears in cell D4, because this is the second house in the list.

You have now linked the combo box to the list of houses and linked the result of the combo box to cell D4. The next step is to retrieve the price from the list.

Retrieving the price from the list

- Select cell C3 and type the formula *=Index(Price,D4)*. The price is automatically inserted.

Using a spinner button

- Delete the contents of cell C4 (Down Payment).

- Click the **Spinner** button on the Forms toolbar.

- Drag out an area near the right of cells A4 and A5 as shown in Figure 10.28.

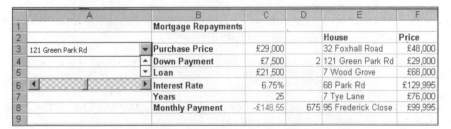

Figure 10.28: The form with controls

- Right-click the spinner control and select **Format Control**. A dialogue box appears which you need to fill in as shown below, with *C4* in the **Cell link** box. Then click **OK**.

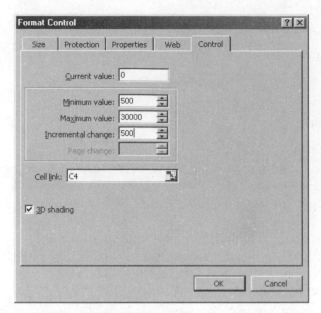

Figure 10.29: Spinner controls

- Click away from the spinner to deselect it and then try it out.

Inserting a scroll bar for interest rates

- Click the **Scroll Bar** button on the Forms toolbar, and drag across cell A6 (see Figure 10.28).

- Right-click the scroll bar and select **Format Control**.

- Fill in the dialogue box as shown below, with *D8* in the **Cell link** box.. This will allow interest rates to vary between 0 and 20%, and the rate will be incremented by .25% each time an arrow is clicked. Click **OK**.

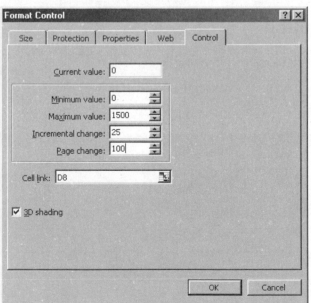

Figure 10.30: Scroll bar controls

- Click away from the scroll bar to deselect it.

- In cell C6 type the formula *=D8/10000*.

- Try out the scroll bar!

Enhancing the form

There are many ways in which you can smarten up the form. You can hide columns D to F, unlock cells that the user will enter data in and protect the sheet, add comments and instructions, and save the form as a template with data fields set to blanks or zeros. Altering the layout, adding colour, borders, changing fonts and font size, naming the worksheet and deleting unused worksheets are all ways of customising the form.

You might also think about using **Goal Seek** to answer such questions as "What house can I afford to buy with a down payment of £2000 and monthly payments of £200?" You may need to allow for the fact that purchasers very often do not pay the full purchase price – the vendor may accept a lower offer. The current model does not cater for that.

This idea could form the basis of a project if you can find a real user with a similar problem – for example an estate agent, a second-hand car dealer or a furniture store.

- Save and close the workbook.

Chapter 11 – Basic Macros

The macro recorder

In early spreadsheet programs, a *macro* was a series of steps that you could create either by recording keystrokes or by writing a simple sequence of macro instructions. In the latest versions of Excel, a macro is much more than just a series of recorded keystrokes. The language used to record macros is a real programming language called Visual Basic for Applications, which you can use to perform complex tasks.

The macro recorder is a good way to start creating macros and learning about Visual Basic. However, recording all the keystrokes involved in a long, complex task will rarely result in a satisfactory macro and you will need to understand the program code behind the macro so that you can edit it to produce the desired result.

We'll start by creating and running some simple macros, and then learn how to edit them and create Visual Basic programs using the macro code as a starting point.

Recording a macro to insert a new line in a table

In Chapter 6 you created the **Atlas Products** workbook containing a table of Products like the one below.

	A	B	C	D
1	**Products**			
2				
3	**ProductCode**	**Description**	**RetailPrice**	
4	A1	Deluxe Edition	£11.00	
5	A2	Standard Edition	£7.00	
6	A3	Economy Edition	£5.00	
7	END OF TABLE			
8				

Figure 11.1: Table of Products

The range which embraces columns A to C was given a name *ProductTable*. Columns A, B and C were named *ProductCode*, *Description* and *RetailPrice* respectively.

We will write a macro to insert a new line just above 'END OF TABLE' ready for the user to enter a new product.

- Open the workbook **Atlas Products**. Delete any extra products you may have added while testing so that the table looks like Figure 11.1. If you haven't got this workbook handy, create a new one, and name Sheet 1 *Products*.

- Name the ranges as described above if you have just created a new worksheet. To do this, drag across column headers A to C and type the name *ProductTable* in the **Name** box. Then select each of the column headers A, B and C in turn and type the relevant name in the **Name** box. Remember to press **Enter** after typing each name. (See Figure 11.2.)

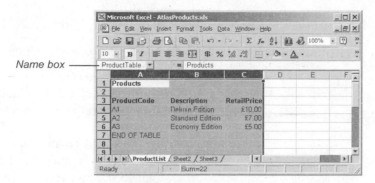

Figure 11.2: Naming the Product Table

- Click any cell outside the table to deselect it. Now you're ready to record the macro!

- From the **Tools** menu select **Macro**, **Record New Macro**. *(Menus are slightly different in Excel 7 but this will not be pointed out each time.)* A dialogue box is displayed.

- Give the macro the name *InsertLine* (no spaces are allowed in a macro name) and type a suitable comment to explain the purpose of the macro.

- *(In Excel 7 click the options button.)* Assign a shortcut key *Ctrl-Shift-I* by clicking in the **Shortcut key** box and pressing Shift-I. Make sure that **This Workbook** is specified in the **Store macro in** box. Click **OK**.

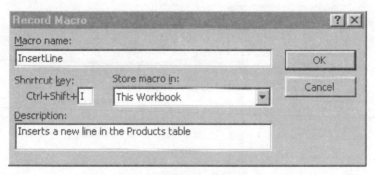

Figure 11.3: Recording a new macro

Every keystroke that you make will now be recorded as part of the macro until you click the **Stop Recording** button.

- Select cell A3.

- Press **Ctrl-Down Arrow** to go to the last row in the table.

- Right-click and select **Insert**. Select **Entire Row** and click **OK**.

- Click the **Stop Recording** button. (If the **Stop Recording** toolbar is not displayed, you can display it by right-clicking any toolbar, selecting **Customize**, clicking the **Toolbar** tab, checking the toolbar name **Stop Recording** and closing the dialogue box. Sometimes toolbars get closed by mistake, and they are not all named on the short list of toolbars.)

Your macro is now recorded and you can try it out. First of all, right-click in Line 7 and select **Delete** to delete your new row.

- Press **Ctrl-Shift-I**. A new line should be inserted.

- If you press **Ctrl-Shift-I** a second time, a new line is inserted above A3. Can you work out why?

- Delete any new rows you have inserted. You can also run your macro be selecting **Tools, Macro, Macros, Run**. Try this now.

- Type details of a new product and make sure your macro runs when there are more than 3 products in the table – it should do!

Changing the shortcut key

- Select **Tools, Macro, Macros, Options**. You can change the shortcut key in the dialogue box that appears. Note that if the shortcut key that you choose is already assigned to another macro, Excel will not warn you and either macro may run when you press the shortcut key.

Examining the macro code

The macro is stored in the workbook, but in a hidden location. In order to see the macro you must use the Visual Basic Editor. *(In Excel 7, the macro is stored in a worksheet named **Module 1**, and you can select the sheet tab to view the code. You will not see the **Project Explorer** window shown in Figure 11.4.)*

- Select **Tools, Macro, Macros,** and select the **InsertLine** macro. Click the **Edit** button. A window similar to the following will appear.

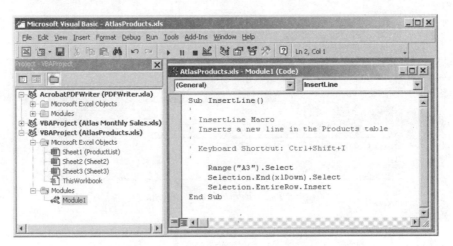

Figure 11.4: The Visual Basic Editor

The **Visual Basic Editor** appears as a new application with a main window called the **Code window**, and the **Project Explorer** window on the left (if this does not appear, select **Project Explorer** from the **View** menu). Notice that application buttons for both Microsoft Excel and Microsoft Visual Basic are now visible at the bottom of the screen and you can switch between worksheet and code using these buttons. Alternatively, if you make the VB Editor window smaller you can see the worksheet window behind it and you can click in it to return to the worksheet.

Syntax of Visual Basic statements

Note that:

- all macros start with a line **Sub *macroname*()** and end with the line **End Sub**;

- any statement preceded by a quote mark (') is a comment for documentation purposes and has no effect on the running of the macro;

- the three lines of the macro starting **Range ("A3").Select** correspond to the keystrokes you used, translated into Visual Basic code. These statements are called the *body* of the macro.

- Each statement in the body of the macro consists of two parts separated by a full-stop. Everything before the full-stop is the *object*, which specifies what part of Excel the statement will affect. The word after the full-stop is the *action* word. If the action word is followed by an equal sign, then it is called a *property*. If it is not followed by an equal sign, then it is called a *method*. All the statements in the above macro are methods.

- If a statement is too long to fit conveniently on one line, type a space followed by an underscore and continue the statement on the next line.

Adding a message to the user

Once a new line has been inserted in the table, you could display a message telling the user to enter the new product.

- Press **Enter** at the end of the line before **End Sub**.

- You probably don't know the syntax of the statement for displaying a message, so make a guess and let Excel help you. Type the word *message* and then right-click. Select **List Properties/Methods**. A list appears starting **Math, Mid** etc – scroll down and eventually you come to **MsgBox**, which is the one you want. Double-click it and then type a space. A prompt appears telling you the syntax of the statement. Type *("Type your data above END OF TABLE")* so that the statement now reads

```
MsgBox ("Type your data above END OF TABLE")
```

- Return to the **Products** worksheet and test the macro again.

Stepping through a macro

You can watch your macro run by stepping through it a line at a time. This is a useful debugging technique when your macro doesn't do quite what you expect.

- Display the Visual Basic toolbar by right-clicking any toolbar and selecting **Visual Basic**. The toolbar appears as shown below (*with small differences in Excel 97 and 7*).

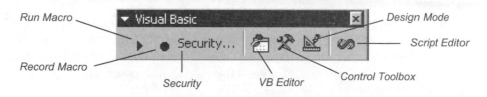

Figure 11.5: The Visual Basic toolbar

- Click the **Run Macro** button on the Visual Basic toolbar.

- With the **InsertLine** macro selected, click **Step Into**.

The Visual Basic Editor appears again and the first statement of the macro is highlighted in yellow. The yellow arrow indicates that this is the next statement that will be executed.

- Each time you press F8, a single statement will be executed. Press it now.

- Drag the Visual Basic window out of the way of the Products table so that you can see what happens as you step through the macro. Keep pressing F8 and watch the arrow move through the macro as each line is executed.

Note that if you don't run a macro to its conclusion you must click the **Reset** button on the top toolbar before you can run it again.

- Save the workbook.

Using the Visual Basic toolbar

We will now create another macro which will run after the InsertLine macro to accept data from the user. First of all we'll try out the keystrokes and see what code is generated. Then we'll edit the code to make it do what we want.

- Start with a Products table that looks like the one in Figure 11.1 containing just 3 products.

- Run the InsertLine macro to insert a new line. (You can run a macro by clicking the **Run macro** button on the Visual Basic toolbar and selecting the required macro.)

- Click the **Record macro** button on the Visual Basic toolbar. Enter the name *InputProduct*, and a suitable description. Don't allocate a shortcut key. Click **OK**.

- The cursor is already in the correct cell, so enter a new Product record, *A4, Test, 12.50*, tabbing between cells and pressing **Enter** after entering *12.50*.

- Click the **Stop Macro** button.

- Now go to the Visual Basic window and examine the code that has been created.

```
Sub InputProduct()
'
' InputProduct Macro
' Allows a user to enter a new product
'
    ActiveCell.FormulaR1C1 = "A4"
    Range("B7").Select          ** needs a relative reference
    ActiveCell.FormulaR1C1 = "Test"
    Range("C7").Select          ** needs a relative reference
    ActiveCell.FormulaR1C1 = "12.5"
    Range("A8").Select          ** needs a relative reference
End Sub
```

Two things need to be altered: firstly, this macro always enters the same data, and secondly, it always puts the data in cells B7 and C7 after putting the new Product code in the current cell. Try running InsertLine followed by InputProduct to see the effect of performing the steps a second time. Then delete the new lines you have created in the Product table – we'll try writing another version of the **InputProduct** macro.

Using relative references in a macro

The statement **Range("B7").Select** was created when you tabbed to the right. But we don't always want to go to B7 – we want to go one cell to the right from whatever cell is currently selected. In other words, we want a relative, not an absolute, cell reference.

*(Excel 7 users should skip to the next section entitled **Using relative references in Excel 7**.)*

- Click the **Run Macro** button on the Visual Basic toolbar. In the dialogue box, select the **InputProduct** macro and click **Delete**. Answer **Yes** when asked if you want to delete the macro.

- Run the InsertLine macro to create a new line.

- Click the **Record macro** button on the Visual Basic toolbar. Enter the name *InputProduct*, and a suitable description. Don't allocate a shortcut key. Click **OK**.

Here comes the clever bit!

You can control whether the macro recorder uses relative references or not by selecting or deselecting the **Relative Reference** button on the **Stop Recording** toolbar at any time during the recording of a macro.

Relative Reference button

- Click the **Relative Reference** button.

- Enter a new Product record as before, *A4, Test, 12.50*, tabbing between cells and pressing **Enter** after entering *12.50*.

- Click the **Stop Recording** button.

- Now examine the code that has been created.

```
Sub InputProduct()
'
' InputProduct Macro
' Allows a user to enter a new product

    ActiveCell.FormulaR1C1 = "A4"
    ActiveCell.Offset(0, 1).Range("A1").Select
    ActiveCell.FormulaR1C1 = "Test"
    ActiveCell.Offset(0, 1).Range("A1").Select
    ActiveCell.FormulaR1C1 = "12.5"
    ActiveCell.Offset(1, -2).Range("A1").Select
End Sub
```

This time the absolute references to cells B7 and C7 and A8 have been replaced by an offset from the current position. For example `ActiveCell.Offset(0,1).Range("A1")` means 'Move one cell to the right and call that cell A1'. `ActiveCell.Offset(1, -2).Range("A1")` means 'Move one cell down, two cells to the left and call that cell A1'.

- Return to the worksheet and run **InsertLine** followed by **NewProduct**. The macro works well except that it puts the same data in both times. The next amendment is to allow the user to input data.

You can't do this by recording keystrokes, so you have to write the Visual Basic code.

- Click the **Run Macro** button on the Visual Basic toolbar and select the **InputProduct** macro. Select **Edit** to display the code.

- Delete the line
    `ActiveCell.FormulaR1C1 = "A4"`

In place of this line, type the word *input*. This is simply a guess – now right-click and **select List Properties/Methods** to see if we are on the right track. Yes – there is a method called **InputBox**. Double-click it and press the space bar. A tip appears telling you what parameters are required.

The tip is not really detailed enough – we need more help.

*(Skip to the section **Using the object browser to get help**)*

Using relative references in Excel 7

The macro recorder does not know automatically whether you want the absolute cell you selected, or a cell relative to where you started. You can, however, tell it whether to use absolute or relative cell references and use the recorder to replace the first incorrect statement.

- On the **Tools** menu, click **Record Macro, Use Relative References**.

This command changes the recorder so that it records all new cell selections *relative* to the original selection. Now you need to replace the statements which I have marked ** **needs a relative reference** in the original code.

- Go to the code window, select the entire line `Range("B7").Select` and click **Delete**.

- Don't move the insertion point. On the **Tools** menu, click **Record Macro, Mark Position for Recording**. This makes Excel start inserting new commands at the mark.

- You want to record the action of moving right one cell – it doesn't matter which cell you start in, so go to any worksheet and select any cell.

- On the **Tools** menu, click **Record Macro, Record at Mark**.

- Press the Right arrow key once to record a relative movement.

- Click the **Stop Macro** button.

- On the **Tools** menu, click **Record Macro, Use Relative References** to clear the check mark next to the command. This returns the macro recorder to the default of recording absolute addresses. Excel remembers the most recent setting until you exit. Each time you restart Excel, the setting is returned to the default of absolute references.

- Activate the module sheet and look at the change. The new statement you recorded looks like this:

```
ActiveCell.Offset(0, 1).Range("A1").Select
```

This means 'Move one cell to the right and call that cell A1'. Edit the rest of the code so that it appears as shown below.

```
Sub InputProduct()
'
' InputProduct Macro
' Allows a user to enter a new product
    ActiveCell.FormulaR1C1 = "A4"
    ActiveCell.Offset(0, 1).Range("A1").Select
    ActiveCell.FormulaR1C1 = "Test"
    ActiveCell.Offset(0, 1).Range("A1").Select
    ActiveCell.FormulaR1C1 = "12.5"
    ActiveCell.Offset(1, -2).Range("A1").Select
End Sub
```

Note that `ActiveCell.Offset(1, -2).Range("A1")` means 'Move one cell down, two cells to the left and call that cell A1'.

- Return to the Products worksheet and run **InsertLine** followed by **NewProduct**. The macro works well except that it puts the same data in every time. The next amendment is to allow the user to input data.

The function **InputBox** will be used to do this.

- Edit the macro so that the code looks like that shown below:

```
Sub InputProduct()
'
' InputProduct Macro
' Allows a user to enter a new product
    ActiveCell.FormulaR1C1 = Application.InputBox _
        ("Enter the new product code: ", "Product Code")
    ActiveCell.Offset(0, 1).Range("A1").Select
    ActiveCell.FormulaR1C1 = Application.InputBox _
        ("Enter the new product title: ","Product Title")
    ActiveCell.Offset(0, 1).Range("A1").Select
    ActiveCell.FormulaR1C1 = Application.InputBox _
        ("Enter the new retail price: ","Retail Price")
    ActiveCell.Offset(1, -2).Range("A1").Select
End Sub
```

Note that:

1. **InputBox** is a *function*. Functions are always written using the general syntax

   Object = function (parameters)

2. The two parameters used by **InputBox** are the **prompt** and the **box title**.

3. The underscore at the end of a line (which must be preceded by a space) indicates that the statement continues on the next line. You can split a line however you like, but not between opening and closing quote marks – or you can type each statement all on one line.

- Test your new macro.

*(Now experiment on getting help with the **Object Browser** in a similar way to that described below, or skip to **Making a macro run other macros**.)*

Using the Object Browser to get help

- Highlight the word **InputBox** and then click the **Object Browser** button.

- In the dialogue box, type *InputBox* in the second list box.

- Click the **Search** button.

- Click the **Help** button (the question mark).

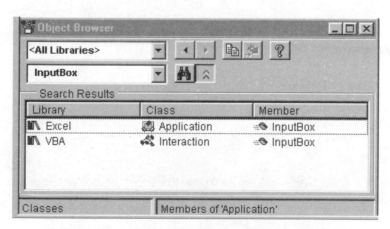

Figure 11.6: Getting help from the Object Browser

The following information is displayed.

InputBox Method

<u>**See Also**</u>   <u>**Example**</u>   <u>**Applies To**</u>

Displays a dialog box for user input. Returns the information entered in the dialog box.

Syntax

expression.InputBox(Prompt, Title, Default, Left, Top, HelpFile, HelpContextId, Type)

expression   Required. An expression that returns an **Application** object.

Prompt   Required **String**. The message to be displayed in the dialog box. This can be a string, a number, a date, or a Boolean value (Microsoft Excel automatically coerces the value to a String before it's displayed).

Title   Optional **Variant**. The title for the input box. If this argument is omitted, the default title is "Input."

Default   Optional **Variant**. Specifies a value that will appear in the text box when the dialog box is initially displayed. If this argument is omitted, the text box is left empty. This value can be a Range object.

Left   Optional **Variant**. Specifies an x position for the dialog box in relation to the upper-left corner of the screen, in points.

Top   Optional **Variant**. Specifies a y position for the dialog box in relation to the upper-left corner of the screen, in points.

HelpFile   Optional **Variant**. The name of the Help file for this input box. If the **HelpFile** and **HelpContextID** arguments are present, a Help button will appear in the dialog box.

HelpContextId   Optional **Variant**. The context ID number of the Help topic in **HelpFile**.

Type   Optional **Variant**. Specifies the return data type. If this argument is omitted, the dialog box returns text. Can be one or a sum of the following values.

Value	Meaning
0	A formula
1	A number
2	Text (a string)
4	A logical value (**True** or **False**)
8	A cell reference, as a **Range** object
16	An error value, such as #N/A
64	An array of values

You can use the sum of the allowable values for **Type**. For example, for an input box that can accept both text and numbers, set **Type** to 1 + 2.

Remarks

Use **InputBox** to display a simple dialog box so that you can enter information to be used in a macro. The dialog box has an **OK** button and a **Cancel** button. If you choose the **OK** button, **InputBox** returns the value entered in the dialog box. If you click the **Cancel** button, **InputBox** returns **False**.

If **Type** is 0, **InputBox** returns the formula in the form of text - for example, "=2*PI()/360". If there are any references in the formula, they are returned as A1-style references. (Use **ConvertFormula** to convert between reference styles.)

If Type is 8, **InputBox** returns a **Range** object. You must use the **Set** statement to assign the result to a **Range** object, as shown in the following example.

```
Set myRange = Application.InputBox(prompt := "Sample", type := 8)
```

If you don't use the **Set** statement, the variable is set to the value in the range, rather than the **Range** object itself.

If you use the **InputBox** method to ask the user for a formula, you must use the **FormulaLocal** property to assign the formula to a Range object. The input formula will be in the user's language.

The **InputBox** method differs from the **InputBox** function in that it allows selective validation of the user's input, and it can be used with Microsoft Excel objects, error values, and formulas. Note that **Application.InputBox** calls the **InputBox** method; **InputBox** with no object qualifier calls the **InputBox** function.

Figure 11.7: The InputBox function

There is a lot of information in this Help file which will be useful to you. Note that the **inputBox** function can be used to allow the user to select a cell or range which can be used in a macro, as well as entering text, numbers or formulae.

For the moment, close the Help window and complete your **InputBox** statement as follows:

```
ActiveCell = Application.InputBox("Enter the new product code: ", _
"Product Code", , , , , 2)
```

Notes:

1. InputBox is a function in the above statement, not a method. Functions are always written using the general syntax

```
Object = function (parameters)
```

2. The underscore at the end of the line (which must be preceded by a space) indicates that the statement continues on the next line.

- Edit the macro so that the code looks like that shown below:

```
Sub InputProduct()
'
' InputProduct Macro
' Allows a user to enter a new product

    ActiveCell = Application.InputBox("Enter the new product code: ", _
    "Product Code", , , , , 2)
    ActiveCell.Offset(0, 1).Range("A1").Select
    ActiveCell = Application.InputBox("Enter the new product title: ", _
    "Product Title", , , , , 2)
    ActiveCell.Offset(0, 1).Range("A1").Select
    ActiveCell = Application.InputBox("Enter the new retail price: ", _
    "Retail Price", , , , , 1)
    ActiveCell.Offset(1, -2).Range("A1").Select
End Sub
```

- Test your new macro.

Making a macro run other macros

You've created two macros: one to insert a new line in the Products table, and one to prompt the user for the new product details and enter them in the table. Now you can create a macro that will run those two macros one after the other. We'll write the code for this macro and place it in the same module as the InsertLine macro.

- Click the **Run Macro** button on the Visual Basic toolbar, and select the **InsertLine** macro. Click **Edit**.

- Scroll down to the end of the code, insert a new line after the **End Sub** statement and type the following subroutine:

```
Sub NewProduct()
'Inserts a new line and then prompts user to input record
    InsertLine
    InsertProduct
End Sub
```

- Return to the worksheet and run the new macro using the **Run Macro** button on the Visual Basic toolbar.

- Oh dear! The name of the macro should have been typed *InputProduct*, not *InsertProduct*.

- An error message appears.

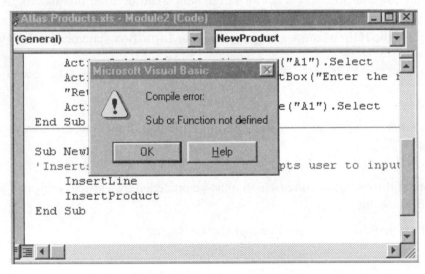

Figure 11.8: An error message

- Click **OK**. The line in error is highlighted. Change it to *InputProduct* and return to the worksheet.

- You won't be able to click the **Run Macro** button again, because you left the macro without running it to completion. Go back to the Visual Basic code, and click the **Reset** button on the toolbar in the VB window.

- Now you can test out the **NewProduct** macro. You may want to remove or change the message in the **InsertRow** macro.

Attaching the macro to a command button

You can create a command button to run your macro.

- Make sure the Forms toolbar is visible. If it is not, right-click any toolbar and select Forms.

- Click the **Button** icon on the Forms toolbar.

- Drag the cursor across about 4 cells, say from the top left corner of E5 to the bottom right corner of F6.

- In the Assign Macro dialogue box which appears, select **NewProduct** and click **OK**.

- Edit the text on the button to read *New Product*.

- Click away from the button to leave Design mode, and then click the button. The macro will run.

The technique of subdividing a complex task into several smaller tasks, recording a macro for each subtask and then writing a macro to call the other macros is a very good one. You are recommended to use it in your project work.

Macro viruses

Since the late 1980s macro viruses have become an increasing problem for users. There are hundreds of different macro viruses in both Word and Excel, written using Visual Basic for Applications.

Some colleges and schools have experienced problems with an Excel macro virus named Laroux B; this overwrites the user's own macros which are by default stored in a hidden file called **Personal.xls**.

Up-to-date, inexpensive anti-virus utility programs such as McAfee's VirusScan will detect such viruses, warn the user and delete them. If you have a home computer, it is essential to have a regularly updated anti-virus utility permanently loaded to avoid being infected with or passing on a virus.

Viruses can easily be downloaded inadvertently over the Internet or via e-mail, so even if you do not transfer disks between school or college you are not safe from viruses, and it will be tears at bedtime if your project is due in a week or so. Be warned!

More information on macro viruses is available from Microsoft's web page

officeupdate.microsoft.com/Articles/antivirus.htm

or alternatively McAfee's

www.nai.com

or Norton's

www.symantec.com

Chapter 12 – Advanced Macros

Data processing

Most data processing is a repetitive operation – each day or week, or minute by minute in a real-time system, new data is added to a transaction file. Sooner or later this data is processed in some way to provide information of some kind, to assist in the daily running of the business or to help management in making strategic or tactical decisions.

In Chapter 10 we looked at creating an Expenses form, and then transferring the data from this form to a database in another workbook with the help of the **Template Wizard with Data Tracking**. This data can then be processed in many different ways to produce information. But if you haven't got this add-in, you can transfer the data to the database either manually or with the help of a macro. That is the task in the next exercise.

Task 12.1: Transfer data from an Expenses form to a database

In this task you will write a macro to add data in one worksheet to a simple flat-file database held in a second worksheet. This data could subsequently be analysed to produce useful information.

We will start with a new workbook and create a simple Expenses form in case you haven't got the one created in Chapter 10.

- Open a new workbook and save it as *Expenses Database*.

- Type headings as shown in the figure below.

- Name cells as follows:

E3	*EmployeeNum*	B6	*CarMiles*
B4	*MeetingNum*	E6	*Amount*
E4	*MeetingDate*	B8	*Rate*

- In cell E6 enter a formula = *CarMiles*Rate*

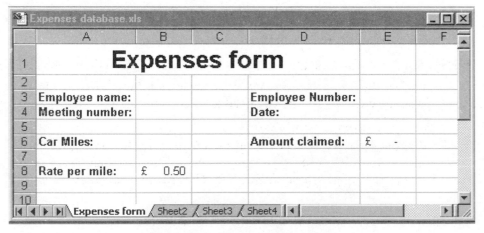

Figure 12.1: Simple expenses form

- Name the sheet *Expenses Form*.

- Enter test data for *S.Hitchcox*, Employee number *123*, meeting number *400* on *January 6ᵗʰ 1999, 150* miles. You may need to format cells for date, currency etc.

- Move to Sheet2 and rename this sheet *Expenses Database*. Save the workbook.

- Enter headings as shown below.

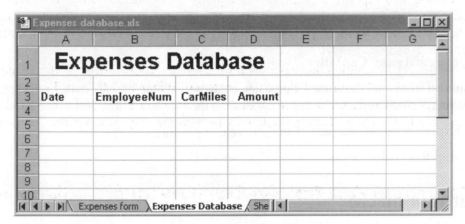

Figure 12.2: The empty database

- Format column A in date format as *dd-mmm-yy* and column D as currency.

For the purposes of this exercise we will only transfer 4 fields: **Date**, **EmployeeNum**, **CarMiles** and **Amount**.

We'll add one row to the database before recording the macro – for reasons to be explained later.

- Add the following line to the first row of the database:

Date	EmployeeNum	CarMiles	Amount
06-Jan-99	111	180	£ 90.00

Recording the macro

- If the Visual Basic toolbar is not already displayed, right-click any toolbar and select **Visual Basic**.

- Click the **Record Macro** button on this toolbar.

- Name the macro *AddToDatabase* and click **OK**. All your keystrokes will now be recorded.

The first thing you need to do is to select the entire database and then move down one cell to the first blank row, ready to paste the data. To do this you need to select any cell in the database – we'll select cell A3.

- First make sure that the **Relative Reference** button on the Stop Recording toolbar is not pressed in. since you always want to select cell A3 as the first step. *(In Excel 7, select **Tools, Record Macro** and make sure that **Use Relative References** is not checked.)*

- Select cell A3 and press **Ctrl-Shift-*** to select the whole database.

- Press **Ctrl-Down Arrow** to go to the last row of the database.

- Now click the **Relative Reference** button before continuing. You want to move down one cell relative to your current position. *(In Excel 7, select **Tools, Record Macro** and click **Use Relative References**.)*

- Press the Down Arrow to move down to the first blank row, cell A4 in this case.

- Click the **Expenses Form** sheet tab, and select **MeetingDate** (cell E4). Click the **Copy** button.

- Return to the **Expenses Database** sheet and click **Paste**.

- Tab to the right to position the cursor in the **EmployeeNum** column, and copy and paste **Employee Number** from **Expenses Form** to **Expenses Database.**

- Similarly, copy and paste **CarMiles**.

- Copy **Amount** from the **Expenses Form** sheet, but this time in the database select **Edit, Paste Special**. Select **Values** to paste the value rather than the formula. Click **OK**.

- Return to **Expenses Form** and press **Esc** to leave Copy mode.

- Click the **Stop Recording** button.

Trying out your macro

Click the **Run Macro** button on the Visual Basic toolbar to select and run your macro. You will probably get an error message as follows:

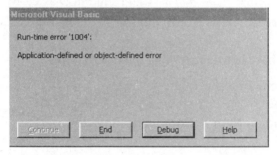

Figure 12.3: Visual Basic error message

- Click the **Debug** button to see what's gone wrong. The code is shown with the line in error highlighted. (If you don't get an error message, just go to the code window.)

```
Sub AddToDatabase()
'
' AddToDatabase Macro
' Macro recorded 08/12/98 by Heathcote
'

'
    Range("A3").Select
    Selection.CurrentRegion.Select
    Selection.End(xlDown).Select
    ActiveCell.Offset(1, 0).Range("A1").Select
    Sheets("Expenses form").Select
    ActiveCell.Offset(-2, 2).Range("A1").Select    (**Change range to MeetingDate)
    Selection.Copy
    Sheets("Expenses Database").Select
```

```
      ActiveSheet.Paste
      ActiveCell.Offset(0, 1).Range("A1").Select
      Sheets("Expenses form").Select
      ActiveCell.Offset(-1, 0).Range("A1").Select      (**Change range to EmployeeNum)
      Application.CutCopyMode = False
      Selection.Copy
      Sheets("Expenses Database").Select
      ActiveSheet.Paste
      ActiveCell.Offset(0, 1).Range("A1").Select
      Sheets("Expenses form").Select
      ActiveCell.Offset(3, -3).Range("A1").Select      (**Change range to CarMiles)
      Application.CutCopyMode = False
      Selection.Copy
      Sheets("Expenses Database").Select
      ActiveSheet.Paste
      ActiveCell.Offset(0, 1).Range("A1").Select
      Sheets("Expenses form").Select
      ActiveCell.Offset(0, 3).Range("A1").Select      (**Change range to Amount)
      Application.CutCopyMode = False
      Selection.Copy
      Sheets("Expenses Database").Select
      Selection.PasteSpecial Paste:=xlValues, Operation:=xlNone, SkipBlanks:= _
          False, Transpose:=False
      Sheets("Expenses form").Select
      Application.CutCopyMode = False
   End Sub
```

Basically, what has gone wrong is that we are using relative references not only in the **Expenses Database** sheet, but also in the **Expenses Form** sheet, where we should be using absolute references. We need to replace all these relative references with cell names.

Also notice that the first statement selects cell A3 but we haven't specified on which sheet. We should add a statement to select the correct sheet in case we run the macro from some other sheet.

- Copy the statement **Sheets("Expenses Database").Select** from lower down in the code and paste it above the first statement underneath the comment lines.

- Find the line
    ActiveCell.Offset(-2, 2).Range("A1").Select and edit it to read *Range("MeetingDate").Select*

- Change the other lines as indicated in italics in the code listing above, removing the **ActiveCell.Offset** in each case.

- Click the **Stop Macro** button on the toolbar and return to the **Expenses Database** worksheet. Delete any fields that have been incorrectly copied by the macro but leave one line of data under the headings.

- Now try your macro again. This time it should work correctly. However, it needs more testing!

Debugging a macro

- Clear all the data from the Expenses database and run your macro again. Oops! You get an error message and if you look at your worksheet you'll find you're on the bottom line of the worksheet.

- Look at the code and you will see that the line which caused the error is
    `ActiveCell.Offset(1, 0).Range("A1").Select`

- Stop the macro by clicking the **Stop Macro** button.

- Return to the worksheet. We need to step through to find out what's going on.

- Click the **Run Macro** button on the Visual Basic toolbar, select the **AddToDatabase** macro and click **Step Into**. The code window appears with the first statement highlighted.

- Keep pressing F8 until the statement **Selection.End(xlDown).Select** is highlighted. This is the next statement that will be executed. Have a look at the worksheet to see what it looks like – the database headings are selected.

- Return to the code and press F8 again. Check the worksheet. Aha! It has jumped to cell A65536. Press F8 one more time and the error message appears as the cursor can't move down any more.

The code worked perfectly when there was at least one line of data, but if the database is empty, we need to skip the line **Selection.End(xlDown).Select**.

If..Then..Else..Endif statements

What is needed is an **If..Then..Else..Endif** statement.

- Click **End** in the error message window, and above the statement **Selection.End(xlDown).Select** insert the lines

```
' Check for empty table
If Range("A4") <> "" then
```

- Below the statement **Selection.End(xlDown).Select**. insert the line

```
End if
```

- Try running the macro again. This time it should work!

- From the **Expenses Database** sheet, run the macro again. It works now however many rows are in the database. It has one annoying characteristic, however – the screen flickers as the macro moves between sheets as it runs. We can cure this.

Hiding operations from the user

- At the top of the macro, add the lines

```
' Hide operations from the user
    Application.ScreenUpdating = False
```

Yes, it's that simple. Try running the macro again and bask in its seamless operation.

Task 12.2: Use a Do..Until loop to implement a conditional format

Performing a loop in a macro

There are three basic constructs used in any programming language
- **Sequence**, in which one statement follows another
- **Selection**, where one statement or group of statements is selected based on some condition, as in an **If..Then..Else..End If** statement
- **Iteration**, which means performing a group of statements several times or until some condition is met. This is what is meant by 'performing a loop' – you go round and round the same set of statements.

As an example of a loop, in this task we'll apply a conditional formatting to the column containing the Amount in the Expenses database. We'll give a yellow background to all cells containing an amount greater than or equal to 100.

- First of all, add some more data to the database as follows:

Date	EmployeeNum	CarMiles	Amount
06-Jan-99	123	150	£ 75.00
07-Jan-99	123	200	£ 100.00
08-Jan-99	123	150	£ 75.00
09-Jan-99	136	250	£ 125.00
10-Jan-99	147	28	£ 14.00
10-Jan-99	136	50	£ 25.00
14-Jan-99	152	300	£ 150.00

- Now start by recording a macro that formats a single cell. Click the **Record Macro** button, and name the macro *FormatAmount*.

- Make sure that the **Relative References** button is not pushed in.
  *(In Excel 7, select **Tools, Record Macro** and make sure that **Use Relative References** is not checked.)*

- Click the **Expenses Database** sheet tab to make it the active worksheet.

- Select cell D5, and use the **Fill Color** button to colour this cell yellow.

- Press the Down Arrow to move down one cell, and stop the macro.

- Have a look at the code that this macro generated, given below.

```
Sub FormatAmount()
' FormatAmount Macro
'
  Sheets("Expenses Database").Select
  Range("D5").Select
    With Selection.Interior
        .ColorIndex = 6
        .Pattern = xlSolid
    End With
    Range("D6").Select
End Sub
```

It's quite a good start but we forgot to change to relative references before moving down one cell.

- Alter the line

```
Range("D6").Select
```

to

```
ActiveCell.Offset(1,0).Range("A1").Select
```

- Now add the required **If..Then..Else..End If** statement.

The macro now reads:

```
Sub FormatAmount()
' FormatAmount Macro
'
    Sheets("Expenses Database").Select
    Range("D5").Select
    If ActiveCell >= 100 Then
        With Selection.Interior
            .ColorIndex = 6
            .Pattern = xlSolid
        End With
    End If
    ActiveCell.Offset(1, 0).Range("A1").Select
End Sub
```

Now we want to introduce the loop so that the macro will keep moving down one cell, checking the contents, turning the background yellow if greater than or equal to 100, until it reaches an empty cell.

- Add the two statements shown in bold below, and indent the code so that **If**s line up with **End If**s, **With**s with **End With**s and so on.

```
Sub FormatAmount()
' FormatAmount Macro
'
    Range("D5").Select
    Do Until ActiveCell = ""
        If ActiveCell >= 100 Then
            With Selection.Interior
                .ColorIndex = 6
                .Pattern = xlSolid
            End With
        End If
        ActiveCell.Offset(1, 0).Range("A1").Select
    Loop
End Sub
```

- Test your macro!

Auto_Open and Auto_Close macros

When you open a workbook, Excel automatically runs any macro named **Auto_Open**. You could use an **Auto_Open** macro to make a particular sheet active on opening, set a default pathname, open other workbooks, set up custom menus and toolbars.

You can look at the **Auto_Open** macros in the sample project to see how most of these tasks are done. In the next chapter we'll look at how to set up custom menus and toolbars.

The **Auto_Close** macro executes automatically when you close the workbook.

Chapter 13 – The User Interface

Creating a full-screen menu

Having a full-screen menu which is displayed automatically when the user opens the application workbook, or even when Excel is opened (using an AutoExec macro) is quite a neat way of displaying all the options in the application. An example of a menu is shown below:

Figure 13.1: A full-screen menu

Task 13.1: Create a full-screen menu

In this task you'll create the menu shown above, and attach macros to the first and last options. It's best to create all the macros that you need before you create the front end menu, but if they are very simple you can create them at the same time as you place the command buttons on the menu.

- Open the **Expenses Database** workbook created in the last chapter.

- Drag the Sheet3 tab to the left of the **Expenses Form** worksheet and rename it *Main Menu*.

- Type headings, select a suitable font and enlarge the text, merge and centre it across the screen.

- From the **Insert** menu select **Picture, Clip Art** and place a graphic on the page. It will probably be larger than you want, so right-click it, select **Format Picture**, select the **Size** tab and make it about 3cm high.
  (In Excel 7, look for a suitable .bmp or .wmf file in a folder such as C:\winword\clipart.)

- If the Forms toolbar is not visible, make it so by right-clicking any toolbar and selecting Forms.

- Click the **Button** icon on the Forms toolbar and drag out a button on the screen.

- A dialogue box will open, asking you for the macro name that this button is to run. Type the name *EnterExpenses* and click **Record**. Click **OK** in the next dialogue box.

- Click the **Expenses Form** tab. Clear all the cells in Column B and cells E3 and E4, leaving the formula in E6. Then select cell B3 ready for the user to start entering data and click the **Stop Recording** button.

- Return to the **Main Menu** sheet and edit the button caption to *Enter Expenses*.

- Place a second button and click **OK** without recording a macro. Edit the text on the button to *Monthly Analysis by Employee*.

- Place the third button for **Exit Application**, naming the macro *QuitApplication*. Click **Record** and record an empty macro by clicking the **Stop Recording** button.

- Edit the macro **QuitApplication**, inserting a line **ActiveWorkbook.Close** after the comments.

- Edit the caption on the button and save your work.

- Remove the gridlines by clicking the **Toggle Grid** button on the Forms toolbar.

- Test the **Exit Application** button – you can cancel before actually closing if you haven't saved your latest changes. If the workbook closes, open it again!

Creating custom buttons and toolbars

Instead of, or as well as, having a full-screen menu you could have custom toolbar buttons, either on an existing toolbar or on a new, specially created toolbar.

Task 13.2: Add a custom button and a custom toolbar

We'll create a brand new toolbar with a button to run the macro **FormatAmount**.
(Instructions for Excel 7 users are given in the next paragraph.)

- Right-click any toolbar and select **Customize**. Click the **Toolbars** tab in the Customize dialogue box.

- Click the **New** button, type *BigCo* as the name for the new toolbar, and click **OK**.

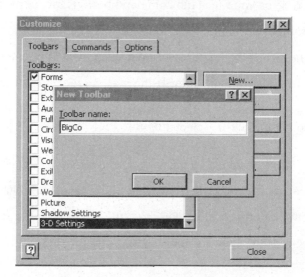

Figure 13.2: Creating a new toolbar

A new, empty toolbar appears.

- In the Customize dialogue box, click the **Commands** tab. You can add any existing toolbar buttons to the new toolbar, or you can add a custom toolbar button that will run a macro.

- From the **Categories** list, select **Macros**. From the **Commands** list, drag the **Custom Button** item onto the BigCo toolbar.

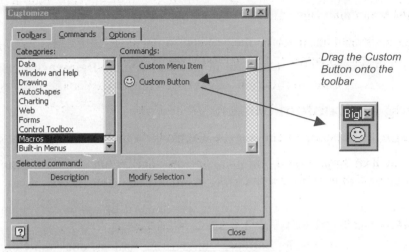

Figure 13.3: Adding a custom button to the new toolbar

Now that the button is on the toolbar, you can customise it. It needs to be given a name (which will appear in the Screen Tip when you hold the mouse over the button) and assigned to a macro.

- Right-click the button. On the shortcut menu, replace the default name **Custom Button** with the name *&Format Amounts.*

Figure 13.4: Using the shortcut menu to name the button and assign a macro

- Click **Assign Macro** on the shortcut menu. Select **FormatAmount** and click **OK**.

- You can change the button image from the shortcut menu by selecting **Change Button Image**.

*(Skip the next paragraph and go on to **Testing the custom button**.)*

Adding a custom toolbar in Excel 7

- Right-click any toolbar and select **Toolbars**.

- In the **Toolbar Name** box, type the name *BigCo*. Click **New**. Your new tiny toolbar will appear somewhere on the screen.

- In the **Customize** dialogue box select **Custom**.

- Drag one of the buttons onto the new toolbar.

- Select the macro **FormatAmount** in the **Macro Name/Reference** box and click **OK**.

Testing the custom button

You can add as many custom buttons as you like to your new toolbar.

- Click **Close** in the Customize dialogue box, and try out your new button. You'll need to set the Fill colour back to **No Fill** before testing in order to see the button working.

- You can dock your toolbar wherever you like – it fits quite conveniently at the end of the standard toolbar.

If you want to put a custom button on an existing toolbar, click the **Commands** tab in the Customize dialogue box and drag the custom button on to an existing toolbar, placing it close to an existing button. To remove a button, simply drag it off the toolbar while the Customise dialogue box is open.

*(In Excel 7, right-click any toolbar and select **Customize**, select **Custom** in the dialogue box and drag a button onto an existing toolbar.)*

Adding a custom menu

Most of the toolbar buttons have an equivalent command on a menu, so that the user can choose whether to use the button or the menu command. To modify a menu, you open the same Customize dialogue box that you used for adding a button.

Task 13.3: Add a custom menu to the menu bar

In this task you'll create a BigCo menu which will have two options – one to enter expenses (using the macro **EnterExpenses**) and one to highlight amounts greater than or equal to 100 (using the macro **FormatAmount**).

(Excel 7 users should skip to the next paragraph.)

- Open the **Expenses Database** workbook if it is not already open.

- Right-click any toolbar and select **Customize**. Click the **Commands** tab.

- In the **Categories** list, select **New Menu**. In the **Commands** list, select **New Menu** and drag it onto the menu bar just to the right of the **Help** menu.

- Right-click the new menu and change its name to *BigCo Menu*. Insert an ampersand (&) before the B to turn B into a 'hot key', and press **Enter**. (The letter B will appear underlined in the menu bar, and the user can select it by typing Alt-B instead of using the mouse.)

- You can now copy the toolbar button directly to the menu. With the Customize dialogue box still open, hold down the Ctrl key while you drag the custom button onto **BigCo Menu**. (Drop it on the blank 'tab' of the menu's first line.)

- The second option, **Enter Expenses**, does not have a toolbar button so has to be added in a different way. In the **Categories** list, click **Macros** and in the **Commands** box, select **Custom Menu item** and drag it onto the new menu. You can choose whether to put it above or below the existing option.

- Click **BigCo Menu** and right-click the new item **Enter Expenses**. Click **Assign macro** and in the dialogue box, select the **EnterExpenses** macro. Click **OK**, and close the **Customize** window.

- Test out your menu items.

*(Excel 97 users skip to **Deleting and restoring menus**)*

Adding a custom menu in Excel 7

- Click the **Menu Editor** button on the Visual Basic toolbar. The **Menu Bars** list should display **Worksheet** as the default menu bar.

- In the **Menu Bars** list select **(End of Menu Bar)** at the bottom of the list and click **Insert**.

- In the **Caption** box, type *&BigCo Menu* (but do not press **Enter**). That creates the menu - now you need to add the menu items.

- Select the **(End of Menu)** label in the **Menu Items** list (the middle list) and click **Insert**. **&BigCo Menu** now appears in the **Menus** list.

- In the **Caption** box type *&Format Amounts*. In the **Macro** list, select **FormatAmounts**.

- Select **(End of Menu)** again in the **Menu Items** list to add the second menu item to the menu, and click **Insert**.

- In the **Caption** box type *&Enter Expenses*. In the **Macro** list select **EnterExpenses**.

- Click **OK** to close the window.

- Test your menu items!

Deleting and restoring menus

*(Excel 7 users can skip this paragraph since the custom menu will only be visible in the application workbook for which it was created. The **RestoreMenu** macro will not work in Excel 7.)*

When you leave your application it is desirable to restore the menu bar to its default state. Excel has several built-in menu bars, depending on whether a worksheet, chart, Visual Basic module is currently active, or no document is open. The name of the menus are **xlWorksheet**, **xlChart**, **xlModule** and **xlNoDocuments**.

You can delete the BigCo menu from the worksheet menu bar using the following subroutine:

```
Sub DeleteMenu()
'Deletes the custom BigCo menu
MenuBars(xlWorksheet).Menus("BigCo Menu").Delete
End Sub
```

When you start up the application, you want the menu to appear. The following subroutine restores the custom menu:

```
Sub RestoreMenu()
'Restores the BigCo menu
MenuBars(xlWorksheet).Menus.Add Caption:="&BigCo Menu", restore:=True
End Sub
```

Hiding, displaying and positioning toolbars

You can use Visual Basic code to display or hide either Excel's built-in toolbars or your custom toolbars. The **Visible** property of a toolbar controls whether or not Excel displays the toolbar. You can specify the position of a toolbar by using the **Position** property; the toolbar can be floating or in one of several docked positions. The table below shows Excel's predefined constants for a toolbar's **Position** property.

Constant	Effect
xlTop	Places toolbar in top docking area
xlBottom	Places toolbar in bottom docking area
xlLeft	Places toolbar in left docking area
xlRight	Places toolbar in right docking area
xlFloating	Floats toolbar

The following subroutines display the **BigCo** toolbar in the top docking position and hide it.

```
Sub DisplayToolbar()
' Display and position the BigCo toolbar
With Toolbars("BigCo")
    .Position = xlTop
    .Visible = True
End With
End Sub

Sub HideToolbar()
' Hide the BigCo toolbar
Toolbars("BigCo").Visible = False
End Sub
```

You can also hide Excel's built-in toolbars if you wish – for example the statement

```
Toolbars("Standard").Visible = False
```

will hide the standard toolbar.

The code for displaying the required menus and toolbars should be placed in an **Auto_Open** macro, and statements to restore menus and toolbars to their default state should be placed in an **Auto_Close** macro.

For example:

```
Sub Auto_Open
'Display the custom toolbar
    DisplayToolbar
End Sub

Sub Auto_Close
'Hide the custom toolbar
    HideToolbar
End Sub
```

Part 4

Tackling the Project

In this section:

Chapter 14 – Project Ideas

Introduction

The first problem in tackling a Computing or Information Technology project is to come up with a suitable subject. You need to find a friend, relation, Club Secretary or Treasurer, Scout Treasurer or local business person who has a 'problem' which could be solved using Excel. It isn't necessary for them to actually use the system when you've finished it, though that would be a bonus both for them and for you.

Finding a genuine user is the first step in producing a good project. It is almost impossible to do a proper analysis and evaluation on a made-up problem, and you will not be able to get real user feedback which is helpful in improving your design and implementation and will result in a better project all round.

Using a problem set by the teacher for several people in a class will almost certainly limit the amount of independent analysis, design and implementation work that you can do.

Input-Process-Output

Take heed of these words written by the Principal Moderator in the Report on the Examination 1998: "An increasing number of projects were seen where the candidate concentrated upon the user interface but the solution did not actually do anything. Functionality of input/processing/output took second place to cosmetics… splash screens, combo boxes, list boxes, menus and buttons calling macros were created to provide an impressive front end but little or no real data processing was done."

Such projects will not score very good marks. You should, therefore, look for an application in which data is

- **input**, preferably on a regular basis (daily, weekly, monthly or even annually),

- **processed** in some way (added up, summarised, averaged, sorted, filtered, consolidated, used in scenarios or Goal Seeking, transferred to a flat-file 'database' worksheet from which a PivotTable is created, minced or scrambled), and finally

- **output** in the form of a report or chart of some kind.

Using advanced features of Excel

You are unlikely to do very well if your project consists of a single sheet containing some labels, numbers and basic formulae. Like diving, some of the marks go on 'difficulty'. Try to include at least half a dozen of the following features:

- **Template creation;**
- Linking worksheets/workbooks;
- Lookups (looking up values from a table in one sheet and inserting in another sheet);
- Inputting data into a dialogue box or form and transferring the data to another sheet;
- Advanced functions (Vlookup, If, Rand, Pmt, Index etc);
- Form controls such as dropdown lists, combo boxes, command buttons;
- PivotTables;
- Goal Seek and Solver;
- "What if" scenarios;

- **Customised macros, including AutoExec, Auto_Open, Auto_Close;**
- **Customising of toolbars or menu bar;**
- **Cell protection;**
- **Auditing tools to show data dependency.**

Here are some ideas to get your mind working along the right lines. Then go out and find your own user!

Preparing budgets

Spreadsheets are frequently used by new companies who are devising a business plan to show to their accountant or their bank manager, perhaps in the hopes of getting a start-up loan. Established companies also prepare budgets to help them plan a business strategy for the coming year. A school or college teacher or administrator may prepare a budget to see whether the school can afford to send students on a trip to France. The secretary of the Social Committee may prepare a budget to see how much to charge for the annual dinner dance.

Spreadsheets are ideal for this task because it is so easy to alter a few figures and see what effect the changes have on profits (or losses).

Project Idea 1: Prepare a budget for a school trip

This could be for any regular event. Create a blank template with headings and formulae, a front end menu, possibly a custom toolbar or menu, and customised macros to help the user get the required output.

Input: Number of pupils, cost of hiring coach, train fares, cross-channel ferry, cost of accommodation, amount each student will pay.

Processing: Profit/Loss on trip. What-if scenarios to establish effect of changing variables, goal-seek to establish break-even point.

Output: Scenario report. Maybe a comparison with last year's trip.

Project Idea 2: Prepare an annual budget for a business

Have you any friends who are about to start, or have recently started a new business? It could be anything from a new Training company to give computer courses, to setting up a coffee kiosk on the local commuter station or a hamburger stall at the annual County Show.

When preparing a budget to show to a Bank Manager, you need to prepare four different items:

- **Opening Balance Sheet**
- **Profit and Loss Account**
- **Cash Flow Statement**
- **Closing Balance Sheet**

To illustrate how these are set out, an example is given below of these reports for a proposed business which will deliver Computer Training courses.

Mr Pelham, who is proposing to start up the business on 1st March 1999, intends to start with an initial investment of £20,000, half of which he hopes the Bank will lend him. He has used Excel to work out the following figures to show the Bank Manager.

The Opening Balance Sheet is set out as follows:

Opening Balance Sheet as at 1st March 1999

Assets		Liabilities	
Cash in bank	20,000	Capital	10,000
		Bank Loan	10,000
Total	**20,000**		**20,000**

Figure 14.1: Opening Balance Sheet

Mr Pelham has worked out the income and expenditure figures for the first 4 months (better if he had done it for 6 months or even a year) based on a certain number of courses each week, an estimated number of people on each course, the charge per person and so on. All these variables are held in a separate part of the workbook, and used in formulae in the Profit and Loss Account.

Profit and Loss Account for the period of 4 months ended 30th June 1999

	March	April	May	June	Cumulative Total
Income - total invoiced sales	2,880	5,760	9,600	11,520	29,760
Direct costs					
Course material	-720	-1,440	-2,400	-2,880	-7,440
Salaries	-1,200	-1,800	-2,400	-2,400	-7,800
Total Direct costs	-1,920	-3,240	-4,800	-5,280	-15,240
Indirect costs					
Hardware depreciation over 2 yrs	-400	-400	-400	-400	-1,600
Marketing	-2,000	-1,500	-1,500	-1,500	-6,500
Rent, electricity etc	-600	-600	-600	-600	-2,400
Redecoration, rewiring of premises	-1,000	0	0	0	-1,000
Total indirect costs	-4,000	-2,500	-2,500	-2,500	-11,500
Less: Total costs	-5,920	-5,740	-7,300	-7,780	-26,740
Net Profit/Loss (Income - Total costs)	-3,040	20	2,300	3,740	3,020

Figure 14.2: Profit and Loss Account

You will note that in order to account for the reduction in value of computer equipment over a period of time, Mr Pelham has decided to charge the Profit and Loss Account with £400 per month. This charge is technically known as *depreciation*.

Now although Mr Pelham starts making a profit (on paper) in the second month, he may still run into difficulties if he has to pay for a lot of equipment and so on in advance, and his customers don't pay their bills on time. Many businesses which are profitable on paper go bankrupt – it's all a question of Aged Debtors, and the more Aged they are, the worse your situation is likely to be. Similarly, businesses can have a significant problem if they have too much unsaleable stock or high overheads.

A *Cash Flow Statement* shows how much money Mr Pelham will actually have in the bank at the end of each month – if it's negative, the Bank could close him down at any time!

Cash Flow Statement for the 4 months ended 30th June 1999

	March	April	May	June	Cumulative Total
Actual cash received in bank	720	3,600	6,720	10,080	21,120
Actual cash paid out of bank					
Computers	-10,000	0	0	0	-10,000
Advertisements	-2,000	-1,500	-1,500	-1,500	-6,500
Rent	-1,800	0	0	-1,800	-3,600
Redecoration	-1,000	0	0	0	-1,000
Salary	-1,200	-1,800	-2,400	-2,400	-7,800
Course materials	-720	-1,440	-2,400	-2,880	-7,440
Total cash paid	-16,720	-4,740	-6,300	-8,580	-36,340
Net cash flow (Cash In-Cash Out)	-16,000	-1,140	420	1,500	-15,220
Opening bank balance	20,000	4,000	2,860	3,280	**4,780**
Plus or Minus net cash flow	-16,000	-1,140	420	1,500	
Closing bank balance	**4,000**	**2,860**	**3,280**	**4,780**	

Initial Investment   *Carry forward*   *This is derived from Opening Cash Balance – Net Cash Flow*

Figure 14.3: The Cash Flow Statement

All Profit & Loss and Cash Flow Statements are based on assumptions. You have to think about these assumptions very carefully and make them as realistic as possible.

The main assumption that Mr Pelham has used is that 25% of customers will pay up front, and the rest will pay in 30 days time – if they don't pay up, the business could be in trouble! Notice that he started with £20,000, and although his business is making a profit month after month, after 4 months he only has £4,780 in the bank.

The Closing Balance Sheet shows the position after 4 months. The two sides must balance.

Closing Balance Sheet as at 30th June 1999

Assets		Liabilities	
Cash in bank	4,780	Capital	10,000
Debtors (See Note 1 below)	8,640	Bank Loan	10,000
Rent paid in advance (See Note 2 below)	1,200	Profit and Loss Account	3,020
Stock (computers etc) (See Note 3 below)	8,400		
Total	**23,020**		**23,020**

Note 1: **(Debtors)** Total Invoiced Sales £29,760 (from Profit and Loss Account) less Actual Total Cash Received £21,120 (from Cash Flow Statement) = £8,640.

Note 2: **(Rent paid in advance)** Rent actually paid £3,600 (from Cash Flow Statement) less Rent charged £2,400 (from Profit and Loss Account) = £1,200.

Note 3: **(Stock – computers etc.)** Cost of computers £10,000 (from Cash Flow Statement) less Hardware depreciation £1,600 (from Profit and Loss Account) = £8,400.

Figure 14.4: The Closing Balance Sheet

Input: Estimated expenses, salaries, number of courses, price of each course, people on each course, percentage paying on time, etc. These figures can all be held in a worksheet and referenced in the calculations.

Processing: Profit/Loss and cash balance after a period of months. Goal-seeking, What-if scenarios.

Output: Opening and Closing Balance Sheets, Profit and Loss Account, Cash Flow Statement, Scenario report.

Expenses claims forms

Project Idea 3: Travel claims system

Another common use for a spreadsheet is keeping track of expenses. I've used this idea as an example in Chapter 10. The original specification for this example was given to me by a friend who works for B.T. and was as follows:

Travel claims specification

Employees of a large company have to record details of their journeys so that they can reclaim the costs involved. For each claim, they need to record the date, details, an account code against which the expense is reclaimed, the mileage travelled and the resultant cost claimed and other costs, which are hotel bills, food bills, train fares, parking costs and "other". "Other" costs must have a code associated with them.

The initial version of the spreadsheet should simply tabulate all these. Totals should be added at the bottom of each relevant column, plus total per line and overall total. The next step is to calculate mileage costs from miles travelled (using a fixed cell location for the rate per mile). Next is to track claims made/paid/yet to be sent (this will allow data filters to be set so we can print out only those yet to be sent – subtotal can also be introduced). After that I'd look at using a form to input the data. I do this using Data Form so that my formula for mileage costs is copied down the "database". After that you could introduce pivot tables to summarise claim values against account codes. For me, the *piéce de resistance* would be to summarise miles travelled by the month in which the journey was made and draw a graph of that. This can be put on the same graph as "expected" miles, which would assume an annual mileage of 2500 (a tax break). Users can therefore see whether they are doing enough company miles. (I do this with database formulae, although pivot tables could be used.) The key "presentational" aspect is to avoid zeros messing up the graphs – it's necessary to ensure that months in the future have no graph point associated with them.

Input: Details of journey, name/employee ID.

Processing: PivotTables to summarise data, charts, tracking claims made/paid/yet to be sent.

Output: Total expenses per journey per employee, total weekly/monthly/annual company expenses, monthly miles travelled by an employee, etc

This spec is not 100% clear, nor is it intended to be. You need a real user with a similar problem if you want to use this idea!

Keeping accounts

Project Idea 4: Club Accounts system

All organisations like Sports Clubs, Scouts, small businesses making curtains or cleaning windows need to keep accounts. Basically you need to have a list of 'Nominal codes', such as (for a Scout group)

> Subscriptions
>
> AGM Expenses
>
> Camps
>
> Dance
>
> Jumble Sales
>
> Equipment
>
> Affiliation fees

and accounts such as

> Bank (Current Account)
>
> Bank (Deposit Account)
>
> Cash

Every time the Treasurer is asked for a cheque or cash, or handed cheques or cash, he/she makes a double entry in an accounts book, showing which account is to be credited (e.g. Jumble if the money came from Jumble Sale profits) and which account is to be debited (e.g. Cash if the money came in cash). You must be able to make transfers between Bank Accounts, and you must be able to add new Nominal Codes.

You would need to consult a Club Treasurer to find out more details!

Input: Nominal codes, opening balances, transactions.

Processing: Preparation of annual accounts using, perhaps, consolidation or PivotTable report. Clearing down at the end of the year and transferring balances ready for next year.

Output: Annual accounts.

You would do well to have a look at an Accounts package such as Sage Sterling before you embark on this, because you may decide this is a more suitable package. If you decide to go ahead in Excel you will get an idea of an Accounts system works.

Invoicing and sales summaries

Project Idea 5: Invoicing and sales system

Someone running a small business such as making dresses, curtains, Christmas and Birthday cards, printing T-shirts or anything along these lines, may like to have a system which allows them to create and print out an invoice, and then have the invoice details added to a database from which monthly and annual sales summaries can be produced. The sample project at the end of this section does something rather similar although it is specific to a particular user, as indeed your project should be. (The sample project does not create invoices – it uses invoices created in an Accounts package as input documents.)

Input: Invoice details.

Processing: Add invoice figures to year-to-date database of sales. Use PivotTable reports to calculate summary data.

Output: Invoices, weekly/monthly/annual sales summaries.

Quotation systems

Project Idea 6: Produce a quotation for a job – e.g. Tree-felling, re-upholstering, loose chair covers, curtains, catering for a dinner party or building a conservatory.

Input: Job details.

Processing: Calculate costs, add profit margin, calculate quote.

Output: Printed quotation.

Another idea falling into this category might be the calculation of the price of a new car or computer, depending on the extras required. As well as (or instead of) calculating the price you could calculate loan repayments. An example using a similar idea is given in Chapter 10.

Student grades system

Project Idea 7: Keep track of student grades

Many college lecturers use a spreadsheet to record marks for the classes they teach, so that they can produce neat lists on demand for visiting moderators and exam boards. They can also easily pick out recalcitrant students and write stiff memos to their tutors or letters to parents. They can calculate average marks quickly to put on termly reports, and assign a grade A-E, N, U depending on the mark. There is really quite a lot of scope in this idea if you can prevail upon your teacher to act as your own personal user. Maybe you have a parent or friend of the family who could use such a spreadsheet.

Input: Student names and marks. (Student names might be obtained from the College SIMS system as a **.csv** file.)

Processing: Calculate totals, averages and grades, pick out failing or brilliant students, goal seeking to calculate marks required to pass, etc

Output: Class list, individual student report, list of failing students.

Inappropriate projects

Finally, here's some advice on what ***not*** to choose.

- Payroll, which is a very complex business and, unless you have first-hand experience of a payroll system, best avoided;
- One-off problems such as one week's expenses for a Youth Club;
- Problems with too much scope such as an attempt to computerise an entire major business, taking in stock control, ordering, invoicing, paying suppliers, payroll and so on;
- Essays comparing different software or describing how to customise and install software.
- Projects which would be better tackled using other software, e.g. a database type of project.

Chapter 15 – The Systems Life Cycle

Introduction

Project work and theory should go hand-in-hand on any course and this one is no exception. In order to produce a satisfactory project report you need to know something about the systems life cycle and the techniques used in each stage. The basic stages in the traditional cycle (excluding ongoing maintenance) form the basis of what you are expected to do for your project, and they are shown in diagrammatic form below.

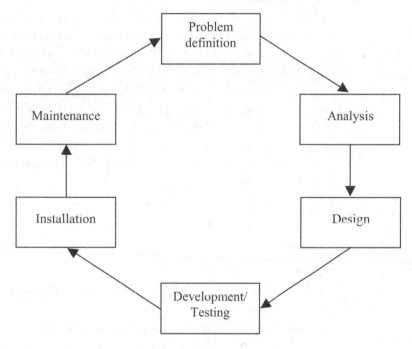

Figure 15.1: The Systems Life Cycle

Problem definition

In the last chapter we talked about choosing a suitable project. In a working environment, of course, the Systems Analysts would not be casting about looking for suitable projects to keep them busy – some alert manager or employee would perceive the need for change or innovation and be suggesting ways in which I.T. could drive the company forward. In that case, as in your current situation, the first requirement is to *state the problem* in writing clearly and unambiguously. This can be referred to as the *Terms of Reference*.

Analysis

During this stage you will be expected to:

- Investigate and report on the existing system and problems associated with it;

- Specify objectives for the new system (e.g. better customer service, faster and/or more accurate operation, ability to handle increased volume of business, better management information);

- Specify the input, processing and output of the new system;

- Specify the performance criteria (quantitative and qualitative) of the new system;

- Prepare a plan for implementing the new system within a set time scale.

Finding out about the current system

There are basically three ways of finding out about the current system, any or all of which you might use in your project work:

1. Interviews

Fix up an interview with the prospective user of the system, who may or may not be known to you – quite likely it could be a parent or friend. You should first of all make a list of questions you intend to ask, and write down the answers. It is not necessary or recommended to include a transcript of the interview in your project report – just summarise the findings, making it clear how you got your information.

Here are some general suggestions for questions that might form the framework of an interview. Of course, you have to be flexible and follow a line of questioning, but it helps to have a basic plan if you are not going to waste your own time and that of the interviewer.

- Can you give me a brief description of the problem you had in mind?
- How does the current system work?
- How would the new system be different?
- Have you any sample input documents I could look at, and possibly have a copy of?
- What form would the output take? Would hard copy be required? How should it be laid out? Have you any samples I could look at or have a copy of?
- What volume of data is involved (e.g. how many invoices daily, how many club members, how many transactions weekly?)
- Are records ever removed from the system to be 'archived'?
- What hardware and software do you have available for the new system to be run on?
- How expert are you (or whoever will use the new system) at using PCs, Windows, Excel or whatever software is installed?

2. Questionnaires

Questionnaires are useful in some circumstances if the new system has a large number of potential users. The questionnaire has to be very carefully worded in order to obtain exactly the information you require, and of course many people won't bother to fill them in. Don't include a hundred copies of returned questionnaires with your project – one sample is enough, with a summary of the results.

3. Observation and inspection of documents currently used

Spending some time with the user or in the user's organisation is always a good way of finding out how things actually work. If you have firsthand experience of the task that you intend to computerise you are likely to understand the problems associated with it, and the pitfalls to avoid in your new system.

Possibly the single most important part of the Analysis in your project work is showing the relevant source documents to your teacher and explaining them. If you can do this with ease you probably have a good understanding of the scenario. If however you are unable to describe the purpose of your source documents, you probably need to stop and take some advice from your teacher.

From the teacher's point of view, it is often very difficult to grasp what a student's project is all about from a written or verbal explanation. Laying a source document in front of them will at the very least, shed some light on what you are going to attempt.

Data flow diagrams

One important task of systems analysis is to find out:

- where the data originates,
- what processing is performed on it and by whom,
- who uses the data,
- what data is stored and where,
- what output is produced and who receives it.

One way of recording all this information is to use a **data flow diagram (DFD).** You are encouraged to include such a diagram in the Analysis section of your project report.

There are only four symbols used in data flow diagrams, and they should not be confused with any other type of flowcharting symbols.

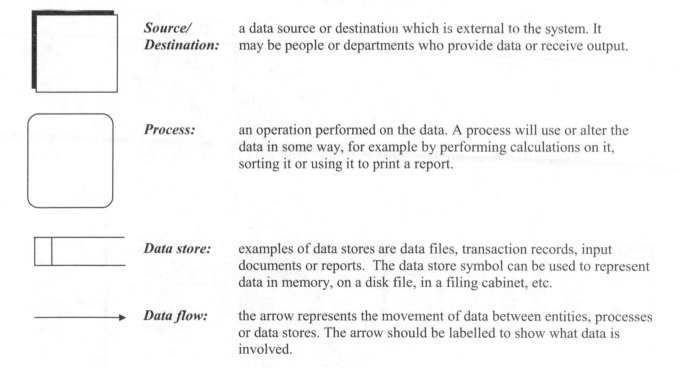

Source/ Destination: a data source or destination which is external to the system. It may be people or departments who provide data or receive output.

Process: an operation performed on the data. A process will use or alter the data in some way, for example by performing calculations on it, sorting it or using it to print a report.

Data store: examples of data stores are data files, transaction records, input documents or reports. The data store symbol can be used to represent data in memory, on a disk file, in a filing cabinet, etc.

Data flow: the arrow represents the movement of data between entities, processes or data stores. The arrow should be labelled to show what data is involved.

Figure 15.2: Symbols used in Data Flow Diagrams

When drawing data flow diagrams, you should stick to the following conventions:

- Do not draw data flow lines directly between data stores and external entities: there should be a process box between them to show the operation performed (e.g. print a report)

- Label the data flow lines so that it is clear what data is being transferred.

Levelled DFDs

It is often impossible to represent a complete business system in a single diagram, so two or three levels of data flow diagrams may be used, each showing more detail. A Level 0 DFD represents the entire system as one process, and is also known as a **context diagram**.

Example: *A Club sends out annual reminders to members to pay their subscriptions. When they receive payment they make a note of this and renew the member's subscription for another year. An analysis of member types (Family, Junior, Senior) is made to be presented at the Annual General Meeting.*

The context (Level 0) data flow diagram (DFD) can be drawn as follows:

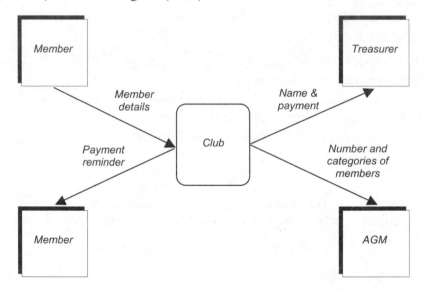

Figure 15.3: A context diagram or top level DFD (Level 0)

A Level 1 DFD can then be drawn showing a process to handle each incoming data flow and a process to generate each output data flow.

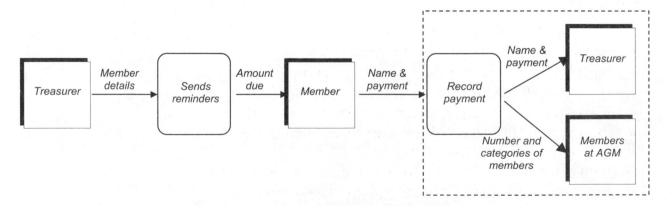

Figure 15.4: Level 1 DFD

146

A context DFD or a Level 1 DFD containing only two or three processes might form part of the Analysis documentation in your project.

A Level 2 DFD may show part of this system in greater detail, and could be included in the Design section of your project. Perhaps the system under consideration only covers the part of the DFD shown within the dotted lines in the previous diagram. The next level of detail may show data stores and more detail of the processing involved, as illustrated below:

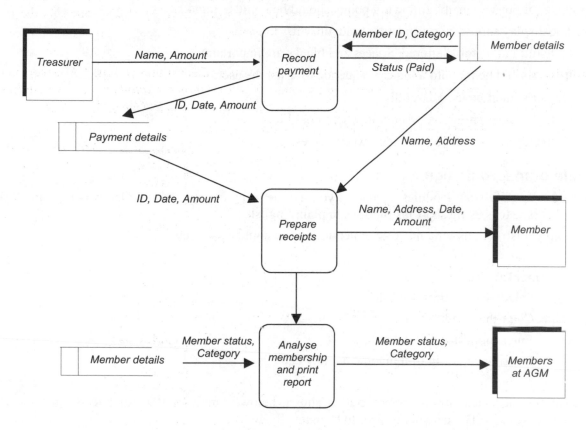

Figure 15.5: Level 2 DFD

Design

The systems designer will consider

- ♦ **output:** content, format, sequence, frequency, medium (e.g. screen or hard copy) etc;
- ♦ **input**: documents, screens and dialogues;
- ♦ **files or workbooks**: contents, record layout, organisation and access methods;
- ♦ **processing**: the programs and procedures needed and their detailed design;
- ♦ **security**: how the data is to be kept secure from accidental corruption or deliberate tampering or hacking;
- ♦ **testing strategies**: how the system is to be thoroughly tested before going 'live';
- ♦ **hardware**: selection of an appropriate configuration.

User Interface

A good user interface design is an important aspect of a successful system. The design must take into consideration:

♦   **who** is going to use the system - members of the public, experienced computer users or novices;

♦   **what tasks** the computer is performing; e.g. repetitive tasks or variable tasks such as switching between a word processor, spreadsheet and database

In particular, careful **screen design** can make a huge difference to the usability of a system. When designing an input screen, the following points should be borne in mind:

♦   The display should be given a title to identify it;

♦   It should not be too cluttered. Spaces and blanks are important;

♦   Items should be put into a logical sequence to assist the user;

♦   Colour should be used carefully;

♦   Default values should be written in where possible;

♦   Help facilities should be provided where necessary.

Module or macro design

You need to specify what modules or macros you will be using in your system. One way of doing this is to write out the steps using short instructions in plain English.

For example, instructions for a macro to enter an invoice could be written

EnterInvoices
Select the Invoices worksheet
Clear the current data
Enter today as the default date
Position cursor in first invoice number cell

The code for the actual macro comes out as shown below – most of it automatically generated by recording keystrokes. The comments have to be manually added.

```
Sub EnterInvoices()
' Goes to the invoice sheet, clears the form, enters today's date
' and positions cursor
    Sheets("Invoices").Select
    Range("InvoiceLines").Select
    Selection.ClearContents
    Range("InvoiceDate").Select
' Set default date to today on data entry form
    ActiveCell.FormulaR1C1 = "=TODAY()"
    Range("C4").Select
End Sub
```

Test strategy

A test strategy will typically include:

♦   **Module testing** to test every macro or procedure in the system under different conditions, using valid, invalid and extreme data;

♦   **Functional testing** to ensure that the test tries each menu item under different conditions;

- ♦ **System testing** to test the system from beginning to end;
- ♦ **User testing** which is likely to throw up errors and weaknesses if you have not fully understood the requirements of the system.

Prototyping

Prototyping involves building a working model of a system in order to evaluate it, test it or have it approved before building the final product. When applied to computer systems, this could involve, for example, designing basic worksheets, a user interface or front end with buttons that don't actually do anything, and a sample report showing what will be produced (or at least the headings) when the processing has been done. The user can then experience the 'look and feel' of the input process and suggest alterations before going any further.

Sometimes prototypes are simply discarded before the real system is started, and in other cases the prototype may be developed into a working system.

Prototyping is a useful development tool, especially when you are inexperienced with the software and are still experimenting with Excel's capabilities, but it should not be used as a substitute for thinking out the design before you start on the implementation. Even prototypes have to be designed properly.

Development

This stage involves the actual implementation of your design using the computer. The word 'implementation' is confusing because it is sometimes used to mean doing the practical computer work involving creating workbooks or templates and writing formulae, macros etc and other times it means actually getting the system up and running on the user's hardware.

In the mark scheme for the project, 'Implementation and Testing' implies the former – getting the project to actually do what it's supposed to do.

Testing is an important part of development and should be done in accordance with the test strategy and test plan written in the Design phase.

Installation

This involves installing the system on the user's computer – this will very likely not form part of your project, although user testing and obtaining user feedback should be done.

Evaluation

An evaluation of what has been achieved and how well the system meets the performance criteria is an essential part of the system life cycle. Evaluation will take place not only at the completion of a system; it is an ongoing process, and sooner or later it will lead to problems or inadequacies being recognised, and the whole systems life cycle will start again.

Chapter 16 – Writing the Project Report

Introduction

This chapter will give you some advice on how to set about writing the project report. Remember that the moderator will not actually see your system running – the report has to provide all the evidence of what you have achieved.

It will help you to look at the sample project as you will see how the report could be laid out and get some idea of what should be included in each section.

The mark scheme

Turn to the Appendix at the end of this book, which contains the AQA instructions and guidance for project work. You will see that the mark scheme in Section 20 is divided into five sections: **Specification**, **Implementation**, **User Testing**, **Evaluation** and **User Documentation**. You could organise your project report into these five major sections, but you may choose to vary this. Analysis and Design, for example, may be included in the mark schemes for other specifications. Spend some time familiarising yourself with the mark scheme so you know exactly what you are aiming for. Ultimately the decision on how best to structure the report is yours.

Creating an outline for your project

Word has a useful feature called **Outlining**. This feature enables you to create an outline for your entire project, breaking it down into sections and sub-sections, which you can then fill in as you build up your project. You can easily add, delete or rearrange headings at any stage, and at the end of it all you will be able to create an automatic Table of Contents.

Task 16.1: Create an outline for your project

In this task you will use Word's Outline feature to create an outline for your project. You can do this even before you have selected your project. It will help you to get a clear idea of the kind of task you should be setting yourself.

- Open a new document using the *Normal* template and save it as *Project.doc*.

- Click the **Outline View** button at the lower left corner of the Word window.

Outline View

Figure 16.1: The Outline View button

- The Outline toolbar pops up, the Style box displays Heading 1 style, and a fat minus sign appears in the left margin.

Figure 16.2: The Outline toolbar

- Type your first heading *Specification* and press **Enter**.

- Now type the first subtopic heading, *Description of the Problem*. It also gets Heading 1 style, just like the first heading. Since you want it to be a subtopic, click it and then click the **Demote** tool on the Outline toolbar. That makes it a Heading 2 style.

- Type the other headings for the Specification section. These could include:
  Input
  Processing
  Output
  Test Strategy
  Test Plan
  Test Data and Expected Outcomes

- Press **Enter** after *Test Data and Expected Outcomes*, click the **Promote** tool and type the next major heading: *Implementation*.

- The headings in the Implementation section will obviously depend on what you are implementing. Most of the marks in this section will be given for the actual implementation which you will demonstrate to your teacher. Useful evidence of the implementation should also be present in the user documentation.
  In this section, you can include, for example:

  Overview of the Solution

  Advanced Software Features Used

  Description of the User Interface

  Justification of Hardware Used

  Justification of Software Used

  Project Log

  Description of Difficulties Encountered and Solutions Found

  Do not follow these suggestions slavishly – they may not be appropriate for your particular project. Take note of Section 19.1.2 in the AQA Mark Scheme if you are following this specification:

  "Documentation is expected on the implementation work completed, which will contribute to the assessment of whether the candidate fully employed their package skills in an effective and appropriate manner. Also, that the selections of the chosen hardware and software facilities have been fully justified in relation to the solution developed. The project log recommended in the specification for Module 3 is expected to contribute towards the evidence for this aspect."

- Add these headings and subheadings to your outline. At this stage your screen should look something like Figure 16.3.

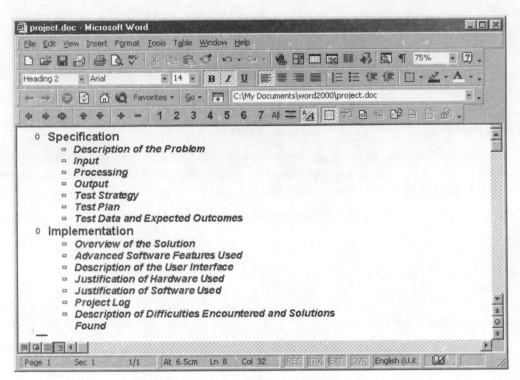

Figure 16.3: Outline for Analysis and Design

- Now enter the headings for the next four major headings: *User Testing*, *Evaluation* and *User Documentation*. These are all at Heading 1 level.

This completes the project outline. Naturally, you will probably want to amend it as you develop your own ideas.

Reordering topics

If you decide that you want to change the order of topics in your project, do the following:

- Select for example *Project Log*. To move it up to the top of the Design section, click the Move Up button several times until it reaches the top of the section.

Adding numbers to the headings

- Select **Format, Bullets and Numbering**.

- Click the **Outline Numbered** tab and select a numbering format or customise one to your own liking. Your outline will appear something like Figure 16.4.

Note: If you decide to move your outline headings up or down it's a good idea to remove the numbers first and then re-apply them.

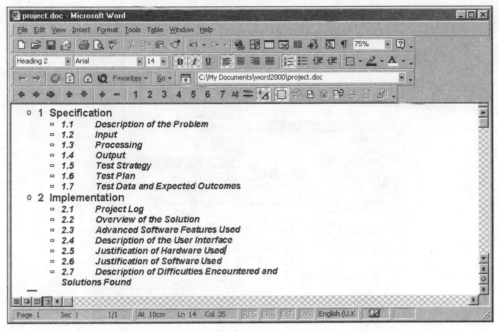

Figure 16.4: Adding numbers to an outline

Turning the outline into a document

The outline IS the document. Just click the **Normal View** button at the bottom of the window, and start entering text. You may want to change the indent and make a new style for the document text.

Adding a header and footer

You should add a header and footer to your project documentation. For example, the header could contain the Project title and the Section title, and the footer could contain your name and the page number.

- Insert page breaks between each of your major sections by pressing **Ctrl-Enter** wherever you want a page break.

- With the cursor at the beginning of the project outline, select **View, Header and Footer**.

- On the left hand side of the header, type your project title.

- Tab twice to get to the right hand side of the header. We need to insert a field here so that the name of the section is inserted.

- Select **Insert, Field**. In the **Categories** box select **Links and References**. In the Field Names box, select StyleRef.

- After the word STYLEREF, enter the style name "Heading 1" in quotes as shown in Figure 16.5.

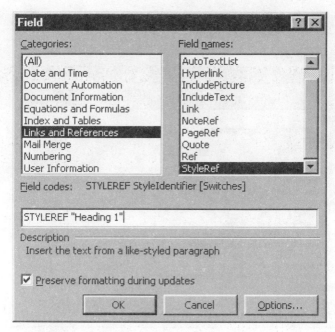

Figure 16.5: Inserting a field into the header

- Click **OK**. The header should appear as in Figure 16.6.

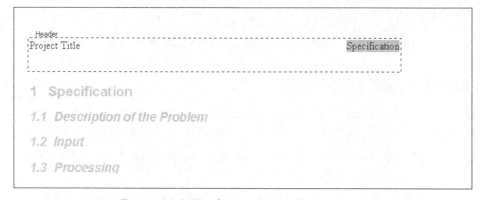

Figure 16.6: Header containing Section name

- Click the **Switch between Header and Footer** button and insert your name.

- Tab once or twice and insert the page number using the **Insert Page Number** button on the Header and Footer toolbar.

Inserting a Table of Contents

You can now insert a Table of Contents at the beginning of your project. This can be automatically updated at any time by clicking in it and pressing F9.

- Insert a page break in front of the heading *Specification*. (You can do this by pressing **Ctrl-Enter**)

- Click the **Normal View** button in the bottom left of the Word window (or select **View, Normal**).

- With the cursor at the beginning of the document, click **Insert, Index and Tables**.

- Click the **Table of Contents** tab. Leave the other defaults as shown in Figure 16.7.

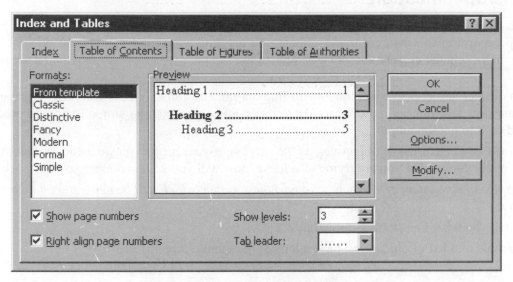

Figure 16.7: Inserting a Table of Contents

- The table of contents will appear as shown below.

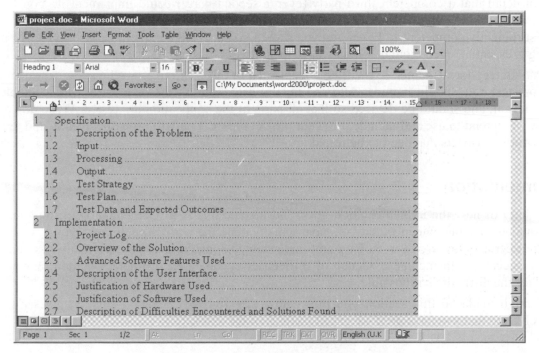

Figure 16.8: The Table of Contents

- You can change the styles of TOC1, TOC2 etc. which are used in the Table of Contents using **Format**, **Style**.

- You can also change the styles of Heading 1, Heading 2 etc.

That's about it for your project outline. In the next few paragraphs we'll flesh out each section.

Analysis/Specification

Excel is a suitable software package to use for either a Minor or a Major project. The project will be written up according to whatever mark scheme you are following, and you should be very careful to follow the mark scheme closely. Do not assume that the sample project has exactly the headings that you should use.

In the last chapter advice was given on how to find out information about the current system, and how to draw a data flow diagram to show where data comes from, what data is stored and what processes are performed on it to get the output.

Try to write a good clear list of objectives, as the success of your project may depend on this. After all, if you don't really know what you are trying to achieve, how will you know whether you have achieved it?

"The objective of my system is to create a user-friendly system which will be more efficient, save time and be easy to use."

Does this tell you what I am setting out to build?

For an example of a list of objectives, have a look at the sample project.

Design

This forms part of the 'Specification' section in the AQA mark scheme for an AS project. You must establish and document the input, processing and output requirements. The design should be specified in sufficient detail that a competent third party (even a second party) could implement it. You MUST do some design work on paper before you start implementing. If you feel you are unable to do so, then you are not sufficiently competent in Excel and you should go back and complete Parts 1 and 2 of this book! Planning is essential, even though you may have to alter your design if it doesn't work.

Your test strategy (see Chapter 15) will be documented in this section, as well as your test plan and test data. Your test data should include valid and invalid data, data on the boundaries of acceptable values where relevant, and should be devised so that all parts of the application are tested. Write down the test data that you intend to use and include it in your project report. You will probably need to add to it as you discover further aspects that need to be tested.

Implementation

Keep a diary of how the implementation goes, and include this in a 'Commentary on Implementation'. This provided valuable evidence that you have actually done the work. Explain why you have performed a task in a certain way or why you have not implemented something as you originally designed it. It is perfectly acceptable to include evidence of difficulties encountered in implementation, and to discuss reasons for the difficulties if possible.

To gain high marks in this section you must show that you have actually solved the user's problem effectively, and that you have used advanced features of the software.

Testing

You must show evidence of testing in the form of screenshots or printed output. This output must be cross-referenced to the original test plan – it is a complete waste of time and paper including page after page of output with no meaningful comment as to what it is supposed to show. Handwrite on the output, use a highlighter pen, or any other means to help the reader understand what your test is designed to show, and how it actually shows it.

Evaluation

Refer back to the objectives and state to what extent these have been achieved. Also give some suggestions as to how the system could be enhanced, or what its weaknesses were – it's no good pretending that a rather feeble project is exactly what the user always wanted for Christmas, the moderator is unlikely to be fooled. Much better to show that you realise there are weaknesses and write about how you feel it could be improved. Honesty pays!

User documentation

This is for a non-technical user and should explain clearly all the functions of your system. Use plenty of screen shots to illustrate the text. These can also provide valuable evidence of the fact that your system actually works. Many moderators look at the User Guide early in the moderation process to help them understand the project better.

Technical documentation

(This is not required for an AQA 'AS' Level Project.)

You should include a separate section or manual for technical documentation which might show, for example, the formulae used on each sheet, all cell names, and macro listings. It could also include instructions for installation, how to unprotect worksheets to make alterations, and hardware or software requirements.

Handing it in

You must include a title page and a Table of Contents, and number every page, by hand if necessary.

Don't spoil it all by handing your project in as a collection of loose pages paper-clipped together, or stuffed into a single plastic pocket intended for a single sheet. Take pride in what you have achieved – spend 50p on a plastic folder in which the pages can be securely held.

Heed this advice from the 1998 Examiner's report:

"All projects must be securely bound; a thin folder or punched holes and treasury tags work well. Slide binders are often inhibiting to reading all the text, or they come off in the post. Ring binders, lever arch files and individual plastic pockets must not be used at all. They add unnecessary bulk and weight. The practice of using multiple sheets in poly pockets should cease."

Well! That tells it like it is! If you can't follow simple instructions on how to bind a project, what hope is there for you? Very little, I should say.

Don't forget to include a signed cover sheet giving your name, candidate number and centre number.

Best of luck!

Part 4: Tackling the Project

158

Appendix A

Sample Project

Atlas Publications

Daily Picking List

Project by:
A. Student
Any College
1998

Table of Contents

*You MUST number your pages and include a Table of Contents. This one was created automatically using Word's **Insert, Index and Tables**.*

Analysis

Introduction

Atlas Publications is a small publishing company publishing road atlases which are sold by three different methods:

- to wholesalers, who in turn sell them on to retailers (bookshops etc);
- to retailers such as bookshops, service stations, shops specialising in car accessories;
- to individual members of the public who order directly by phone or mail in response to advertisements.

Atlas Publications uses a specialised Accounts package to enter orders, prepare invoices and keep records of customer accounts. Each day they accept orders by phone, fax, e-mail or regular mail and prepare invoices accordingly. There are normally about 5-15 orders each day. These invoices, together with an extra copy of each one, are then mailed the same day to Penco Warehouse, a separate organisation which stores large quantities of books for hundreds of different publishers. Penco packs and dispatches the books, enclosing one copy of the invoice with the books and keeping the other copy for their records.

A 'Picking List' report has to be enclosed with the invoices sent daily to Penco, telling them the total number of each title that has to be dispatched that day. The warehouse covers several acres and a forklift truck driver has to be sent to collect the correct number of books from the specified 'bins' and take them to the dispatch area where they are packed and collected for delivery by Securicor.

At the end of each month Atlas Publications receives an invoice from Penco for their services, based on the sales value of books dispatched that month.

The current system

The user (Mr Jones, the owner of Atlas Publications) was interviewed to ascertain how the current system of producing Picking Lists works, and exactly what are the requirements of the new system.

Mr Jones does not want any changes to the current method of recording customer orders and printing invoices using the software package Sage Sterling. However, the Picking List as described above cannot be generated by this system in the format required by Penco warehouse, and producing this by hand is time-consuming and prone to error.

At present the Picking List is prepared by adding up the total quantity of each book from the invoices, and entering the figures on to a photocopied form. Sometimes the sales clerk uses a spreadsheet as a calculator just to make sure the addition is correct, but there is no set method of preparing the report.

Mr Jones would also like to be able to get instant information on total monthly sales, which is not available from the Sage Accounts system in the format in which he would like it.

Samples of an invoice **output** from Sage but used as an **input** document for the Picking List, and a copy of the Picking List, are shown on the next two pages.

Create and use styles for section and paragraph headings. Then you will be able to automatically generate a Table of Contents. 11 or 12 point Times Roman is a good choice for body text. (The text here is 11 point)

Include an introduction to give some background information about the organisation.

Then give an overview of what the project is about.

You should interview the user and write a summary of what you discovered.

Discuss the problems with the current system, and why changing it would be beneficial.

Source document 1: Invoice

The day's invoices are used as the input documents in the production of the Picking List.

Show actual samples of input and output documents currently used. Explain aspects of the documents that need clarification.

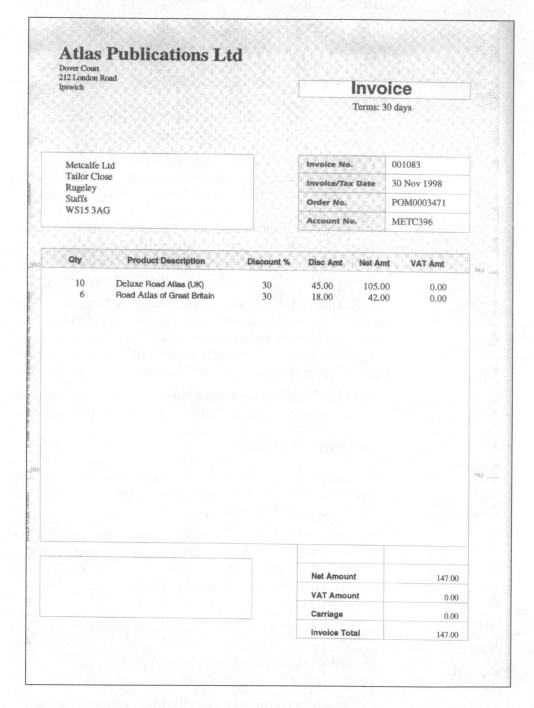

Atlas Publications Ltd
Dover Court
212 London Road
Ipswich

Invoice

Terms: 30 days

Metcalfe Ltd
Tailor Close
Rugeley
Staffs
WS15 3AG

Invoice No.	001083
Invoice/Tax Date	30 Nov 1998
Order No.	POM0003471
Account No.	METC396

Qty	Product Description	Discount %	Disc Amt	Net Amt	VAT Amt
10	Deluxe Road Atlas (UK)	30	45.00	105.00	0.00
6	Road Atlas of Great Britain	30	18.00	42.00	0.00

Net Amount	147.00
VAT Amount	0.00
Carriage	0.00
Invoice Total	147.00

Notes: VAT and Carriage are not charged on books. These items automatically appear on invoices generated by Sage Sterling.

The data that will be input to the new system from the day's invoices are **Product Code** (not shown but as there are only three different products, the staff have them memorised), **Quantity** of each item and **Invoice Total**.

Atlas Publications Ltd

Dover Court
212 London Road
Ipswich

Picking List   Date:

Title	Bin No	Total copies
Deluxe Road Atlas (UK)	AP001	
Road Atlas of Great Britain	AP002	
Towns of England	AP003	

Total Number of invoices:

Notes: The Picking List is currently filled in by hand after adding up the quantities of each title sold and counting the number of invoices (normally about 5-15 daily). Every weekday a Picking List is sent to Penco with two copies of each invoice, except on the very rare occasions when there are no orders.

The Bin numbers are supplied to Atlas by Penco but these never change. Warehouse staff at Penco need to know the Bin Numbers so they know where to find the books to be dispatched. They take the Picking Lists from different publishers and drive around the warehouse loading up the specified number of each book to take to the Dispatch area where the books are packed.

Objectives of the new system

The list of objectives must specify the actual purpose of the system – i.e. what tasks it will perform

The Accounts manager would like a new system which will perform the following functions:

♦ allow data from the invoices (quantity of each book and total invoice value) to be recorded quickly and accurately;

♦ calculate totals and produce a picking list from this data automatically;

♦ produce monthly sales summaries;

♦ produce a chart showing monthly sales over the past year, and indicating predicted sales based on these sales figures;

♦ The system must be robust and easy to use.

Data flow diagram (Level 1)

The following diagram illustrates in outline the process of ordering, invoicing and dispatching books.

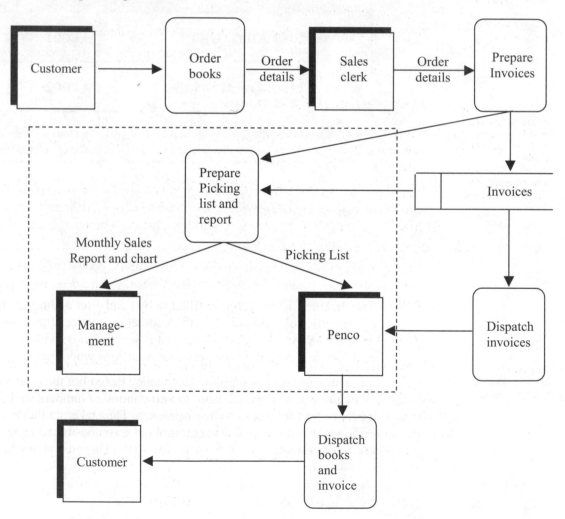

Boundaries of the system

The dotted line in the above diagram shows the part of the whole system that is to form this project.

Performance Indicators

The following performance indicators will be used:

1. It should not take longer than 30 seconds to enter each invoice.
2. Data entry should be made so simple that the resulting Picking List is 100% accurate.
3. The Picking List will be produced in one operation by the user – for example selecting from a menu or clicking a button on a customised toolbar.
4. The monthly sales summary and chart will be produced in a similar way, using a menu item or a button.
5. The system must cater for any number of titles to be added at a future date as the company expands.
6. It must be impossible to accidentally erase formulae, headings etc.
7. The system should be easy to use for anyone with a rudimentary knowledge of Excel.

The Performance Indicators will be used to 'benchmark' the new system.

There is no point having a new system which performs the tasks set in the objectives, but is no better than the existing system.

A good set of performance indicators is crucial to writing the Evaluation!

Hardware and Software

Include a discussion of the hardware, which version of the software you will be using for development and which version the user has, if different.

Atlas Publications has a Pentium PC with 128 Mb of RAM and 15 Gb hard disk. Windows 2000 and Office 2000 are loaded on this PC. A laser printer is used for hard copy.

Development work will be carried out partly on a school network and partly on a standalone Pentium similar to the one described above. All the files will need to fit on a 3½" floppy disk for easy transportation between home and school. (They may need to be compressed.)

The school network stations are 120MHz Pentium PCs with 16Mb of RAM attached to a laser printer. There are no user areas on hard disk, so floppy disks are used to store student work.

User's Skill Level

The user's skill level is relevant to the final design.

There will be two users of this system. Mr Jones, the owner of the firm is very computer-literate and has a good basic knowledge of Excel. However he does not do the day-to-day entry of invoices and the production of the Picking List report. This is done by Mrs Nicholson, an employee who is familiar with Windows 95 and has some knowledge of Excel which she uses occasionally for entering simple lists of numbers and formulae.

Design

Choice of software

This system will be implemented using Excel 97. This package is ideal as it includes many features which can be used in customising the application, such as:

Summarise the advanced features that you plan to use.

- Ability to create a blank template;

- Ability to link product details entered in one workbook with invoice details entered in a second workbook through a table lookup;

- Pivot tables to create monthly summaries;

- Sophisticated report facilities with the ability to format text, set margins and page layout, import a company logo if desired and preview before printing;

- Charting facilities including the ability to add a trend line;

- Ability to protect worksheets and workbooks so that the user cannot accidentally destroy formulae or headings;

- Formatting to help make it clear to the user where to enter data;

- Macros to automate various functions;

- Macros which will execute automatically on opening and closing workbooks;

- Customised menus and toolbars;

- Auditing tools to help ensure that there are no errors in the workbook

Worksheet design

System overview

A data flow diagram is an excellent way of showing where data comes from, what data is stored, what processing is carried out, what output is produced and who receives the reports.

Refer to Chapter 14 for guidelines on drawing DFDs.

The system will be based on two workbooks; a Products workbook containing details of all products and a template containing a number of separate worksheets for data entry, reports and summaries. (See below, **Detailed Design**, for details.) At the beginning of each year the user will be able to open a new workbook based on this template and enter daily invoice data, which will be accumulated day by day over the year. Reports and charts will be produced from this accumulated data by means of options on a custom menu stored in the template. In addition, a front end menu will enable the user to choose which task they wish to perform – e.g., enter data from invoices (which are used as **source** documents in this system), print a monthly sales summary or chart. A Level 2 data flow diagram of the system is shown below.

Data Flow Diagram of proposed new system

```
End user          Product          Input and          Product
(Atlas            number, title,   store              number, title,        Products
Sales             Bin Number       product            Bin Number
Clerk)                             codes and
                                   titles
                                                       Product
                                                       title, Bin
                                                       Number

End user          Date, invoice    Input              Date, invoice number, product
(Atlas            number, product  invoice data        number, title, Bin number,        Invoice list
Sales             number, quantity,                    quantity, sales value
Clerk)            sales value

                  Month, product   Calculate          Print daily
                  number, title,   monthly            picking list
                  quantity, sales  summary
                  value
                                                                              Product title, Bin
                                                                              number, quantity,
                  Monthly summary                                             number of invoices
                  data             Prepare                                    Picking list
                                   charts

                                                                              Penco
                  Manage-          Monthly sales
                  ment             and trend
                                   Charts
```

*A hand-drawn
sheet is an
enormous help to
the moderator. At
the end of this
project you will find
a page of blank
worksheets that
you can photocopy
and use for this
purpose. Cut out
individual sheets
and glue them to
an A3 sheet.*

Detailed design

On the next page a diagram shows the connection between and two workbooks **Atlas***yy***.xls** (a new workbook opened at the beginning of each year, based on the template **AtlasProject.xlt**) and **Atlas Products.xls**.

The diagram also shows the interconnection between the 5 sheets in **Atlas***yy***.xls**.

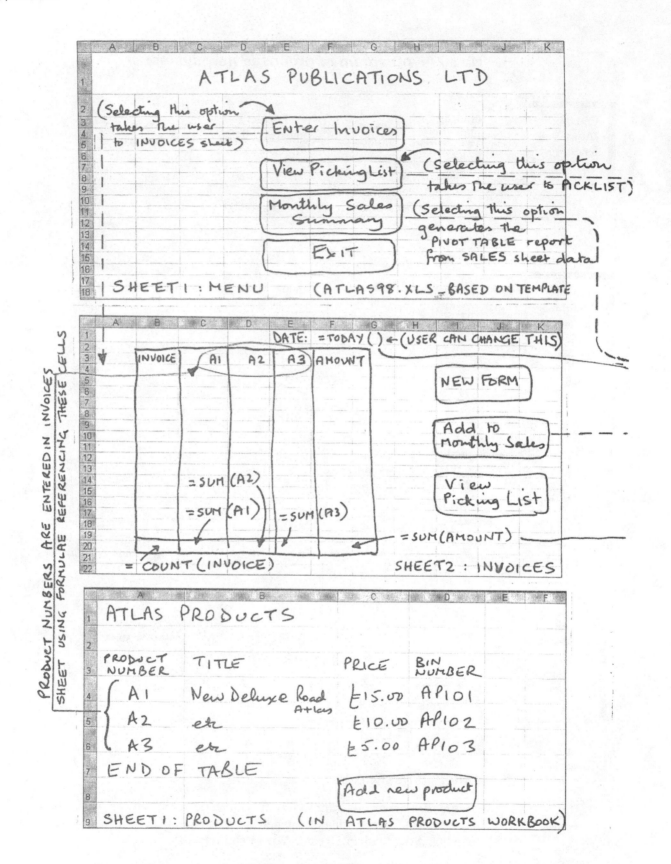

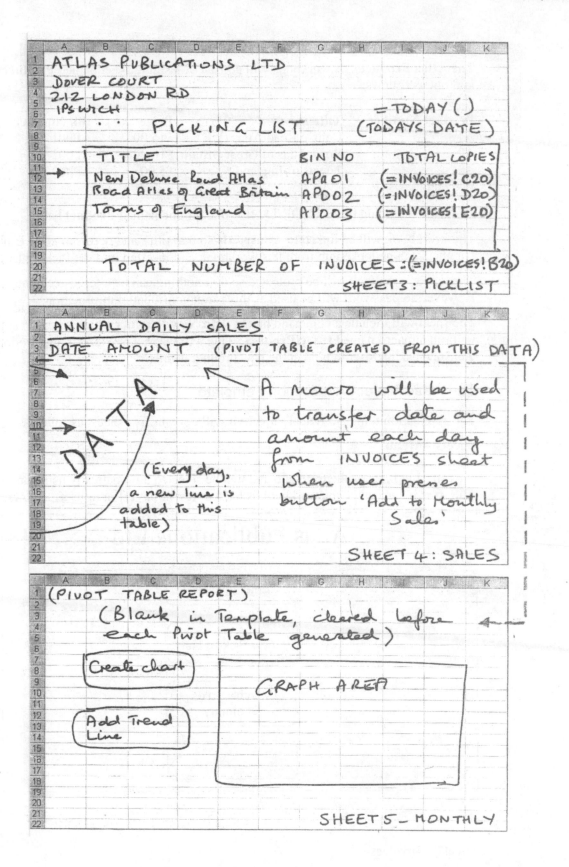

ATLAS PUBLICATIONS LTD
DOVER COURT
212 LONDON RD
IPSWICH

PICKING LIST   =TODAY( )
                 (TODAYS DATE)

TITLE	BIN NO	TOTAL COPIES
New Deluxe Road Atlas	APA01	(=INVOICES! C20)
Road Atlas of Great Britain	APD02	(=INVOICES! D20)
Towns of England	APD03	(=INVOICES! E20)

TOTAL NUMBER OF INVOICES : (=INVOICES! B20)

SHEET3: PICKLIST

ANNUAL DAILY SALES

DATE AMOUNT (PIVOT TABLE CREATED FROM THIS DATA)

DATA

(Every day, a new line is added to this table)

A macro will be used to transfer date and amount each day from INVOICES sheet when user presses button 'Add to Monthly Sales'

SHEET 4: SALES

(PIVOT TABLE REPORT)

(Blank in Template, cleared before each Pivot Table generated)

Create chart

Add Trend Line

GRAPH AREA

SHEET 5 — MONTHLY

The **Atlas Products** workbook

The **Atlas Products.xls** workbook will consist of a single sheet named **Products**, laid out as follows:

Product Number	Title	Price	Bin Number
A1	Deluxe Road Atlas (UK)	£15.00	AP001
A2	Road Atlas of Great Britain	£10.00	AP002
A3	Towns of England	£5.00	AP003
END OF TABLE			

Describe each workbook to explain your hand-drawn design in more detail.

The table including the END OF TABLE line will be named **ProductTable**.

This workbook will be linked to **Atlas*yy*.xls** so that titles and corresponding Bin Numbers can be looked up from this workbook and inserted into the Picking List.

The whole workbook will be protected so that nothing can be altered accidentally. However no password will be used as this is not confidential information.

The sheet will include a command button **Add New Product** which when pressed will run a macro named **InsertProduct**. This will insert a new line in the Products table and ask the user to type in the new product details.

The **AtlasProject** Application Template

The application template **AtlasProject.xlt** will contain five sheets as follows.

Sheet1 - Menu

This sheet will act as the front end and will be selected automatically using an Autoexec macro when the workbook is loaded. It will have 4 options as follows:

A front end menu provides a pleasing user interface and is quickly created.

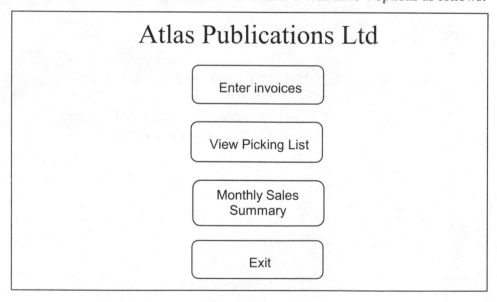

Sheet2 – Invoices

This is where the daily invoices will be entered. It will be laid out as follows:

DATE:

Invoice number	A1	A2	A3	Amount
(16 blank rows for invoices)				
Count(Invoices)	Sum(ProdA1)	Sum(ProdA2)	Sum(ProdA3)	Sum(Amount)

(Cells and ranges used in formulae will be named)

The user will copy the details from invoices (a sample of which is shown in the Analysis section) to this sheet. All cells will be locked apart from the ones where data is entered, meaning that it will be impossible to overwrite formulae, and data entry will be faster because tabbing will automatically move to the next unlocked cell.

There will be three command buttons on the form:

New Form - to clear old data from the form ready for today's invoices, and to enter the default date *=Today()* (Macro **NewForm**)

Add to Monthly sales - to automatically add the date and total sales value to the list of daily sales on Sheet 4 (Sales) (Macro **AddToMonthlySales**)

View Picking List – to go to sheet 2 (**PickList**) where the figures will have automatically been copied from the totals on this sheet (Macro **ViewPickingList**).

Sheet3 – PickList

This sheet will take the form of the Picking List which will have formulae linking it both to the **Atlas Products** workbook for the Product titles and Bin numbers, and the **Invoices** worksheet from where it will get the totals. It will be as follows:

Picking List   Date:

Title	Bin Number	Total copies
(link to Atlas Products workbook)		=Invoices!TotalA1
		=Invoices!TotalA2
etc		

Total number of invoices: = Invoices!TotalInvoices

The user will be able to print this using the standard **Print** button after checking that all is correct.

Sheet 4 – Sales

This sheet will contain all the daily sales amounts for the current year. It will have just two columns:

	Date	Amount
e.g.	05 Jan 1999	£678.00
	06 Jan 1999	£1,087.00
	etc.	

The day's data will be automatically added to this list when the user presses the **Add to monthly sales** button on the **Invoices** sheet.

Sheet 5 – Monthly

This sheet will hold a PivotTable that will show year-to-date monthly sales. The user can create the PivotTable report by selecting the option **Monthly Sales Summary** either from a custom menu (**Atlas**) on the menu bar or from the front end menu. This runs a macro called **MonthlyPivot** which groups the sales totals by month.

The user can produce a chart and trend line from these figures using the standard Chart button and following instructions in the User Manual, as this is a very straightforward procedure.

Note: Formulae and cell names used in the worksheet are shown in the Technical Manual which follows the User Manual (Figures 6 to 9).

Data entry and Validation

Entering Products

*Data validation is important – and easy to implement. Select **Data, Validation** from the menu bar (not available in Excel 7).*

Products are entered or edited extremely rarely – they will be entered initially by the application designer, and thereafter only when a new product is published. There is therefore no need to have any special validation procedures.

Entering invoice data

Date will be validated as a valid date between 1/11/1998 and 31/12/2020. Normally the user will not need to enter the date, as the default formula =**Today()** is inserted into the Invoices sheet when the user selects the **Enter Invoices** option on the Main Menu, but occasionally the user may enter a batch of invoices the day after they were printed (e.g. on a Saturday morning), and will then enter yesterday's date.

Invoice number will be validated and only whole numbers between 1 and 99999 will be accepted.

Quantities of each product will be validated and only whole numbers between 1 and 300 will be accepted.

Amount will be validated and must be between £2.00 and £3000.

Macros

Use short instructions in plain English to describe your macros.

The following macros will be used:

InsertProduct

Unprotect the sheet
Insert a new line above 'END OF TABLE'
Ask user to enter each new field
Protect sheet

EnterInvoices

Select the Invoices sheet
Clear the invoice form
Select the date cell and set it to Today()
Go to first data entry cell

ViewPickingList

Select the Picking List sheet

AddToMonthlySales

Select the Invoices sheet
Copy the date
Select the Sales sheet
Select cell A3 (top left of the list)
Select all the list *(by pressing Ctrl-Shift-*)*
Go to the last cell in the left column
(Switch to relative references here)
Move down one cell to the first blank cell
Paste the date
Select the Invoices sheet
Select the cell containing the invoice total
Select the Sales sheet
Move right one cell
Paste
Exit Cut/Copy mode *(by pressing Esc)*

MonthlyPivot

Delete the current name SalesTable which does not include the latest additions
Select the whole of SalesTable
Name it
Clear the existing PivotTable from Monthly sheet
Create the new PivotTable
Group the date by months

Auto_Open (Runs automatically when the Atlas workbook is opened)

Set default path
Open Products workbook
Make Atlas workbook active
Select the menu sheet

Auto_Close (Runs automatically when the Atlas workbook is closed)

Closes all open workbooks

Security

Both the Atlas Products workbook and the Atlas template will be protected so that data can only be entered in unlocked cells. However the user does not want a password attached to either workbook in case she forgets it. Therefore the workbooks can be unprotected using **Tools Unprotect**, but accidental alterations will be prevented (provided the user remembers to protect a sheet after making necessary alterations.)

Test Strategy

The test strategy used will include:

♦ Unit testing to test each macro under different circumstances;

♦ Functional testing to test each menu item and command button under different circumstances;

♦ Using the Auditing toolbar to help ensure that every formula is correct;

♦ Testing the effects of inputting invalid and extreme data;

♦ System testing by running through a sequence of tests which test every menu item;

♦ End-user testing to establish whether the system meets the end-user's requirements.

Test Plan

The following tests will be performed

1. Open a brand new worksheet using the Atlas template **AtlasProject.xlt** and save it as *Atlas99.xls* for the year 1999, or *Atlas00.xls* for the year 2000, etc.

2. Test the **Enter Invoices** button.

3. Add invoice data for Jan 5th (see test data set 1).

4. Test the **View Picking List** button on the Invoices sheet.

5. Print out the Picking List.

6. Test the **Add to Monthly Sales** button on the Invoice sheet.

7. Test the **New Form** button on the Invoices sheet.

8. Attempt to add an invoice with invalid date 30/02/99, invoice number that is not numeric, quantities that are not numeric, amount not numeric. Error messages should be displayed in each case.

9. Try to enter data in a locked cell. This should not be possible.

10. Add invoice data for Jan 6th – Mar 6th (see test data set 2).

11. Test the **Monthly Sales Summary** button on the main menu. The total sales figures should be

Jan: £2100   Feb: £1872.75   Mar: £1650

12. Test the **Create Chart** button, which displays a message telling the user to delete any existing chart, select the month names and sales totals, press the **Chart** button on the standard toolbar and then select **Finish** for an instant chart.

13. Test the **Add Trendline** button.

14. Test the **Exit** button on the main menu. Save as Atlas99.

15. Open the Atlas Products workbook.

16. Attempt to add a new product without using the **Add New Product** button (should be impossible).

17. Attempt to edit a product (should be impossible without first removing protection).

18. Test the **Add new Product** button. Add a new product *A4*, *Highways and Byways, &8.50, Bin AP004*. An error message should be displayed as the Price is invalid.

19. Enter the new product correctly.

System Testing

20. Open Atlas99 again. (The model will need to be changed to accommodate the new product, but this will not be done here).

21. Enter invoices for April (see Test data set 3). Press **Add to Monthly Sales**.

22. From the Main Menu, select **View Picking List**.

23. From the Main Menu, select **Monthly Sales Summary**. This test ensures that the old PivotTable is deleted before the new one is created.

24. Create the Monthly Sales chart with trend line.

User Testing

25. The user will test all the normal functions of the system.

26. User will test the editing and addition of a new product, and the process of altering the Atlas model to insert the new product on the invoice form and Picking List.

Using the Auditing toolbar

27. Display precedents and dependents on Invoice sheet.

28. Display precedents and dependents on Picking List sheet.

29. Display precedents and dependents on Monthly Sales sheet.

The purpose of these tests is to ensure that all formulae are correct and refer to the right cells.

All evidence of testing is given in the 'Commentary on Testing' below.

Test Data and Expected Outcomes

The following test data will be used:

Test data set 1: Invoices for January 5th 1999

Invoice number	A1	A2	A3	Amount
1001	10	20		£300
1002	100		25	£1200
1003		30	10	£200
Totals 3 invoices	*110*	*50*	*35*	*£1700*

Test data set 2: Invoices for January 6th 1999 to Mar 6th 1999

Date	Invoice number	A1	A2	A3	Amount
6 Jan	1004		50	20	£400
Total sales for Jan:					*£2100*
7 Feb	1025	100	10	25	£1550.75
8 Feb	1026		30	10	£200
	1027	12	2	1	£122
Total sales for Feb:					*£1872.75*
6 Mar	1200	50			£450
	1201	100		70	£1200
Total sales for Mar:					*£1650*

Test data set 3: Invoices for April 5th-6th 1999

Date	Invoice number	A1	A2	A3	Amount
5 Apr	1300	10	20		£300
	1301	90		25	£1000
	1302	50	30	10	£900
Totals 3 invoices		*150*	*50*	*35*	*£2200*
6 Apr	1303	10			£90
Total sales for Apr:					*£2290*

Schedule of Activities

The Schedule of Activities is a required part of the project. It could go at the beginning of the Design section.

You can hand-write the comments each week as you work on your project.

HAVE YOU BACKED UP YOUR PROJECT AND THE DOCUMENTATION?

Week	Task	Home/ School	Comment
1 Jan 18	Interview user, find out current system and establish requirements, user skills, hardware, software.	H	Could not get to the user in week 1 so I continued going through the Excel tutorial.
2 Jan 25	Write up analysis section.	S	Saw Mr Jones and he told me the requirements. Typed them up.
3 Feb 1	Draw data flow diagram, design the workbook(s).	S	Decided to use a template with various sheets.
4 Feb 8	Create prototype (menu and worksheet for entering invoices, not macros) and show it to user.	H	Had a lot of problems implementing my design and getting the macros to work. It seems rather clumsy.
5 Feb 15	Continue writing up design section, including front end menu, validation of data, test plan, macros.	H/S	Showed Mr Jones progress so far but unfortunately he doesn't like it and has made some suggestions which mean basically starting again.
6 Feb 22	Implement the system.	H	It's going better with the new design, which I have now written up. Have not started writing any macros yet.
7 Mar 1	Test system. Try installing on user's PC.	H	Still implementing and testing as I go. Many errors showing up. Can't get the Chart macro to work.
8 Mar 8	Get user to test system and get user feedback. Make final modifications.	S	Have modified the design somewhat to get it to work, and run through the test plan taking screen shots as I did it. Corel Capture brilliant for this.
9 Mar 15	Write user and technical manuals.	H	Showed it to Mr Jones and tried out the installation procedure which worked fine, installing it in recommended directory.
10 Mar 22	Write evaluation, finish all documentation, buy a folder, hand in.	S	Printer needs new cartridge, PC crashed, panic stations. Forgot Table of Contents. Help!

Implementation and Testing

Commentary on Implementation

Choice of project

A commentary on Implementation is extremely helpful to the Moderator in assessing your work. It provides evidence of the work done and you can use it to justify design decisions and show continuing user involvement.

A friend of the family suggested this project to me and I thought it sounded suitable. After interviewing the user I felt that maybe the problem was too simple and did not offer enough scope for an 'A' Level project. However, as it contains the basic elements of Input – Process – Output, has a real end user who will be able to use the system and give feedback on it, and can be implemented within the 2 months available for this project, I decided to go ahead with it.

Initial design decisions

My first decision was to use only one template with 2 worksheets. Sheet1 (Invoices) would be used for entering the details of the daily invoices, which would be added to the end of all the other invoices for the year. E.g.

Date	Invoice Number	Product Number	Product Title	Bin Number	Quantity	Sale Price

Sheet2 (Products) would be used for keeping records of all the products. When entering invoice details, Product Title and Bin Number would be looked up from the Product table using **Vlookup**.

I then realised that at the end of each year, I would need to delete all the invoices but leave the products. If I added a new product during the year it would be added to the Products sheet in the current workbook but not to the template, which would be unsatisfactory. My first change therefore was to have 2 workbooks, one for Products and a template for Sales containing only headings, formulae and macros. A new Sales workbook based on the template would be opened at the start of each year.

To get the Picking List I needed a PivotTable report summing the sales amounts for the desired day. A second PivotTable report would be used for the Monthly sales. One problem was that the PivotTable report did not produce the data in the format required for the Picking List, although all the figures were there and could easily be transcribed by hand to a photocopied form.

I produced a prototype based on this design and showed it to the user. The prototype had a menu, a sheet for entering the invoice details and non-working buttons so I could explain how things would work. Unfortunately although it used many advanced features of Excel and did some clever things Mr Jones did not like it as he could not see instantly what the day's sales total was, and he wanted a simple formula showing the total quantity of each product as invoice details were entered. So it was back to the drawing board.

Final design

My final design is as shown in the Design Section. The input of invoices is very simple but it only allows for a maximum of 16 invoices to be input in one day. I could have increased this to say 25 or more but then the totals would not be visible on the screen. I asked the user about this and he said they never had more than 15 invoices, and if they did, couldn't he just insert a few more rows? I agreed that he could do this (he would first have to unprotect the form but it would not affect the way the model worked).

A second problem is that with the new design although it is easy to add a new product to the Product workbook, the Sales template and workbook model would have to be altered to accommodate the new product. Again, the user felt that he would only rarely add new products and would be able to make the necessary alterations if instructions were given.

I originally intended to write a macro to produce the chart and trend line, but I could not get this to work as the macro needs to know the name of the chart, which is automatically generated by Excel as Chart 1, Chart 2 etc each time a new chart is created. Therefore the macro worked the first time the user tries it but not a second time unless Excel is first closed down. As it is quite simple to create the chart and trend line I decided to make the macro give instructions to the user in a message box, and he is quite happy with that.

Commentary on testing

Tests 1-5 (opening a new worksheet, testing the **Enter Invoices** button, adding invoice data for Jan 5th, Testing the **View Picking List** button and printing the Picking list) performed as expected. (See evidence below.)

OK, so some things may just be beyond you! It really doesn't matter, and it's much better to be honest about it. If the moderator doesn't know how to do it either you are not likely to be penalised. Find an alternative way of solving the problem, even if it's not quite so clever.

'Test performed as expected' is worthless without the evidence to prove it.

Your greatest aid at this stage is a good screen capture utility, which will store each screenshot in a file as you work through the tests. Later, you can paste them into your report.

You can use a separate page for each test outcome if this is easier – the test results don't have to be shown in one contiuous report.

Tests 2 and 3

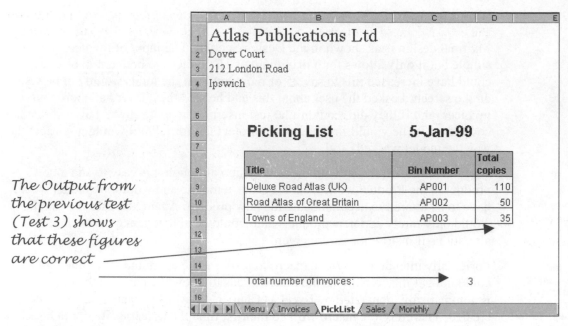

The Output from the previous test (Test 3) shows that these figures are correct

Test 4

Test 6 resulted in a runtime error in Macro **AddToMonthlySales** – it didn't work when the sales list was empty. I added an IF statement to test for this condition and it worked OK. I then adjusted the template.

Figures from the invoices of Jan 5ᵗʰ (see output, Test 3) are correctly transferred to SALES sheet

	A	B	C
1	**Annual daily sales**		
2			
3		**Date**	**Amount**
4		5-Jan-99	£1,700.00
5			

Test 6

Test 7 worked fine. All data was cleared from the entry form, as expected.

All data cleared from yesterday's form

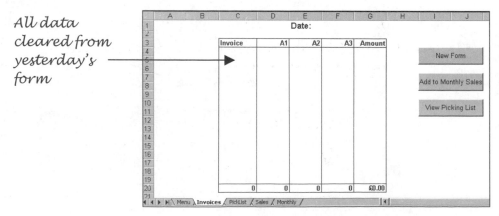

Test 7 – Test the New Form button

Test 8 worked OK but gave the standard Microsoft error message so I customised the error messages using **Data, Validation**. The new messages are shown below.

Customised error messages

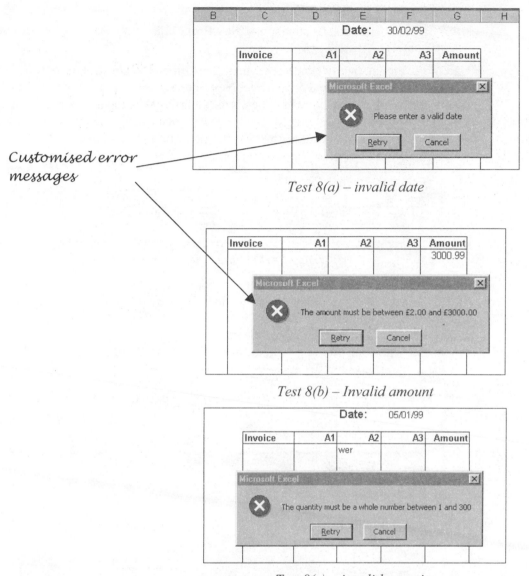

Test 8(a) – invalid date

Test 8(b) – Invalid amount

Test 8(c) – invalid quantity

Test 9 worked OK. The user could not enter data in a locked cell.

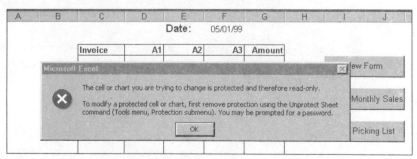

Test 9 – Try to enter data in a locked cell

Test 10. I added the invoice for January and then tried the **Monthly Sales Summary** button. The macro **MonthlyPivot** which creates the PivotTable report failed at the line

ActiveSheet.PivotTableWizard SourceType:=xlDatabase, SourceData:= _

"SalesTable", TableDestination:="**[NewProj.xls]**Monthly!R1C1", TableName:= "PivotTable2"

which was automatically generated when I performed the keystrokes, because I had originally created it while using a sheet **NewProj.xls**. As it is not necessary to specify the workbook name when the current workbook is the one being used, I solved this problem by deleting the workbook name. The Pivot table was then created correctly. (The headings need to be right-aligned.)

Results are correct (see Test data set 2

	A	B	C	D	E	F
1	Sum of Amount	Date				
2		Jan	Feb	Mar	Grand Total	
3	Total	£2,100	£1,873	£1,650	£5,623	
4						

Test 11 – Monthly Sales Summary

Test 11 worked correctly but the figures needed formatting to currency, zero decimal places. I created a new macro called **FormatTotal** to do this and inserted a statement at the end of the **MonthlyPivot** macro to call it. I also realised that I should have put a title at the top of the page to improve the appearance of the report, but with time pressing I did not want to have to change all the macros and test them again. So I left it.

Tests 12 and 13 worked OK, displaying messages to guide the user in producing chart and trend line.

This message appears when the 'Create Chart' button is pressed

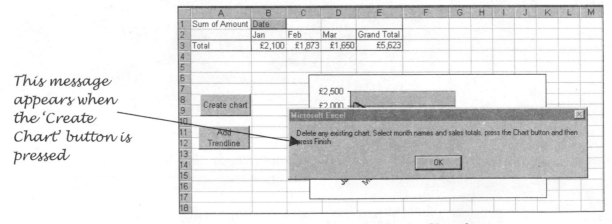

*Test 12 – Press the **Create Chart** button*

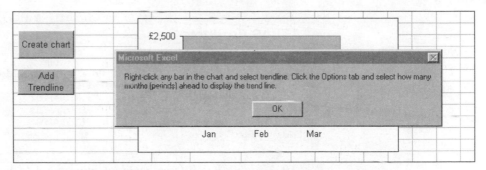

Test 13 – Press the Add Trendline button

Tests 14-19 worked OK. The **Add New Product button** removes the sheet protection ready and inserts a new row. Protection is re-applied in the Auto_Close procedure as soon as the user closes the Atlas Products workbook.

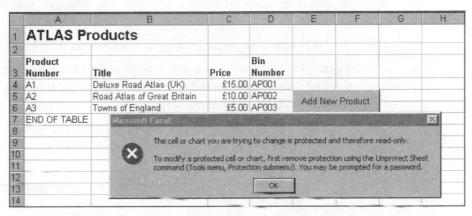

Tests 16 and 17 – attempting to add or edit product in protected sheet

invalid data - & instead of £ entered

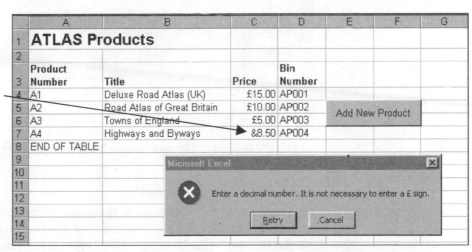

Test 18 – Attempting to add a new product with invalid price (an ampersand was typed instead of a £ sign in the Price field for new product A4)

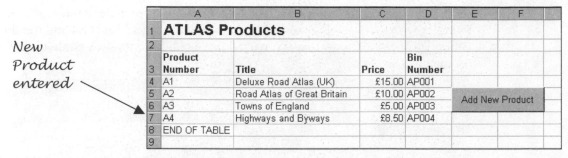

New
Product
entered

Test 19 – Adding a valid new product using the Add New Product button

Test 20 opened Atlas99 again.

Test 21 did not work quite correctly as the old invoice details were left in the form. When they were cleared using **New Form**, the default date was also cleared. I cured this by making the **EnterInvoices** macro delete the old data and insert the default date ready for today's invoices. The new data was then inserted with no problem.

Test 22 (select the View Picking List button on the Main Menu) worked OK

Tests 23 (test Monthly Sales Summary) and **24** (user produces chart and trend line) worked fine except that the screen flickered in an annoying way as the macro ran. I solved that by putting in the statements

```
' Hide the intermediate operations from the user
    Application.ScreenUpdating = False
```

in the MonthlyPivot macro.

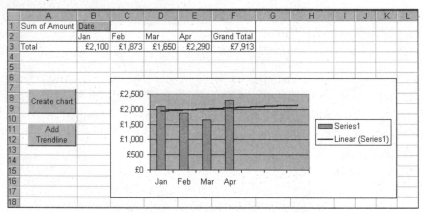

Test 23 and 24 – The new monthly summary, chart and trend line

User testing

When Mr Jones tested the system, he noticed that when he changed a product code and title, the product code did not change in the heading on the Invoice form. I have now replaced the text in the headings with formulae referencing the Atlas Products workbook.

It's a very good idea to get the user to test your system. If he finds no errors or weaknesses the moderator will be deeply suspicious.

He liked the front-end menu, but wanted the gridlines put back in the Invoices worksheet. After discussion we agreed I should put gridlines within the invoice form but not on the background.

He did not like the **Create Chart** and **Add Trendline** command buttons on the Monthly worksheet, as he expected them to actually create the chart and trend line, not just give instructions. I have replaced these buttons with cells containing comments. (See Output Test 25a and b below.)

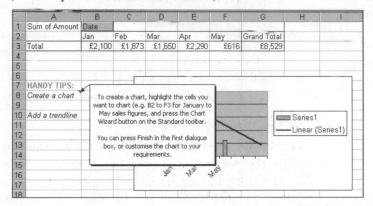

Test 25a – help on producing a chart

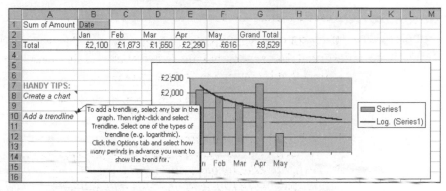

Test 25b – help on producing a trend line

You'll almost certainly need to make some changes to your design after user testing so don't leave this stage too late. Describe the changes you make. Many Brownie points here!

I also realised while watching Mr Jones test the system that it would be quite easy to forget to press the **Add to Monthly Sales** button after entering the day's invoices. I decided to display a message in the **ViewPickingList** macro to remind the user to do so, as the Picking list would always be printed. (Output Test 25c below)

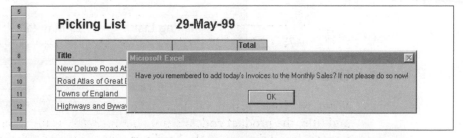

Test 25c – a message reminds the user to add to Monthly sales

We went through the steps of adding a new product and making the necessary adjustments to the Atlas template and the whole process took about 10 minutes. He felt that this would be quite straightforward. We discussed the possibility of catering for future titles by adding a few extra blank rows and columns in the Products worksheet and corresponding rows, columns and formulae in the Atlas workbook but decided it was unnecessary and would look messy. (Output Test 26a and b below)

Product number has been edited to B1, Bin Number to AP101

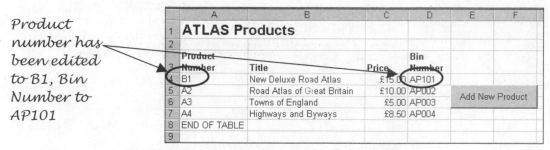

Test 26a – Product A1 has been edited so that its code is now B1 and the Bin number is AP101 instead of AP001, and a new product has been added.

Edited product no. automatically appears on INVOICES sheet

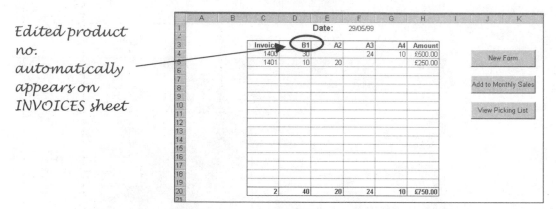

*Test 26b – the Invoices sheet has been altered to include the new product. The edited value (B1 instead of A1) is automatically picked up from the linked **Atlas Products** workbook*

Mr Jones decided he would like to have the Total Invoice value displayed on the Picking List, though this was not originally specified. This was very easy to add. (Output Test 26c below)

Edited Bin Number automatically appears on Picking List

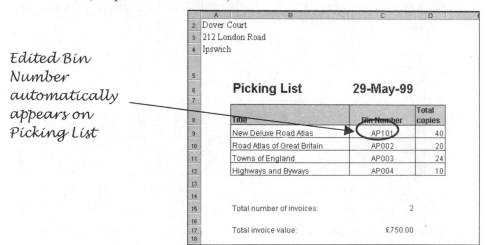

Test 26c – New Picking List showing new and edited products and Total Invoice value – note the altered Bin number AP101 is correctly inserted

Using the Auditing toolbar

The Auditing Toolbar is a genuinely useful way of picking out errors in your formulae. Do use it and document your use of it.

I used the auditing toolbar to trace dependents and precedents of each cell containing a formula. The Invoice sheet appeared as shown below. For example the formula in cell D3 comes from the Products sheet, and the formula in cell C20 is calculated from C4 to C19 and gets pasted to the Picking list sheet

The test threw up the fact that A2 and A3 had no precedents and had been typed as constants. This was incorrect so I changed the contents of these cells on the template.

This shows that cell D3 contains a formula referencing another worksheet. Cells E3 and F3 do not contain formulae - this is an error and needs correcting.

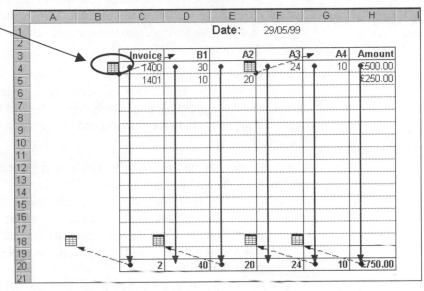

Test 27: Checking formulae on the Invoices sheet.

HAVE YOU BACKED UP YOUR PROJECT AND THE DOCUMENTATION?

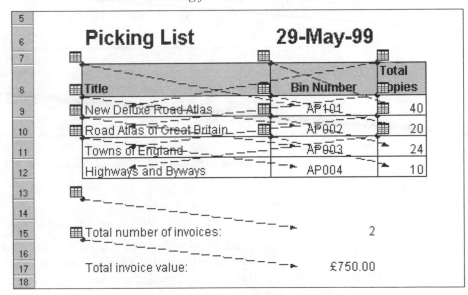

Test 28: All cells correctly reference another sheet.

Test 29 did not reveal anything as the data is converted to values by the macro **AddToMonthlySales** when it is added to this sheet so there are no formulae to audit.

Evaluation

The Evaluation is worth 20% of the marks, so it is not something to be done at 1am on the night before your project is due in.

Go through the Performance Indicators specified in the Analysis section and state honestly how well each of them has been achieved.

Looking back at the Objectives and Performance Indicators specified in the Analysis, the following have been achieved:

1. Trials showed that it took the user only about 15 seconds to enter data from each invoice, well within the 30 seconds specified. This means that data entry for a day's invoices (say 8 on average) will take only about 2 or 3 minutes.

2. The data entry form is very easy to use. Because all cells are locked except those in which data is entered, it is possible to tab from cell to cell. Today's date is automatically entered as the default when the **Enter Invoices** option is selected for the main menu, and the cursor is left in the correct cell to enter the first invoice number.

3. The Picking List is viewed by selecting the button on the **Invoices** sheet. The user found this very convenient and liked being able to perform a visual check on screen before pressing the Print button. It would be possible to incorporate the company logo on this report and this is an enhancement that could be added at a future date.

4. The monthly summary was easily produced from the main menu by pressing the **Monthly Sales Summary** button. The chart showing monthly sales is not produced automatically but requires the user to use the Chart wizard. Instructions on how to follow this simple procedure are given in a 'Handy Tip' which appears on the Monthly Sales Summary screen when the user place the cursor over the cell indicated. The trend line is produced in a similar way. Mr Jones was rather amused that by picking different options, he could make the trend line go up or down – he suggested that he would use one to show the Managing Director how well things were going, and the other to show the Sales staff that the company would soon be bankrupt if they did not improve their efforts.

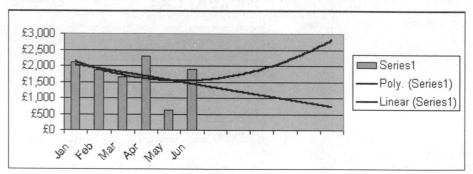

The trend is whatever you want it to be!

He suggested that as sales fluctuate during the year, it would be more useful to have a month-by-month comparison with last year's sales. This would involve copying the figures from December's Sales Summary to cells in the next year's Monthly sheet.

Mention also the limitations of your project and future enhancements that could be made.

5. The system of adding new titles is not ideal as it involves the changing of the actual workbook template and current workbook. Although this takes only 10 to 15 minutes, following instructions given in the User Manual, I would have preferred this not to be necessary. My initial design did not require the model to

Use your critical facilities – you will gain very few marks for an evaluation which simply implies that all the performance indicators were amply satisfied and there is nothing more that could be done.

If everyone was satisfied with their first efforts we would still be driving Model T Fords and watching black and white TV.

be changed when new products were added, but the process of entering the daily invoices and producing the Picking List was not as clear and simple for the user. The user felt he would rather have an extremely straightforward day-to-day system, at the expense of some complication in the very occasional addition of a new product.

6. The worksheets are all protected so that it is impossible to accidentally change anything. The user has to manually unprotect the **Products** worksheet in order to edit an existing product (which should happen very rarely) but if he forgets to protect it again, this is automatically done in an Auto_Close macro when the **Atlas Products** workbook is closed.

7. The day-to-day system is extremely easy to use. The one thing that could go wrong is that the user could forget to add the day's invoice totals to the Monthly Sales figures (by pressing **the Add to Monthly Sales** button). I have added an 'Alert' message to the macro which produces the Picking List, which will be done as a matter of routine, to remind the user to do so. Users could circumvent this message by clicking the Picking sheet tab instead of using the command button, but they would have to be particularly perverse to do this and not remember to add to monthly sales. Just the action of selecting the Picking List button or sheet tab will be enough after a few days to remind them of the correct procedure.

I could hide the sheet tabs so that the user is forced to use the command buttons. I would then have to add either a custom menu on the menu bar or button on the toolbar to return to the main menu, which at present is done by clicking the menu tab. On balance I decided to treat the user like a responsible adult and allow him to use the sheet tabs if he wants to.

I noticed that if a new worksheet is opened in say April 1998 and goes into the next year (January 1999), the Monthly Summary shows January sales before the previous year's sales. This is how the PivotTable grouping function works as it does not take the year into account. My solution to this is to tell the user to start a new worksheet in January of each year.

HAVE YOU BACKED UP YOUR PROJECT AND THE DOCUMENTATION?

I could smarten up the Picking List report by importing the company letterhead and logo, and this is an enhancement which I will implement if asked to do so. The Monthly Sales Summary also needs a heading, which means adjusting the MonthlyPivot macro and would not be hard to do.

Include a letter from the user if possible. This MUST however be genuine, preferably on headed paper — a badly spelt and ungrammatical letter written by yourself or a friend will reflect badly on both you and your school or college.
It is not unknown for an Examination Board to return such letters to a school's Head Teacher.

A letter from Mrs Nicholson, who does the daily Picking List, is shown on the next page.

Letter from user

Atlas Publications Ltd

Dover Court
212 London Road
Ipswich

3rd March 2000

To whom it may concern

I have today used the Excel spreadsheet for the first time, adding today's sales to those already posted by other members of staff.

It was a straightforward process and the sales were quickly entered.

I was then able to proceed to the display of the information contained in the spreadsheet in its various forms:

- the pick list and the daily and monthly sales totals,
- the display of information in graphical form suitable for presentation to different audiences – salesmen, directors, etc.

I think that this is a useful addition to the means of analysis and presentation of information available to the company.

D. Michelson

User Manual

Introduction

The User Manual should explain to the user how to use your system.
You should NOT be explaining how to use features of Excel.

This system has been especially written for Atlas Publications to automate the production of the Daily Picking List and to provide additional management information in the form of monthly sales summaries.

It uses Excel 2000 and runs well on a Pentium PC running Windows 2000. The two workbooks take only a small amount of memory – less than 100K, which will increase as more data is input over a year.

Installation

The installation procedure is given in the Technical Manual.

Starting a new workbook

You should start a new workbook on the first working day in January each year, though of course you can start using the system at any time of year.

- Load Excel and select **File, New**. Select the **AtlasProject** template and click **OK**. A new workbook will open containing all the worksheets, headings and formulae for your system.

- You may see a message telling you that the workbook you are opening contains macros. You can prevent this message appearing every time you load the file by unchecking the box **Always ask before opening workbooks with macros**. You will then be asked to confirm this in a dialogue box as shown below. However, caution is advised here because you are leaving your disk open to infection from other workbooks containing viruses. If in doubt, leave the box checked.

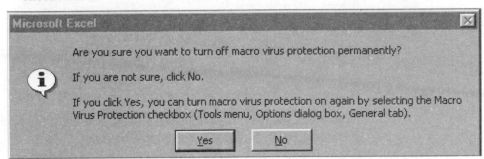

- Another message appears telling you that the workbook contains automatic links to information in another workbook. Click **Yes** to update all information.

- Save this file as *Atlasyy (yy* stands for the current year, e.g. *Atlas99* in 1999) in the directory **My Documents\SampleProj2**, or whichever directory the system was installed in.

- You're ready to start using the system!

Backups

But before you do, backup must be mentioned. At least once a week, take a backup of the two workbooks, **Atlas Products.xls** and **Atlas*yy*.xls** and store the backups in a safe place. They will easily fit on a floppy disk.

At the end of each year, take a final backup and label it carefully. Then open a brand new workbook for the New Year.

Opening an existing file

- Click **File** on the menu bar. Look at the list of most recently used files – most likely **Atlas*yy*** will be top of the list. Click it to open. If **Atlas*yy*** is not listed, click **Open** and select from the appropriate directory (e.g. directory **My Documents\SampleProj2**).

Entering daily invoices and printing the Picking List

Take the user through each menu option, using screenshots to illustrate.

When you open a new or existing Atlas workbook, you will see on your screen the main menu.

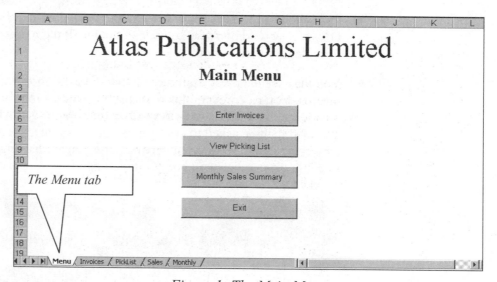

Figure 1: The Main Menu

Notice that the **Menu** tab is selected at the bottom of the screen. You can return to this menu at any time by clicking the **Menu** tab.

- Click the **Enter Invoices** button on the Main Menu. The **Invoices** screen will appear, with the default date already added, ready for you to start entering data from the day's invoices . Use the tab key to tab between fields and enter all the day's invoices. You will not be allowed to make any invalid entries, though of course the computer can't stop you entering 100 when you mean 10, so use a visual check every now and then.

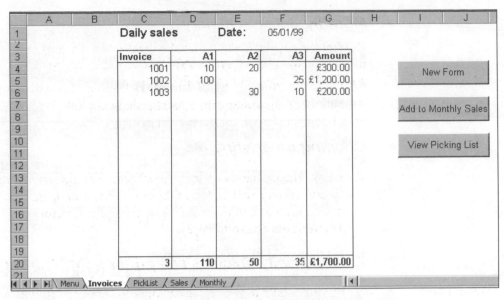

Figure 2: Entering data from the day's invoices

- When you have finished entering the day's invoices, click the **Add to Monthly Sales** button. This adds the day's sales total to the list of all the year's invoices, which is used for the Monthly Sales Summary report.

- Next, click the **View Picking List** button. This will take you to the Picking List screen, (shown below in Figure 3) and will display a reminder message just in case you have forgotten to add to monthly sales. Click **OK** and if the Picking List looks correct (it should be!) press the **Print** button on the standard toolbar to print it.

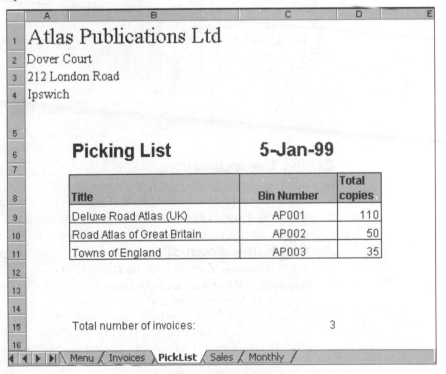

Figure 3: The Picking List

Monthly Sales Summary

- Click the **Menu** tab (see Figure 1) to return to the Main Menu.

- Click the **Monthly Sales Summary** button. This will automatically produce the summary, an example of which is shown below.

	A	B	C	D	E	F
1	Sum of Amount	Date				
2		Jan	Feb	Mar	Grand Total	
3	Total	£2,100	£1,873	£1,650	£5,623	
4						

Figure 4: The Monthly Sales Summary

- If you would like to see a chart of the monthly sales, select the cells to chart, including the headings (e.g. B2 to D3 in the above example) and press the **Chart Wizard** button on the standard toolbar. You can click Finish in the first dialogue box to produce a basic chart, or customise it by following the Wizard's simple instructions.

- To add a trend line to the chart, select any of the bars for Jan, Feb etc., right-click and select **Add Trendline**. There are various types of trend line to choose from. Click the **Options** tab and select the number of periods ahead you want the trend line to cover.

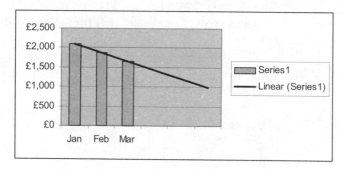

Figure 5: Chart with trendline

Exiting the application

- From the main menu select **Exit**. This will close all open workbooks. You will be asked if you wish to save changes if you have not already done so.

Adding a new product

- Open the **Atlas Products** workbook.

- Click the **Add New Product** button and a new line will be inserted in the list ready for you to enter data. Type the details of the new product. Do not enter a £ sign in the Price field – it will appear automatically as you tab out of the field.

Note: You will have to make alterations to the Atlas template and workbook when you add a new product. The steps are explained in the Technical Manual.

Technical Manual

Installing the system

The system is supplied on a floppy disk which contains two files:

- A template workbook **AtlasProject.xlt**:

- A workbook named **Atlas Products.xls**, which already contains the three titles currently produced by Atlas.

The template needs to be copied to the default templates directory, normally

C:\Program Files\MSOffice\Templates

This can be done using Explorer.

The **Atlas Products.xls** workbook must be copied to a subdirectory of the **My Documents** folder.

- Create a new subdirectory in the **My Documents** folder and name it **SampleProj2**.

- Copy **Atlas Products.xls** to this folder.

If for any reason you want to store the application in a different folder, you will need to change one line in the Auto_Open procedure held in the AtlasProject.xlt template. The line is:

DefaultPath = "C:\My Documents\SampleProj2\"

Change this line to specify the directory you have chosen to store your application.

When you have done this, put the original floppy disk away in a safe place in case you ever need to use it again.

Editing the Products workbook

The process of adding a new product is explained in the User manual. If you wish to *edit* an existing product, you must first unprotect the workbook.

- From the Tools menu select **Tools, Protection, Unprotect Sheet**.

- Make the required changes.

- Protect the sheet again by selecting **Tools, Protection, Protect Sheet**.

Any changes to existing products will automatically be reflected in the **AtlasProject** template and workbook. However if you add a new product, you will have to change the template and current Atlas workbook yourself, following instructions given below.

Adjusting the template after adding a new product

- Open the **AtlasProject.xlt** template (the **Atlas Products.xls** workbook opens automatically) and size both workbooks so that they are both visible on screen.

- In the **Atlas Products** workbook, name the cell containing the new product code, e.g. if the Product code is A4, name the cell *ProductCode4*. To do this, select the cell, type the name in the Name box and press Enter.

- Name the other cells in the row e.g. *A4Title, A4Price, A4Bin*.

- In the **AtlasProject** template, click the Invoices tab and unprotect the sheet. Insert a new column to the left of the Amount column. Use the Format Painter to format it the same as the preceding column. The file is not password protected.

- Select the cell which is to contain the new product code. Type an = sign, and drag the new Product code from the Atlas Products workbook to the Formula bar. The formula will be something like

  = 'Atlas Products.xls'!ProductCode4

- Insert the Sum formula at the bottom of the column. That completes the changes in this sheet.

- In the **Picklist** sheet, you need to add an extra row to the Picking List, format it using the Format Painter and insert new formula in a similar way to that described above.

- Save and close the template.

- As well as changing the template, you must make exactly the same changes in the current workbook.

Worksheet design

Somewhere you must show the formulae and names used in the worksheet. This could be in the Design (hand-written) if you prefer.

The screenshots below show the names and formulae used in the various worksheets

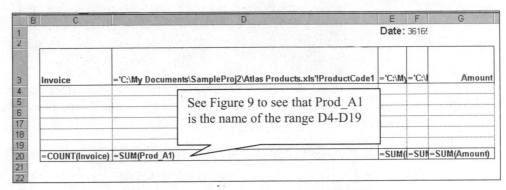

Figure 6: Formulae in the Invoices worksheet

The formulae which are not visible are similar

e.g. In cell E3 the formula refers to ProductCode2 instead of ProductCode1.

The pathname shown in the formulae is the one that was used during development. However if the user chooses to install **Atlas Products.xls** in a different directory, the only change that needs to be made is to change the default pathname in the **Auto_Open** procedure in the **AtlasProject.xlt** template as explained in the Installation instructions. The formulae in the workbooks will adjust automatically.

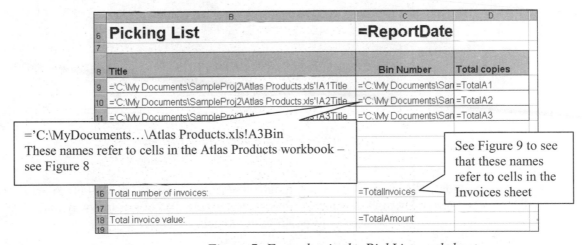

Figure 7: Formulae in the PickList worksheet

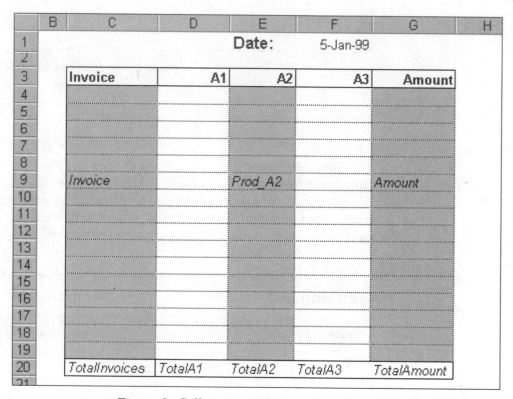

Figure 8: Cell names in the Product worksheet

Figure 9: Cell names in the Invoices worksheet

(The shaded areas denote a range name, e.g. Range C4 to C19 is named Invoices. Range D4 to D19 is named Prod_A1. Naming the cells in this way makes the formulae as shown in Figure 6 easier to comprehend.)

(8,000 words)

Macros

Print listing of your macros, well documented with comments. Use hand annotation to show where you have customised code rather than just recording keystrokes.

The following macros are used in the Application.

```
Sub Auto_Open()
'
' This macro was not created using recorded keystrokes.
' It was written using VB code.
' It runs automatically when the main Atlas template or
workbook is opened
'
    Dim SaveBook, DefaultPath, Workbookname As String
' Save the name of this workbook so that it can be made
active again
' after opening the Atlas Products workbook

    SaveBook = ActiveWorkbook.Name

' Hide the intermediate operations from the user
    Application.ScreenUpdating = False
' Set default path name so that Excel can find the Atlas
Products file
' If the user wants to install in a different directory,
' this line will have to be changed to the specified
directory
  With Application
    DefaultPath = "C:\My Documents\SampleProj2\"
  End With
' Open the Atlas Products file
    Workbookname = DefaultPath & "Atlas Products.xls"
    Workbooks.Open Workbookname
'Make the Atlas workbook the active workbook again
    Workbooks(SaveBook).Activate
'Display the menu
    Sheets("Menu").Select
End Sub


Sub Auto_Close()
'
'Executes automatically when workbook is closed
    Workbooks.Close
End Sub



Sub EnterInvoices()
' Goes to the invoice sheet, clears the form,
' enters today's date and positions cursor

' NewForm macro clears the form
    NewForm

' Set default date to today on data entry form
    ActiveCell.FormulaR1C1 = "=TODAY()"
    Range("ReportDate").Select
End Sub

Sub AddToMonthlySales()
```

```
' Adds the current invoice to the list of invoices held in
'   the Monthly sheet
'
' Hide the intermediate operations from the user
    Application.ScreenUpdating = False

    Sheets("Invoices").Select
    Range("ReportDate").Select
    Selection.Copy
    Sheets("Sales").Select
    Range("A3").Select
    Selection.CurrentRegion.Select
'move down one cell and see if the table is empty
'if it is not, go to the last cell in the table
    If Range("A4") <> "" Then
        Selection.End(xlDown).Select
    End If
    ActiveCell.Offset(1, 0).Range("A1").Select

    Selection.PasteSpecial Paste:=xlValues,
Operation:=xlNone, SkipBlanks:= _
        False, Transpose:=False
    ActiveCell.Offset(0, 1).Range("A1").Select
    Sheets("Invoices").Select
    Range("TotalAmount").Select
    Selection.Copy
    Sheets("Sales").Select
    Selection.PasteSpecial Paste:=xlValues,
Operation:=xlNone, SkipBlanks:= _
        False, Transpose:=False
'Turn off Copy mode
    Application.CutCopyMode = False
End Sub

Sub MonthlyPivot()
'
Creates a Pivot table report from daily sales data and groups
it by months
'
' Hide the intermediate operations from the user
    Application.ScreenUpdating = False

'Name Sales Table range
    Sheets("Sales").Select
    Range("A3").Select
    Selection.CurrentRegion.Select
    ActiveWorkbook.Names("SalesTable").Delete
    Selection.Name = "SalesTable"
'
'Clear existing pivot table
    Sheets("Monthly").Select
    Range("A1:P5").Select
    Selection.Clear
'
'Create new pivot table
'
    Sheets("Monthly").Select
```

```
      ActiveCell.Range("A1:Q9").Select
      Selection.ClearContents
      Sheets("Sales").Select
      ActiveSheet.PivotTableWizard SourceType:=xlDatabase,
SourceData:= _
          "SalesTable", TableDestination:="Monthly!R1C1",
TableName:= _
          "PivotTable2"
      ActiveSheet.PivotTables("PivotTable2").AddFields
ColumnFields:="Date"

ActiveSheet.PivotTables("PivotTable2").PivotFields("Amount").
Orientation = _
          xlDataField
      ActiveSheet.PivotTables("PivotTable2").PivotSelect
"Date[All]", xlLabelOnly
      Selection.Group Start:=True, End:=True,
Periods:=Array(False, False, False, _
          False, True, False, False)
      ActiveSheet.PivotTables("PivotTable2").PivotSelect
"Date[All]", xlLabelOnly
'     Format the cells containing monthly sales totals to
currency, 0 dec.pl.
      FormatTotal

End Sub



Sub NewForm()
'
' Clears the Invoices Data Entry form
'
      Sheets("Invoices").Select
      Range("InvoiceLines").Select
      Selection.ClearContents
      Range("ReportDate").Select
      Selection.ClearContents

End Sub



Sub ViewPickingList()
'
' Selects the Picking List sheet and displays a reminder to
the user
'
      Sheets("PickList").Select
      MsgBox ("Have you remembered to add today's Invoices to
                the Monthly Sales? If not please do so now!")
End Sub
```

HAVE YOU BACKED UP YOUR PROJECT AND THE DOCUMENTATION?

You may photocopy these blank worksheets to use in your Design documentation. Cut them out and arrange them on an A3 sheet, and design your sheets using different coloured pens for cell names and formulae, highlighter pens to show protected or unprotected cells, arrows to indicate links between sheets, etc.

	A	B	C	D	E
1					
2					
3					
4					
5					
6					
7					
8					
9					
10					
11					
12					
13					
14					
15					
16					
17					

	A	B	C	D	E	F	G
1							
2							
3							
4							
5							
6							
7							
8							
9							
10							
11							
12							
13							
14							
15							
16							
17							
18							
19							
20							

Appendix B
AQA Project Guidelines

19   Guidance for Setting Centre-Assessed Component

19.1   AS Module 3

Coursework: Task Solution   In the AS Module 3 project, emphasis will be on the full exploitation of particular generic application software and the advanced facilities available within them. The project will be a self-contained problem. The emphasis in the project will be on the candidate's ability to produce a high quality implementation to the problem.

It is anticipated that teachers will introduce candidates to problem-solving techniques involving the use of a range of generic software facilities. These will include relational databases, spreadsheets, document processing, desk top publishing, multi-media presentations and graphics packages. However, teachers may well wish to introduce other types of software or packages and are encouraged to do so.

For successful completion of this module, candidates will be expected to devise and test a solution to a task-related problem that provides them with adequate scope to employ appropriate and advanced package skills. **The criteria are so devised as to genuinely provide an opportunity for candidates to learn and progress throughout the duration of the project rather than only provide an assessment point at the end of the module.** The standards expected from this project are to be maintained but, the software tools for completion of the work are not restricted to a single package. Candidates should focus on the issue of "appropriate tools for the task" and if this requires the use of facilities from two or more generic packages then this is deemed to be wholly appropriate.

Great emphasis in the marking criteria has been placed on the issue of planning for testing, the methods of completing this testing and assessment of results, and, while the main focus remains on the acquisition and use of software skills, candidates are required to show an appreciation of whether their solution is appropriate in the context of the problem and for the IT solution as a whole.

In completing a project, the candidate will be required to undertake the following processes.

> The definition of a problem in information technology terms.
>
> The derivation or specification of information technology tasks.
>
> The completion of appropriate design work from which to implement the solution.
>
> The determination of a schedule of activities.
>
> The determination of a plan for testing, which should be clearly documented.
>
> The implementation and testing of a solution, which will involve the use of advanced functionalities of the package(s) in the most efficient way to achieve the desired results.
>
> Evaluation of the solution against the requirements of any potential user.

Candidates are required to provide a written commentary of these processes in document form.

Specification

The following comments on the method of assessment should be read with reference to the module specification and the assessment criteria.

From a clear statement of the problem to be solved, with background information, there should be an appropriate specification given. This specification, depending on the problem area, should reflect the end-user's requirements of the solution, the desired outcomes (as an implementation free specification) and any constraints or limitations on the development of the solution, e.g. human and physical resources.

The input, processing and output needs, which match the requirements specification, must be clearly stated, although the format of this section will vary according to the software solution available. For example, a database solution will need a database design from which to complete the project.

Before implementation, the candidate should produce an appropriate test strategy. This should address the elements which need to be completed as progress is made towards the solution, the type of test to be carried out and the desired outcome from which success or otherwise can be measured.

In addition, an effective and full testing plan should be devised. The testing plan should include, for each element, the test data to be used, the reasons why this data has been selected and the expected outcomes.

From this section, the candidate is expected to have a clear understanding of the exact nature of the problem to be solved and the steps that will be needed to achieve this solution. The candidate should be aware of the need for testing, to be able to select appropriate tests for the various stages and be clear on the success criteria for those stages.

Implementation and Testing

The ultimate goal of these sections is for the candidate to produce an effective solution to be problem stated. This is one which satisfies the requirements specification and specifically, can be operated in the proposed environment and the interface provided maps well to the skills of the intended end-user. It is expected that the candidate will make sensible and appropriate use of data capture and validation procedures, data organisation methods, output contents and formats and user interfaces. This will of course be dependent upon the software selected and/or available for the completion of the solution.

It is very much in the spirit of this specification that candidates will implement and test in a modular fashion and that the evidence for this aspect, and that of the Testing section, may well be presented together. Candidates are expected to consider the limitations of not just the whole solution but individual aspects and gain further credit by identifying improvements, designing new test criteria, implementing and testing again as the project develops.

For example, on completion of part of a project where data is input, it may become apparent that validation is needed where none was previously considered. Further credit is then available if the candidate corrects this, implementing an improved version and making appropriate tests.

This approach is designed to be more conductive to candidates learning throughout the duration of the coursework whilst still providing an appropriate form of assessment.

Documentation is expected on the implementation work completed, which will contribute to the assessment of whether the candidate fully employed their package specific skills in an effective and appropriate manner. Also, that the selections of the chosen hardware and software facilities have been fully justified in relation to the solution developed. The project log recommended in the specification for module 3 is expected to contribute towards the evidence for this aspect.

The results of any testing activities should be fully documented with hard copy evidence available, where practicable, this being cross-referenced to the original test plans.

Evaluation

A written evaluation is expected at the conclusion of the project. This should reflect the candidate's own awareness of the effectiveness of their solution in meeting the initial requirements specification. The candidate, regardless of success, is expected here to show an awareness of the criteria for a successful information technology solution and how well their solution maps to the selected criteria. This assessment should discuss any remaining limitations of the solution and the reasons for these constraints.

User Guide

The candidate is expected to produce extensive user documentation which is appropriate for the solution and also the hardware and software available. This may include on-line help in some format in addition to paper-based user guides and manuals. It should cover all aspects that are relevant to the solution but it is expected that this will always include normal operation of the software solution and common problems that have been found to occur along with the solutions. Regardless of the nature of the user guides or help provided, the material presented should always be appropriate to the needs of the end-user.

20   Assessment Criteria

20.1	Introduction	
	Assessment of project work	It is necessary to provide a structure for the assessment of project work so that all teachers are, in general, following a common procedure. Such a procedure will assist with the standardisation of assessment from centre to centre. Each project is therefore to be assessed in accordance with the criteria set out below. In assessing candidates, centres must ensure that comparable standards are observed between different teaching groups. Each centre must produce a single order of merit for the centre as a whole.

20.2	Criteria for the assessment of Unit 3	The following categories are to be used in the assessment of the project. The criteria for marking these categories are listed below. The project is marked out of a total of 60.

Specification	13 marks
Implementation	20 marks
User Testing	12 marks
Evaluation	6 marks
User Documentation	9 marks
Total	**60 marks.**

Specification (13 marks)

11-13   A detailed requirements specification has been produced for the identified problem, which matches the needs of the stated end-user(s).

The input, processing and output needs, which match the requirements specification, are clearly stated.

Effective designs have been completed which would enable an independent third party implementation of the solution.

An appropriate test strategy has been determined. An effective test and full testing plan has been devised. The testing plan includes the test data and expected outcomes and directly relates to the requirements specification.

8-10   A detailed requirements specification has been produced for the identified problem, which matches the needs of the stated end-user(s).

The input, processing and output needs, which match the requirements specification, are stated.

Designs have been completed but lack detail so as not to allow an independent third part implementation of the solution or, are inefficient in relation to the problem stated.

A test strategy has been determined and testing plan have been devised but are limited in scope or do not relate to the requirements specification stated.

4-7   A requirements specification has been produced for the identified problem but does not fully match the needs of the stated end-user(s) or lacks detail and clarity.

The input, processing and output needs are stated but do not fully match the requirements' specification or are not sufficiently clear.

Design work has been attempted but is incomplete and does not reflect an efficient solution to the problem stated.

A test strategy has been determined but is either incomplete or does not relate to the requirements specification stated. The testing plan is either vague or missing.

1-3   The requirements specification is vague or missing.

The input, processing and output needs are only vaguely considered or are absent.

There is little or no design effort.

The test strategy and testing plan are vague or missing.

0   The candidate has produced no work.

Implementation (20 marks)

16-20	An effective solution has been developed which is operable in the proposed environment by the intended end-user. Appropriate data capture and validation procedures, data organisation methods, output contents and formats and user interface(s) have been used. Generic and package specific skills have been fully employed in an effective and appropriate manner. The selection of the chosen hardware and software facilities has been fully justified in relation to the solution developed.
11-15	A solution has been developed which is operable in the proposed environment by the intended end-user but has some inefficiencies. There is evidence of the use of some appropriate data capture and validation procedures, data organisation methods, output contents and formats and user interface(s). Generic and package specific skills have been fully employed but not always in an effective and appropriate manner. The selection of some of the chosen hardware and software facilities has been justified in relation to the solution developed.
6-10	A partial solution has been developed, but those aspects completed are useable by the intended end-user. There is some evidence of the use of some data capture and validation procedures, data organisation methods, output contents and formats and user interface(s). Generic and package specific skills have been employed but not always in an effective and appropriate manner. The selection of some of the chosen hardware and software facilities has been only vaguely justified in relation to the solution developed.
1-5	A solution has been developed which is very limited and is not practically operable in the proposed environment by the intended end-user. Few, if any, data capture and validation procedures, data organisation methods, output contents and formats and user interface(s) have been used. The generic and package specific skills used are simplistic and/or were not always applied appropriately. The selection of the chosen hardware and software facilities are not justified in relation to the solution developed.
0	The candidate has not implemented the system.

Testing (12 marks)

9-12	The test strategy and test plan previously devised have now been followed in a systematic manner using typical, erroneous and extreme (boundary) data. The results of testing are fully documented with outputs cross-referenced to the original plan. Corrective action taken due to test results will be clearly documented.
5-8	The test strategy and plan devised have been followed in a systematic manner but using only normal data. The results of testing are partially documented with some evidence of outputs cross-referenced to the original plan. There is some evidence of corrective action taken due to test results.
1-4	The test strategy and plan devised have been followed in a limited manner using only normal data. There is little or no documentation of the results of testing. There is little or no indication of corrective action required due to test results.
0	There is no evidence of testing.

Evaluation (6 marks)

4-6   The effectiveness of the solution in meeting the detailed requirements specification has been fully assessed with the candidate showing full awareness of the criteria for a successful information technology solution. The limitations of the solution have been clearly identified.

1-3   The effectiveness of the solution in meeting the original requirements specifications has only been partly assessed with the candidate showing only partial awareness of the criteria for a successful information technology solution.
The limitations of the solution are vague or missing.

0   There is no evidence of evaluation.

User Documentation (9 marks)

7-9   There is extensive user documentation for the solution which covers all relevant aspects including normal operation and common problems and is appropriate to the needs of the end-user.

4-6   A user guide is present which describes the functionality of the solution and is appropriate to the needs of the end-user.

1-3   A limited user guide is present which describes only the basic functionality of the solution.

0   There is no evidence of user documentation.

Index

Successful ICT Projects in Word (2nd edition)

by P.M.Heathcote

February 2000   208pp   ISBN 1 903112 25 7

This text, updated for the 2001 syllabus and Office 2000, covers the essential features of Word from basic editing and formatting right through to advanced features such as templates, macros, customised toolbars and menus. It is suitable for students on a number of courses such as 'A' Level or GNVQ ICT, HNC and HND in Business Information Technology and Access to HE.
It gives ideas for suitable projects and explains how to complete each phase from Analysis and Design through to Implementation, Testing and Evaluation. AQA Project Guidelines and a mark scheme are included in an Appendix.

Successful ICT Projects in Access (2nd edition)

by P.M. Heathcote

July 2000   224pp   ISBN 1 903112 27 3

This book, updated for the 2001 syllabus, will help students to complete a project in MS Access, using version 2000, 97 or 7. It covers database design, creating tables, forms and subforms, queries, importing and exporting data to other packages, analysing and processing data, reports, macros and some Visual Basic for Applications. It includes advice on choice of projects and a sample project.

It is suitable for students on a wide range of courses such as 'A' Level or GNVQ ICT, HNC and HND in Business Information Technology and Access to H.E.

Successful ICT Projects in FrontPage

by R.S.U. Heathcote

January 2001   208pp   ISBN 1 903112 28 1

This book is designed to help students on an 'A' Level, GNVQ or similar course to design and implement a Web site using MS FrontPage 2000. It assumes no previous knowledge of FrontPage and takes the reader from the basics such as entering, editing and formatting text and images on a Web page through to advanced features such as writing scripts, gathering data from forms, and making use of active components. A wide range of examples is used to illustrate the different facilities of FrontPage, and a sample project shows students how to tackle and document each stage of project work.

Key Skills in Information Technology (Levels 2 and 3)

by P.M. Heathcote & R.P. Richards

July 2000   224pp   ISBN 1 903112 37 0

This book covers all the topics needed to achieve the Key Skills Certificate in Information Technology at Levels 2 and 3, and explains exactly how the student can build a portfolio of evidence to achieve the qualification. It covers techniques in Windows, Word, Excel, Access, PowerPoint, Internet Explorer and Publisher, and contains advice and examples of activities to demonstrate IT key skill competences. Sample questions are included to give students practice for the externally set test and each chapter is cross-referenced to the relevant key skill specification. It will be a useful text for students doing project work for GCSE Information Technology.

Consult our Web site www.payne-gallway.co.uk *for latest news on titles and prices.*

Software:

Algorithms and Data Structures (2nd Edition)
by P.M.Heathcote and E.Morgan

Published March 1st 1998. Site Licence £90.00 (plus VAT)
ISBN 0 9532490 1 8

This highly popular interactive package can be loaded and run on a network and gives students approximately 10 hours of interactive tuition on how to tackle problems involving data structures. It contains 6 units covering Programming fundamentals, Sorting and Searching, Linked Lists, Queues, Stacks and Trees. A seventh unit tests students on the concepts they have learned.

A Level Computing Interactive Revision
by P.M.Heathcote and E.Morgan

Published March 1st 1998. Site Licence £70.00 (plus VAT)
ISBN 0 9532490 2 6

This popular interactive Revision Aid for A Level Computing contains 12 modules, each consisting of a quiz on one area of the syllabus. A full explanation is given to the student after each question is attempted. A random 10 questions from the bank of 30 questions on each topic are given each time a student attempts a quiz, and the score can be recorded each time on the student's own disk.

Hundreds of centres have already discovered the benefits of our two computer-aided learning packages, written especially for 'A' Level Computing students and unique in the market! The packages are straightforward to install and run, offer excellent value for money and keep students interested and motivated.

The software is supplied on 3½" disks for Windows 3.1, 95, 98, NT Server or 2000 (not MacOS). Schools and colleges may order both the above packages for the special price of £140.00 plus VAT.

Inspection copies of books and a free disk containing a demonstration version of both 'Algorithms and Data Structures' and 'A Level Computing Interactive Revision' are available from our distributors:

BEBC Distribution
P.O. Box 3371
Poole, Dorset
BH12 3YW

Tel: 01202 712909   Fax: 01202 712913   E-mail: pg@bebc.co.uk